Hot Apple Ci

"I love this collection of stories and poems told by great Canadians; stories of real people that transcend the ages. Many of these stories felt like they were a leaf from my own life book. You will find this reading hilarious, therapeutic and inspirational. A must-read for all book lovers."
Randall W. Young, Manager, Artists Relationships, World Vision Canada

"There were contributors with backgrounds from Africa to Europe to the Philippines, from Atlantic Canada to British Columbia to Attawapiskat. It was not long before I was drawn into experiencing the expression of God's grace through challenges of autism, adoption, or abuse; the joys of forgiveness and friendship; and even the setting of priorities with ice cream bars. Some pieces tugged at my heartstrings, others encouraged and some made me smile, even chuckle aloud—thank you Champ! I was reminded that, no matter our background or circumstance, our struggles and victories are universal and we need one another. This is a book to share with a cup of hot apple cider and cinnamon, but it's also good with a glass of cold lemonade."
Dawn Loucks, member, Bayview Glen Church

"I commend these delightful, heartfelt stories from fellow Canadian authors. They are worth your time to read. The Hot Apple Cider series is a great Canadian treasure."
The Rev. Dr. Ed Hird, author of *Restoring Health: Body, Mind, and Spirit*

"Uplifting, heart-warming, and invigorating. Life—real life! Precious, diverse, thought-provoking, worth every minute of it. A pure jewel!"
Claire de Burbure, MD, PhD, Medical & Environmental Health Teacher

"There is a line in a Joni Mitchell song that says, 'the sun poured in like butterscotch and stuck to all my senses.' That's how I felt reading this book. These are tender stories of joy and sorrow, raw and poignant reminders of all that it means to be alive."
Ali Matthews, singer-songwriter

A Taste of Hot Apple Cider

"I loved this Canadian *Chicken Soup for the Soul*. It had me laughing and crying with every story."
Amazon Kindle customer

"I like that most of these are real-life stories or are based on real events. There is some poetry as well. This book is a compilation of stories by Canadian authors but their struggles are common to us all…. What I found is that most of these stories made you feel like you were about to cry, they were that beautiful."
The Rebecca Review

Hot Apple Cider

"A collection of short stories, poetry, and wisdom seeking to heal and mend the soul of the reader after difficult and stressful situations…. Highly recommended."
Midwest Book Review

"Much in the tradition of *Chicken Soup for the Soul*, these delightful readings are like a cozy cup of hot cider. Settle in for a moment of warmth and reflection…. Enjoy!"
Brian C. Stiller, Global Ambassador for the World Evangelical Alliance

A Second Cup of Hot Apple Cider

"The short selections make this a perfect book for even indifferent readers…. Be sure to buy more than one, for you will probably have the urge to share this gem of a collection with others."
Faith Today

"This comforting and encouraging book should be in every home, library, church, and school."
Pauline Christian, President, Black Business and Professional Association

Hot Apple Cider

with Cinnamon

STORIES *of* FINDING LOVE
in UNEXPECTED PLACES

Edited by

N. J. LINDQUIST

That's Life! Communications

Markham, Ontario

Hot Apple Cider with Cinnamon

That's Life! Communications
Box 77001, Markham, ON L3P 0C8, Canada
905-471-1447
http://thatslifecommunications.com
comments@thatslifecommunications.com

ISBN: 978-1-927692-16-5

Cover design and interior layout by N. J. Lindquist.
Cover apple photo © Dionisvera from Shutterstock.com
Interior photos are from Shutterstock.com, Dreamstime.com, and iStockphoto.com

Library and Archives Canada Cataloguing in Publication

Hot apple cider with cinnamon : stories of finding love in unexpected places / edited by N.J. Lindquist.

Issued in print and electronic formats.

ISBN 978-1-927692-16-5 (paperback).--ISBN 978-1-927692-17-2 (ebook)

1. Inspiration--Religious aspects--Christianity. 2. Christian life-- Anecdotes. 3. Spiritual life--Anecdotes. 4. Canadian literature (English)-- Christian authors. I. Lindquist, N. J. (Nancy J.), editor

BV4515.3.H685 2015   242   C2015-906169-5

C2015-906170-9

*This book is dedicated to every individual
down through the ages
who has struggled,
sometimes against overwhelming odds,
to tell his or her story.*

Table of Contents

Foreword

Sheila Wray Gregoire

There is so much sorrow in the world.

Many days, as I lace up my shoes and zip up my fleece jacket to head outside for my prayer walk, my heart is heavy. So much bad news. So much pain. What must God feel when He looks down at us?

But what if that bad news isn't the end of the story? What if there's more going on below the surface—simple stories, that we often don't see?

Yes, there is much sadness and evil in the world, but in the midst of all that sadness there is a simple antidote, and it's just this: Love.

Love your neighbour. It was revolutionary when Jesus said it two thousand years ago, and it can be revolutionary today, too—if we can just grab hold of it.

Choose love.

John Lennon once imagined a world with no heaven—such a world is pretty bleak indeed.

But imagine a world with real love.

That love doesn't have to be shown as big acts! Jesus said bringing a cup of cold water in His name is love. Love is simply shining a light in what is otherwise a very dark world.

This book is all about those acts of love that make the biggest difference. It's choosing to see beyond the old clothes of the lonely old man at your door. It's choosing to let the resentment you felt towards an inadequate father float away as you see his own challenges with new eyes. It's choosing to share balls of yarn with desperate refugees who land in your corner of the world.

In these pages you will find tales of love—love for a parent, for a friend, for a stranger—that span Canadian hockey rinks and African villages and Philippine homes. You will find people choosing hope in the midst of a panicky Alberta hospital room, choosing God in the midst of Alzheimer's, choosing peace in the midst of losing a child.

Those stories brought tears to my eyes—and you'll find yours welling up repeatedly as you read this book. As I've walked and reflected on my reaction to so many of the stories, I've realized I'm not emotional because of the effects of grace and love in sad situations. I'm emotional because each story, in its own way, brings this haunting question: "What did I miss?" In other words, "When did I close my eyes to the opportunity to show love?"

It's so easy to become focused on oneself—to become so busy that each phone call from a lonely friend is an intrusion. It's easy to become focused on our own hurts—how our parents let us down, our friends betrayed us, our spouses left. It's easy to become mad at God. And yet if we give in to that easy road, we miss the blessings—the blessings that only love can bring.

C. S. Lewis wrote, "Humility is not thinking less of yourself; it is thinking of yourself less." Isn't that the recipe for real love?

Real love is seeing your neighbour, your family, and your friends with new eyes. It's deciding to laugh, to love, to live in the knowledge that pain in the world is inevitable, but love is a choice. It's a choice that lights a candle in the darkness. It's a choice that warms us in a cold, Canadian winter, like a cup of Hot Apple Cider on a fall day. And it's a choice that, made daily, will change our lives.

The stories in this book will help you choose love. Every time.

Sheila Wray Gregoire is a blogger, speaker, and the author of seven books on love, including *9 Thoughts That Can Change Your Marriage* and *The Good Girl's Guide to Great Sex*. These days, you can usually find her with her husband in their RV, travelling around North America, birdwatching—and speaking to churches about marriage on the side! Sheila blogs every day at ToLoveHonorandVacuum.com.

http://sheilawraygregoire.com

Introduction

We recently took two of our grandsons to the Royal Ontario Museum. Since the museum is enormous, we asked them to look at the map and choose six areas to visit. One of the areas the boys chose was "Earth's Treasures." They had no idea what that display was about, but liked the name.

So we went to Earth's Treasures, which is, of course, rocks, precious minerals, gems, and meteorites. Since I've always been fascinated by such things, this was a great choice from my perspective.

The Earth's Treasures' area is a large room filled with tall glass cases containing dozens of samples. Some are breathtakingly beautiful. Some are puzzling or amusing. Some are rare and highly valued. Some are very common and yet can become quite intriguing when studied up close.

We marvelled at the beautiful, varied faces of quartz; the weirdness of wulfenite; the awesomeness of calcite and fluorite; the randomness of malachite, mimetite, and vanadinite. We contemplated being miners looking for gold and silver, and not getting fooled by fool's gold. And we puzzled over how one would know that a plain-looking rock was a geode that, when broken open, would display spectacular crystals in its hollow core.

At the end of the large room is a small area with glass cases wedged into the walls at waist-level. This is where the diamonds, rubies, opals, sapphires, emeralds, and other gems are displayed. They, too, are rocks; yet because of their beauty and rarity, they are greatly valued.

No doubt, you're asking yourself what rocks have to do with the Hot Apple Cider books.

Just this. The day after we visited the ROM, I sat down to work on the table of contents for this book, and the first thought that entered my mind was that each piece in this book is like one of those rocks or minerals. Some are amusing, some serious, some plain and straightforward, some intricate and thought-provoking. Some will make you cry, some will make you laugh, some might even make you angry. No two are alike, even though their themes might be similar. Some will resonate with you as you read them now. Some will come to life for you years from now when an experience you've had suddenly lets you see what the author was talking about. One that might be a favourite for you will mean nothing to someone else. And vice versa.

These stories and poems are all treasures, birthed and molded through the lives of the individuals who wrote them, and this book is merely a showcase that enables you to read them.

As the editor, I've spent many hours with these stories and poems, and I'm delighted to present them to you.

N. J. Lindquist

The "Other" First Prize

Nonfiction

Martin Smith

The air was filled with the kind of electric anticipation that usually heralds such historical moments as the first lunar landing, reaching the summit of Mount Everest, or winning a turkey during a bowling tournament. Six eager young lads strode to the starting line, their running shoes brushing against the freshly laid stripes of chalky white lime.

A considerable crowd had formed for the finals of the Grade 2 100-yard-dash at Peace Memorial Elementary School. This was the finale of a long day of track and field action. It was the pinnacle event of the festivities—the apex of a long afternoon whose moments would live on in immortality in scrapbooks and photo albums. This was for the big trophy. No participant ribbon would do.

One of the strapping young contestants vying for the golden cup was an elder sibling of mine, Warren Charles Smith. Mother, on the sidelines, nervously hovered over me and my other brothers, Howard and Lawrence. My father, who had taken the day off from work, held high a large sign made from construction paper covered with the words "Go Warren Go!" Great swells of pride filled our lungs as we saw my brother ready himself. His eyes were focused and his face was confident and sure.

I should mention, at this juncture, that my brother, even at the tender age of eight, was a singular character with a fierce streak of determination and the kind of staggering resolve usually found only in dictators and mad scientists. Even though he was blessed with what one might charitably call "stocky" legs, there was no doubt in his mind that he would be the first one out of the gate and the first one across the finish line.

Prior to the race, Warren had invested considerable time rattling the confidence of the other eight-year-olds with bruising cruelty. He had insisted that their efforts were doomed to failure and that they shouldn't even bother breaking into a sweat in their pursuit of what was surely going to be a crushing humiliation. His taunts included such pithy lines as "Why don't you just lay back a bit and save yourself from the sobering reality of mediocrity?" and "You know second isn't bad. It's worked for Barney Fife[1] for years."

His verbose peacock-like posturing didn't appear to have impressed the other contestants who, for the most part, normally had no idea what he was talking about. They generally found him humorous.

While the school's track and field day was usually a chaotic blend of sounds, an eerie cloud of suspense had descended upon the track as the start of the big race loomed near. A tangible hush blanketed the crowd as the boys shifted into position. All that could be heard was a soft breeze tickling the decorative pennants that lined the field. The pennants, the kind you usually see at your finer used car lots, flapped in a slow lazy motion as if they were moving through thick mud.

Speaking with melodramatic resonance, Vice-Principal Hyde firmly grasped the megaphone and counted down to the start of the race. In his chubby right hand he held the starter's pistol high in the air. As he reached skyward, all eyes fell upon him. Unfortunately, the activities of the day had not been kind to his armpits.

"Ready!" he crackled.

Beads of gelatin-like sweat dripped from the forehead of Davey Peters, located just to the right of my brother on the starting line.

"On your mark!" Vice-Principal Hyde continued with great proclamation.

On Warren's other side, Michael Curtis's eyebrows twitched.

"Get set!" came the final warning.

Further down the row, Nino Greshner licked his lips.

The throng of parents, grandparents, and siblings leaned forward.

Mr. Hyde applied pressure to the trigger of the gun. It creaked like a rusty door hinge, stiff and reluctant, before it exploded with a deafening boom. The sound mingled with the hollering voice of the vice principal. "Go!"

At the outset, things looked promising for Warren.

Luke Wilson stumbled and fell to one knee.

Davey Peters bolted out fast, but it was painfully obvious that he had forgotten to tie his shoelaces.

Nino Greshner had reacted poorly to the starter's pistol, grimacing and covering his ears. Horrified by his own reaction, he bounded forward with gangly limbs, trying to make up for lost ground.

Roland DiMucci, whose parents shunned the sun like withering vampires, was clad with several layers of clothing including pants more suited to clowning than running. His attire made it impossible to run even a 10-step dash, let alone a full 100 yards. He waddled slowly out of the gate as if on a tightrope during an earthquake.

Only Michael Curtis matched my brother stride for stride. His eyes, like Warren's, were fixed with steely fortitude.

The previous shroud of silence was broken by a bursting cacophony of cheers. Inaudible screams and words of instruction poured out from the swelling masses. Much of it was gibberish, but my memory is singed with phrases like "Move it along, Nino!" "Get the lead out, Luke!" and "Tie your shoelaces, Davey!" This last bit of advice was ill-timed, since a bewildered Master Peters appeared unsettled by his mother's instructions. He floated to the back of the athletes and by mid-race was hopelessly behind.

Warren and Michael scurried on, fiery grit and visions of a trophy dancing in their heads.

And then—this is where the story takes a turn for the worse—Miss Martino's voice rushed forth from the public address system, pouring out words that would haunt my family for years. No, decades. "Boys and girls, we are now serving ice cream at the registration table."

Without losing his pace, my brother Warren appeared to lose all interest in the race. He cut right in front of a befuddled Michael Curtis, and, moving as the crow flies, galloped toward the registration desk. He arrived moments before another eager young person, Karen Bell, who, less than gracefully, ended up on the soft side of her anatomy.

Back on the race course, presumably perplexed by Warren's strategy, Michael Curtis, Luke Wilson, Nino Greshner, and Roland

DiMucci stopped running. Well, to be fair, Roland had already stopped to ask for oxygen. Only the floppy-shoed Davey Peters carried on, inspired by the cackling voice of his mother, snapping at him like a rabid turtle. Lurching across the finish line, Davey raised his arms in the air and unceremoniously tripped over his shoelaces.

The onlookers became frenzied in the confusion. Michael Curtis, still staring off in the distance as my brother devoured an ice cream sandwich, got moving and lumbered across the finish line to finish second. He was followed by Nino, Luke, and, in due course, Roland.

Irate parents swarmed Vice-Principal Hyde with objections and vague accusations of unsportsmanlike conduct. One of the parents used the term *fixed* as if there had been wagers placed on a group of eight-year-olds.

Mrs. Curtis, at first, asked for a *recount* but corrected herself and instead requested that the race be run again.

Mr. Hyde would have none of it. He insisted that the results were final.

In the melee that had played out before us, my father had made his way over to Warren, who had the evidence of vanilla ice cream still on his chin.

"Warren, what were you thinking?" my baffled Dad asked.

"They announced that the ice cream was ready."

"But you were in the middle of a race!" My father was more dumbstruck than angry.

My brother paused for a very long time. He considered the plain facts of the incident. He had, indeed, by elementary school standards, been in a major sporting event. He cocked his head to one side to contemplate what had transpired. And then his eyes flashed with an epiphany. He smiled and looked bravely at my dad. "It's all about priorities!"

"Priorities?" My father quizzed.

"Yes. Priorities."

Warren meandered off, oblivious to the gaping expression of confusion that washed across my dad's face.

Twenty minutes later, Vice-Principal Hyde handed out the prizes. Davey Peters held a trophy that was about half his body

  Hot Apple Cider with Cinnamon

weight. Michael Curtis was given a red second place ribbon and Nino Greshner clutched the third place ribbon as if it were the culmination of his life's aspirations.

The great irony of it all was that each contestant was given a booklet with five coupons for free ice cream at the local Dairy Queen. The lone exception was my now-distraught brother Warren, who was denied the prize because he hadn't actually finished the race. Apparently the pursuit of his *priority* had excluded him from the winnings. As he edged toward tears, my mother patted him gently on the head. Even my father, who was still confounded by what had occurred, soothed Warren's crushed spirit with words of reassurance: "Everything will be okay."

I wasn't so sure. I could see the glumness in Warren's eyes and knew full well that he was doing the math on how much ice cream he had lost.

And then, the most marvellous thing unfolded.

Michael, Nino, Luke, Roland, and Davey approached en masse. They each tore a coupon out of their booklets. One by one, they handed Warren the single coupon.

Without the usual prodding it takes to remind a child to say thank you, Warren expressed gratitude to each of them. His voice was soft and humble. He now had five ice creams. It was one more than each of the other boys had remaining in their booklets.

Michael gave Warren a friendly shoulder punch and said, "That was a great race, Warren. You sure made us laugh."

My mother and father both smiled.

Warren looked up at them.

After doing a quick head count, he said, "There's just enough coupons for everyone else in the family to have an ice cream."

My surprised mother mustered a word of protest. "But—"

"I already had one," he answered.

We all piled into the family car and drove to the Dairy Queen. Each of us savoured an ice cream cone, including Warren. As it turned out, my father just happened to have the exact change for an extra ice cream cone in his pocket.

---

1. The laid-back deputy sheriff from *The Andy Griffith Show*.

Angel at Our Door

Nonfiction

Heather Rae Rodin

Insistent pounding on the door brought me quickly from my kitchen. With three little ones down for a nap, I hurried to answer before they were all awakened prematurely. We had just moved into the neighbourhood and I couldn't imagine who it would be.

Opening the door a crack revealed an old man dressed in dirty clothing, wearing mud-encrusted rubber boots. From his hand hung a torn plastic bag.

"Can I help you?" I asked, hoping he had the wrong address.

"Would ya like to buy some fresh garden vegetables?" His voice was shaky with age but his faded blue eyes were fastened on me with hopefulness.

"Are they from your garden?" Peering inside his shabby bag, I saw mostly dirt, with a hint of carrots.

"Yes." His voice was soft and scratchy. "And I kin get some apples from a tree in my yard. Would ya like some of those too?"

My heart softened at his neglected appearance, and I wondered if he desperately needed the bit of money he was asking for his wares. With a sigh, I gestured him in. "Please step inside and I'll get my purse."

The next day, he knocked at our door again.

This time, my gregarious little four-year-old got there first. "Oh, hello. Would you like to come in for tea?" Heidi's high-pitched-voice carried an adult inflection.

Without hesitating, the old man stepped inside and held out a broken basket with several bruised apples resting at the bottom. "From my tree," he said, removing a worn cap that had seen better days. "Thought ya might like to make a pie."

There was no mistaking the wistful glint in his eye.

The three of us sat at the kitchen table and sipped our tea, Heidi's cup containing a much weaker version. Sheer delight in hosting a visitor was evident in her never-ending stream of questions. "What is your name? Where do you live? Why are your clothes so dirty? Will your mother be mad at you?"

The homeless-looking man chuckled as he attempted to answer each question. His name was Mr. Locket and he lived around the corner. His wife had passed away several years before, and his children all lived far away. He was lonely. His need for companionship had sent him door to door under the ruse of selling vegetables. Ours was the only door opened to him that day.

Eventually, the cookies gone and the interrogation slowing, he struggled to his feet. Shuffling his way to the door, he turned and offered us a cheerful grin and a wave goodbye.

As I watched him limp painfully to an ancient bicycle propped against our house, my heart melted with compassion.

Once on his bike, he wobbled back down the road, perhaps a little less lonely than before. He had promised to return tomorrow, and I knew what I wanted to do.

The next day, the children excitedly awaited his visit. The table was set with china and silver, with fancy napkins folded neatly beside each plate. A small bouquet of garden flowers, picked by little hands, adorned the centre of the table. Tantalizing aromas of cinnamon and sugar filled the house as a steaming apple pie beckoned from the table.

As he entered the kitchen, he took in the efforts made on his behalf, and his eyes filled with unshed tears. He focused on the golden-crusted, sugar-topped, apple pie. Pulling up a chair beside my two little girls, he immediately seemed at home, and we watched with amazement as he devoured half the dessert.

Wiping his whiskery lips, he commented, "Yur pies sure taste a lot better'n mine!"

My curiosity was piqued. "How do you make your pies?"

"Well, I just cut up them apples and put 'em in a pan. Then I bake 'em."

I smiled. A few simple tips would help him create at least a better version to enjoy.

The next day, we found a basket sitting on the step. Inside were several rosy apples.

Another pie was slipped into the oven that night.

As the days wore on, Mr. Locket became a daily visitor to our active home. In his quiet and gentle way, he endeared himself to each child. I loved to peek around the kitchen door and watch as he sat in our big comfy chair with one or two little ones curled up on his lap, gazing up at him with rapt attention as he read a children's book or told a story.

Mr. Locket became an honorary member of our family. When the wee ones were tucked into their beds for an afternoon nap, he would rest his weary head on the back of the chair and join the babies in slumber. He usually went home when the sun dipped low in the sky, but stayed for dinner if pie was on the menu.

Our lively family antics at the dinner table always brought a smile to his weathered face. Later, as my husband put the children to bed, I'd stand in the doorway watching this dear old friend pedal his way home in the dark.

One day he revealed a hidden passion. "Ya know, I used to go to the library and get books ta read. It helps fill in the long, quiet nights. Don't rightly feel like riding that far any more, though. S'pose you could lend me a book?"

"That's a wonderful idea!" I couldn't believe we hadn't discussed this sooner. I too loved to read and delighted in sharing books. "What if I put a stack beside your chair for you to read during your visits, and then you can take home anything you want to finish?" His answering smile said it all.

It was fun to see which books he selected and watch him disappear between the pages. He still read to the children each day, and the name "Grandpa Locket" slipped effortlessly into our conversations. Both sets of my children's grandparents lived far away, so the children missed having them attend their Sunday school concerts and Christmas pageants. Although extremely deaf, Mr. Locket was now the grandpa that came to "Ooh" and "Ahh" over each little one's part in the programs.

"Did you hear me, Mr. Locket?" Heidi would chirp.

"Well, I didn't rightly hear ya, but I know it was good!"

Heidi would beam, her tiny hand grasping his old gnarled one. The two had become best friends.

Three years after first meeting Grandpa Locket, we learned we were being moved across the country to Ontario. All that night, I tossed and turned. Pink sky began to peek through the window before I'd found a gentle way to break the news to Grandpa Locket.

When he arrived that morning, I took a deep breath and blurted it out. "Mr. Locket," I began, my voice wobbling. "We're going to be moving very soon. We're all very sad. You've become a treasured part of this family and we—we—we'll miss you."

The old man's chin slowly dropped to his chest as reality hit. Moisture glistened in the corners of his eyes, and threatened to escape.

Swallowing the lump in my throat, I took his worn, calloused hands in mine. "I promise to keep in touch with you and write letters regularly. The kids will send you pictures, and I'll ship as many books as you can read." My throat tightened and I couldn't speak any more.

He nodded and softly said, "Thank you for all your kindnesses to an old man. When I was lonely, ya took me in. When I needed a family, ya included me. My life's bin happy cuz of you." He reached down and rested his free hand on Heidi's head, gazing at her as if memorizing every delicate feature.

During our last visit together, we all hugged him tightly.

Without looking back, the old man limped out the door, straddled his rusty bike, and pedalled down the road.

With heavy hearts, we watched the familiar figure disappear around the corner for the last time. As we closed the door, we knew that a part of our lives was drawing to a close and a new stage was beginning, but no matter where we were, we'd never forget this incredibly precious man.

I kept my word and wrote regularly. The kids made him pictures, and I mailed books every month. We never received a letter in return, but somehow we knew he anxiously checked his mailbox every day to see if anything had arrived from us.

About a year later, a small envelope was delivered to our home—a letter from Mr. Locket's daughter. She informed us that our dear old friend had passed away. She'd found the letters, pictures, and gifts that we had sent, carefully tucked away in one of his dresser drawers. "I'm so grateful for your loving care for my father," she wrote. "I can see how much you meant to him, too."

With tremendous sadness, my husband and I shared this news with the children. Although we grieved the loss of our friend, we also felt a sense of joy. Remembering his gentle spirit and spontaneous chuckle made us smile. And how would we ever forget his love for apple pie?

We still feel it wasn't just an old man who knocked on our door that day, but an angel in disguise. We're so grateful for the unexpected love that swept into our lives the moment we opened that door.

  Hot Apple Cider with Cinnamon

Unto Us a Child Is Given

Nonfiction

Catharina den Hartog-Terry

One wintry December evening some years ago, I was sitting quietly, listening to a choir sing Handel's majestic piece, *Messiah*. Some of the words from Part 1— "For unto us a Child is born, unto us a Son is given"[1]—rang in my heart over and over. I knew this was a quotation from the book of Isaiah and referred to Jesus, but I began to ponder the meaning of the words for me.

I remembered Christmas Eves when I was a young choir member, carefully clutching one faltering candle as I followed the procession down the aisle of our darkened church. The magic of the darkness was slowly dispelled as multitudes of flickering lights from everywhere created a massive glow of warmth and light.

Then, at the front of the church, we children stood and gazed at baby Jesus—a smiling plastic doll wrapped neatly in a blue flannel blanket, lying in a roughly hewn wooden cradle with clean hay placed strategically around its face and body. It would be years before I would see a deeper meaning in the life of that baby in the manger.

Now, as an older adult, I pondered the wonder of God's entrusting His own precious Son to be born to an ordinary Galilean girl, Mary, who willingly surrendered her heart, her reputation, and her body to become Jesus' mom here on earth.

I could just imagine the whisperings behind closed doors as Mary tried to share the angelic news, the cost of her "yes" to God, and the implications of her lifelong loyalty to her Son. I thought of the baby's birth in a humble stable with only the comforting presence of her husband, Joseph, and gazing barnyard animals, no doubt curious about this intrusion into their domain.

The harsh ring of our telephone shattered my thoughts and I reached for the receiver.

"Mrs. Terry?" a voice asked.

"That's me," I replied, not recognizing the voice.

"Would you and your husband be willing to care for your newborn granddaughter?"

"I—I—"

I learned that my granddaughter, who'd been born prematurely two months before, was nearly ready to leave the hospital, but it now appeared that her parents were unable to take care of her. Would we be willing to take responsibility?

"I—I'll have to talk this over with my husband," I stammered, struggling for words, not knowing what to say.

"I'll call you back, Mrs. Terry. We'd like a decision by tomorrow, if possible. The baby will be discharged from hospital soon and we wanted to ask you first before we asked anyone else."

That evening when my husband came home from work, I presented the question to him. He looked me straight in the eyes and, without a moment's hesitation, said, "Of course, we'll take her! When is she coming?" The question was settled.

I began to think, *What will I need for a baby?* Years ago, in one of my fits of clutter reform, I had passed along boxes of hand-knitted baby sweaters, booties, and smocked dresses. How I wished I had them now! But, miraculously, as word of our upcoming arrival got out, clothes and baby items began to arrive from everywhere.

"I have too much baby stuff," one young mom said as she presented me with a bag of new clothes, bottles, and more. A neighbour I barely knew delivered a baby swing, which would provide hours of soothing music and motion so I could prepare meals and do some much-needed housework. Other neighbours offered to babysit "any time you need."

Several evenings later, dark-haired, five-pound Esmeralda entered our home and our hearts. Having been a "three-pound-and-something" preemie, she'd been on a regimented schedule during her weeks at the hospital. Feeding, burping, changing, and sleep times, I was instructed, were to occur with strict and frequent regularity. This was something I hadn't even considered. My own babies were definitely not tiny; nor did they need coaxing to feed.

We soon devised a "plan to survive." This included my husband helping me with the dreaded middle-of-the-night feeding, when I was known to stumble around incoherently and ask, "What on earth was I thinking?"

Still, one question remained. Were we, as sixty-something grandparents, the right ones to open our hearts and all we had to little Esmeralda? Or would a younger couple have more to offer this precious little one, already so dear to us? The question was painful and continued to linger in our minds.

One night, after doing the three a.m. feeding, my husband slipped quietly into bed. I snuggled up to him and was surprised to notice he'd been crying.

"What's the matter, sweetheart?" I asked anxiously.

He didn't answer right away. Then, in a hushed voice, he said tenderly, "When I was holding Ezzie and feeding her, it was as if she told me something. She said, 'No matter what the circumstances were that brought me to your home, I want you to take care of me.'"

That settled the question for us. And after that, the other difficulties were easy to overcome.

One forty-something man approached me at Costco and proudly announced, "My wife and I had a baby while in our forties too, you know!"

I chuckled and said enthusiastically, "Good for you! I'm in my sixties, though, and I'll be eighty when Ezzie's grown! So I'd better keep in shape!"

There were other comments that stretched my patience, even though I was always given wisdom to answer. One well-meaning friend felt I'd stolen my husband's golden years of retirement away from him and, because of Ezzie, his lifelong dreams could never be realized.

"He's as committed to her as I am," I informed him. "In fact, at times, even more so. Besides," I expounded, "in Africa there are millions of orphans being cared for by grannies because their parents have died of AIDS. They live in huts with many little ones and no running water. They cook over an open fire and wash the children's clothes by hand. They have no car to run to the store for milk. They milk goats and hoe and weed gardens in order to feed their little ones. Their biggest worries are 'Where is the next meal coming from?' and 'How will I care for the little ones when I get too old or feeble?' God has blessed us with so much," I told him passionately, "why wouldn't we care for her?"

At that moment, Ezzie gave me a knowing smile and put her head on my chest as if to say, "Come on, Oma, rock me to sleep and sing me that song again. Remember? 'Unto us a child is born, unto us a son is given....'"

1. Isaiah 9:6

     Hot Apple Cider with Cinnamon

A Grandmother's Promise

Connie Inglis

Her soft, pudgy
hand reaches
for the straw,
the last straw,
white with green stripes.

"That was the last straw,
Grandma," she says,
slight wrinkles forming
on her brow between
true baby blues.

"Yes, the last straw,"
I repeat, smiling
at her attention to,
her care over,
this last straw.

In time, her concerns
will grow from
straws to friendships,
to school, to boys,
to career choice,

to life…

Silently, I commit
to being there for her,
whenever possible,
with another
box of straws.

Dancing on the Bus

Nonfiction

Lynne Collier

When I was four years old, I spent a special day at the seaside with my great-aunt, Ada, and a bus full of pensioners on one of their frequent day trips. This day, they had gone to Blackpool, a favourite place for an outing in the north of England.

Aunty Ada sometimes took me along on a day trip. She had no children of her own, and I was an only child and quite often lonely. She liked to show me off in my pretty frock and patent-leather shoes. On this trip, as was normal on the pensioner's bus trips, I was the only child.

Evening was drawing in and we were all exhausted from the long day at the seaside, so Aunty Ada dried my feet from wading in the water and we all lined up to get into the coach for the long drive home.

As the coach pulled away from the damp, overcast sands, the adults started singing pub songs, mostly from the Second World War. I knew some of the words because my grandmother owned a tavern, and when I spent weekends at her house, which was adjacent to the tavern, I would lie in my bed listening to the patrons singing and laughing. I loved the sense of friendship the songs created in those who joined in. And I just knew these people were all nice and friendly. That's all that matters, pretty much, when you're four.

I knelt backwards in my seat, peering over the top, so I could watch everyone laugh as they sang, *"On Ilkley Moor Bhat 'At."*[1] Giggling, I grimaced at the words about being eaten by worms.

I fidgeted in my seat until I couldn't restrain myself any longer. I jumped up and pirouetted in the aisle. Arms flinging wildly and toes pointing every which way, I danced up and down the aisle to the old war songs and laments for the fallen heroes. They even threw in a few ancient hymns for good measure.

I skipped and held my pretty new dress like a true ballerina, until I collapsed back into my seat to thunderous applause and shouts of delight. Everyone was smiling and I felt loved and accepted by these strangers who encouraged me to be totally free—to be me.

Usually when I wanted to express my soul and my love for God, which I had yet to understand, I would be told to sit down and behave. But that night, with my great-aunt Ada and a bus full of strangers, I felt accepted and adored—loved as God loves, pure and unconditionally.

The bus rocked as we drove along, down bumpy winding roads, past endless street lamps that created rhythmic flashes of light as we neared home. It began to rain. The drizzle on the window lulled me to sleep as I snuggled against my aunt, feeling content and full of joy.

Years later, as an adult and mother living in Canada, I've been privileged to see this same love poured out onto one of my own children. My two girls grew up without challenges with respect to development and social interaction. My son Benjamin, however, was quite delayed, and was later diagnosed as having autism. He struggled through his childhood, not fitting in with the other children and wondering what he was doing wrong at every turn.

During his time in the public school system, he was teased by the other children and frowned upon by a number of unsympathetic adults. But his Grade 1 teacher was a wonderful, caring woman who took the time to ask why he behaved the way he did. She was determined to understand him and to accept him as he was.

One day he came home with a note from his teacher. She suggested I go to the school library. They were having a sale, and she thought my son would like one of the books.

I couldn't go for a couple of days and was concerned I'd missed the opportunity. When I finally went to the school, his teacher told me that the sale had ended but that the library had saved the book for my little boy. I suspect the teacher had paid for it out of her own pocket.

It was a peek-a-boo book with a place for a photo. On each page there was an outline of an animal and a hole so that the face in the photo appeared to be the face of the animal.

My son loved it! Through that book, he saw that he could be anything he wanted to be: a cat, an octopus, a dinosaur—even a frog!

His teacher had taken the time to observe and understand him and had discovered a way to help him reach out of his own world and join ours through a story-board book. She had shown love to my autistic child just as those strangers had shown love to me on that bus so many years before.

How many of us have struggled with our own unique design because of the lack of freedom to discover and express who we are? No, I didn't turn out to be a prima ballerina (although I did study with the British Ballet Company in our home town for several years before emigrating to Canada). My son, however, was a child actor and performed for seven years with a Toronto casting agency. He is now a published author who writes fantasy and science-fiction![2] Who would have guessed?

> "Your greatest contribution to the Kingdom of God may not
> be something you do, but someone you raise."
> —Andy Stanley

---

1. A popular folk song from Yorkshire, England, sung in the Yorkshire dialect.

2. https://benjaminfrog.wordpress.com

Breaking Alvin's Fast

Fiction

Marcia Lee Laycock

Alvin Ford stopped in the middle of the empty parking lot and leaned on his cane. He pushed his worn cowboy hat back, stared at the boarded-up windows, and sighed. First time in 15 years he wouldn't have his breakfast at the Co-op Diner. He'd known it was closing, of course, but he hadn't really believed it until this minute.

There were only two other places to get breakfast. One always burned his toast, and the other made coffee that tasted like dishwater. He sighed again. Guess he'd try one this morning, the other tomorrow, and then choose.

He turned north and forced his crooked legs to carry him the two blocks to Main Street. Teetering, he passed Alberta's Best Small Town Hardware Store and Hair's to You Beauty Salon. Looking across the street, he spotted a freshly painted sign that read, "Restaurant." It hung over the spot where Jack's Men's Wear used to be.

When did that happen? Alvin wondered. He crossed the street. *Might as well check it out.* The smell of fresh paint assaulted him as he reached the yellow facade. "Liked it better brown," he mumbled. The large plate glass window to the left of the entry was completely gone. Two weathered sheets of plywood covered it. Alvin remembered the display of cowboy boots and hats Jack had always been so proud of.

Two small tables were arranged on the sidewalk in front of the boarded-up window.

Grunting, Alvin stepped through the door, missing the jangle of cow bells Jack used to have hanging there. Small tables and chairs, all empty, filled the gloomy room. He glanced back at the tables on the sidewalk. Early morning sunlight streamed over them. He shuffled back outside. The chair scraped loudly as he pulled it out and sat.

"Morning."

Alvin started at the old man approaching with a pad of paper in his hand.

He was smiling. "What you like? Eggs and bacon special today."

Black hair and moustache, a beard tinged with grey. Black eyes. Olive skin. Long nose. Alvin thought of the news on TV, stories filled with men with black eyes and long noses. He had stopped watching the news. But he needed his coffee.

Alvin jerked the front of his hat down. "Coffee," he said. "Black."

Still smiling, the man nodded. "Come right up."

Alvin watched him hobble away, swinging one leg out and letting it flop down as his body lurched over it.

The smile was still in place when the man returned. "Best coffee this place." He slid the big mug onto the table. "Good strong coffee."

"Yeah, we'll see." Alvin took a sip.

The old man hovered.

Alvin scowled. "Want something?"

The man gave a quick bow. "Sorry, I not mean offence." He hobbled away.

Alvin took another gulp of coffee. Then another, and another. He banged the empty mug on the table.

The man appeared, coffeepot in hand.

Alvin quickly downed the second cup. "That's coffee," he mumbled.

"Yes." The man bobbed his whole body. "Best coffee this place."

Alvin frowned as he considered his options. He decided he wouldn't risk the bacon and eggs. He pushed himself up and took a step toward the door. "How much?"

The man straightened. "No charge. You first customer. Come back, please."

Alvin grunted and shuffled past him without saying thank you.

The next morning, Alvin's mouth watered for that coffee.

The old man brought a mug and coffeepot, setting them down on the small table, his pencil poised above his writing pad.

  Hot Apple Cider with Cinnamon

Alvin squinted at him. "How come you took thet window out?"

The man blinked. "Someone throw rock," he said. "But we need open. Need make money." He looked out onto the street. "In my country, many sit outside for coffee time."

Alvin pushed his hat back. "You got bacon and eggs on special today?"

The man nodded. "Three dollars ninety-nine."

"You know what "over easy" means?"

"Daughter know. She cook good."

Alvin snorted. "Over easy. Not hard, ya hear? And bacon. Crisp."

The man scribbled on his pad. "Not hard," he said. "Crisp." He made his way back inside.

"And more coffee," Alvin called out.

The man turned, smiling from ear to ear. "Best coffee, yes?"

"Not bad."

Alvin watched the people on the street just as he'd watched people in the Co-op every morning for 15 years. Fifteen years. He couldn't believe it had been that long since he'd moved from the farm into town. That meant it'd been eight since Effie passed on. Effie. He lifted the rim of his hat just a bit, then tugged it back into place. No use lingering on that.

He drained his mug just as the man reappeared and placed Alvin's breakfast on the table.

Alvin poked at the eggs.

The man poured more coffee.

Alvin gave a quick nod of his head.

"Over easy, okay?" The man asked, eyes hopeful.

"Yeah. Okay," Alvin said. "Let me eat."

The man bobbed and disappeared.

Alvin ate. Then he sat for a long time, staring at the passers-by. The old man kept his mug full.

When Alvin got up to pay, he tipped his hat back. "You one o' them Arabs?" he asked.

The man hesitated. Then a grin stretched his face and he stuck out his hand. "Osa—" He hesitated, his eyes darting back and forth. "Sammy," he said, followed by a string of words Alvin didn't understand. Alvin didn't shake hands.

The old man's grin faded. He blinked and stammered. "Sam—Sammy," he said. "My name Sammy."

Alvin shifted his cane from one hand to the other, tugged the brim of his hat, and teetered off down the street.

The next morning, Sammy bobbed and grinned as a scowling Alvin sat down at the same table on the sidewalk.

Sammy brought him coffee and bacon and eggs over easy. He refilled his coffee cup, hovering. "You live here long time?" he asked after the third cup.

Alvin grunted. "All my life."

Sammy nodded. "Good to live one place. Children grow well. Wife happy. Yes?"

Alvin's eyes narrowed. "Wife's dead," he said.

Sammy's face folded into grief. "So sorry. So sorry."

Alvin waved his hand. "Long time ago. Over eight years now."

"You have daughter? She cook good?"

"No daughter," Alvin said. "One boy. Lives in Calgary. Never see him."

Sammy's gaze rested on his feet. "Sammy has three boy. Boy dead. Four years now."

Alvin frowned. "You mean you had four boys? One died?"

Sammy shook his head. Alvin saw the thin line of moisture about to spill out of his eyes. "No boy. Boy all dead."

Alvin looked away from the raw grief.

"Bombs," Sammy said.

Alvin's head jerked up and his eyes widened, but he still said nothing.

Sammy poured him another cup of coffee and sighed. "But daughter is good girl, good girl. God is good."

Alvin tugged on the rim of his hat. *Good? What God would take all of a man's sons and still seem good to him?* Alvin thought of all the times he'd cursed God. As far as Alvin Ford was concerned, God was good for nothing.

He left his money on the table.

The next morning, Sammy asked about Alvin's legs.

Mind yer own business, he thought. But when Sammy poured his coffee and just stood there, Alvin answered.

"Horse fell on 'em." He squinted at the old man. "What happen t' yours?"

"House fell," Sammy said.

"A house fell on you?"

Sammy nodded. "Bombs fall, house fall."

Alvin grunted. "Yeah, I guess it would."

Sammy's face brightened. "Over easy?"

"Over easy." Alvin finished the eggs without tasting them, left a tip on the table, and headed home.

He stared at his house for a long time before going in. It wasn't much—a small bungalow his son had found after Alvin's legs were crushed and they had to leave the farm. *Johnny got us a good price on this little house*, he thought. *It's got a good foundation, solid roof.* He grunted. *Long as no bomb gets dropped on it.*

He hobbled inside, the floor creaking as his cane tapped down the hallway. The wall was full of pictures. Effie's doing. She'd taken pictures of Johnny every year. Framed each one their daughter-in-law Elizabeth sent of the grandkids. A new one still arrived every Christmas. Alvin couldn't remember where he'd put them.

The photo of Johnny at his college graduation stared back at him. He took it down and went into the kitchen where the light was better. The boy looked a lot like his mother. *It's the eyes*, Alvin thought. He propped the photo up against the sugar bowl, got to his feet, and went into the living room, the cane muffled by carpeting. He settled in his recliner, stared at the phone for a while, then picked up the directory. Johnny's number was on the inside of the front cover. Alvin dialled.

Elizabeth answered.

Alvin cleared his throat and asked for Johnny.

She sounded surprised. "Johnny's not home, Dad," she said. "But I'm glad you called."

"Where is he?" Alvin asked.

"At work." He heard the smile in her voice. "It's only eleven a.m."

"Oh, yeah. Forgot."

There was silence for a minute. He opened his mouth to say goodbye when she asked, "So, what's new up there?"

"Co-op closed."

"I heard that."

He was surprised she knew. "Found a place with good coffee, though. Guy named Sammy runs it."

"Oh? That's good. That's real good."

"Yeah, well, I gotta go."

"Dad? There's nothing wrong, is there?"

"No, course not." He gripped his cane and shifted in the chair.

"Okay. Well, I… we've been…"

"What?"

She sighed. "We've been thinking about you… praying for you. I've been praying—well, I've been praying that God would send you… someone…"

Alvin heard her take a deep breath.

"Now don't get mad, Dad, okay?" Her words came in a rush. "I've been praying for a friend, someone who'd tell you how good God is."

In the silence, Alvin heard Sammy's voice, talking about losing three sons and saying, "God is good." Alvin shook his head. "Yeah, well, I guess that's okay," he said. "Gotta go now."

"Okay, Dad. John will call when he gets home, okay?"

"Yeah. But not early in the morning. I go to Sammy's in the morning."

"Tonight, then."

Alvin hesitated. "Tell him… tell him I'll wait up."

  Hot Apple Cider with Cinnamon

Storm Stayed

Fiction

Shelley Norman

A white, swirling cloud of snow encircled the old pickup truck. Molly leaned forward over the steering wheel trying to get her face as close to the windshield as possible, not that it improved her ability to see any. She reached out a red-mittened hand to adjust the defroster to a higher setting. The wipers squeaked as they flew back and forth in a vain effort to keep the snow from collecting on the windshield.

Not for the first time that day Molly was grateful she'd taken her uncle's advice and spent the extra money for four-wheel drive when she'd moved back to Canada in the fall.

When Molly had agreed to take this job at her uncle's garden centre, working in the Christmas tree lot for now and in the greenhouses after the new year, she hadn't realized just how bad the weather got in rural Ontario. Uncle Jeff had tried to warn her, but having spent most of her childhood in the southern United States where her parents had been transferred when she was seven, she'd pooh-poohed his warnings of "lake effect snow" and "white-outs." Now she was seeing firsthand just what "snowing horizontally" meant.

Fortunately, she had only one delivery left for today—to Meadow Creek Farms. Since the weather was getting worse, she'd decided to drop it off on her way home. Uncle Jeff had said she couldn't miss the farm: after turning off the highway, just follow Concession 7 for about five kilometres, and there'd be a large aluminum mailbox at the entrance to the laneway.

Molly checked her odometer again. It had been almost five kilometres. Now where could the turnoff be? But all she could see out the windows was white in every direction. In fact, Molly couldn't even be sure where the edge of the road was. *Lord, please keep me safe*, she prayed.

Slowing down to less than a crawl, Molly searched for any shadow that might be a mailbox. Thud! Crunch! She braked and the truck stopped dead.

Great! Molly thought. Pulling her hood up over her red, curly hair, and tugging the coat zipper up as high as it would go, Molly got out of the truck to see what she'd hit. An aluminum mailbox lay crumpled under the front bumper of her truck, the broken post still attached. Wiping the accumulated snow from the box, Molly read the name "Meadow Creek Farms" painted in black on the side. *Great! I've killed the customer's mailbox.*

Climbing back into her pickup, Molly looked over at her dog, Sadie, still sound asleep on her old blanket on the passenger side seat. A rescue dog that Molly had adopted shortly after arriving back in Canada, Sadie was elderly, with soft brown fur, large brown eyes, and floppy ears. The vet said she was most likely some type of spaniel mix. And apparently nothing could wake Sadie from her nap—including mailbox homicide.

Putting the truck in reverse, Molly attempted to back up, but even with the four-wheel drive, she couldn't get it to move.

Great!

Digging in her purse, she pulled out her cell phone and a copy of the delivery slip for the tree. Punching in the phone number for Meadow Creek Farms, she listened to the phone ring, once, twice, three times.

"Hello?" came a breathless male voice.

"Yes, hello. This is Molly from Addam's Garden Centre. I'm delivering your Christmas tree—"

"Oh, don't worry about bringing it out today. There's a terrible snow storm going on. It's not important enough to come out in a storm for."

"Well, actually, I'm already here. I mean, I'm at the end of your laneway. Would it be okay if I just leave the tree here beside your mailbox? Well, what's left of your mailbox?"

"What's *left* of my mailbox?"

"Um, I had a bit of trouble finding your lane and I drove into your mailbox. But you can feel free to send me a bill for the damages. I'm very sorry, by the way. About smashing it."

  Hot Apple Cider with Cinnamon

"That's okay. You didn't get hurt, did you? What about your truck?"

"I'm fine, and so is my truck. But it's stuck, so I'll just call a tow truck to come and pull me out."

"I hate to be the bearer of bad news, but I'm afraid the highway just closed, and you'll have to wait until it reopens to call a tow truck."

"Oh. They close the highway for a snow storm?"

"They do. There's no way you'll be able to get a ride into town either. Tell you what, I'll come down and get you with the snow-mobile and you can stay here until the highway opens."

"Oh. That's very kind of you but not necessary. I've got an emergency kit in the truck. Little Sadie and I will be just fine here until the highway opens."

"You've got a kid with you? You can't stay in a cold truck for what might be hours, if not days. I'll be right there."

"Sadie isn't a kid, she's a—" But he'd already hung up.

Hearing her name, Sadie finally opened her eyes and raised her head to look at Molly quizzically.

"Great," Molly said to her pet, "what have we gotten ourselves into? This guy might be an axe murderer who preys on helpless women and dogs stuck in snow storms."

Sadie tilted her head to the right, raising a furry eyebrow.

"Well, you never know."

Sadie put her head back down on her blanket and shut her eyes. Apparently she wasn't worried.

Molly picked up her cell phone again and dialled the garden centre. "Uncle Jeff," she said when he picked up. "I'm out at Meadow Creek Farms, and the guy here says the highway is closed. He wants me to stay here until the storm is done and the highway opens, and I'm not sure that's a good idea. I don't know this guy. What if he's a psycho or something?"

Uncle Jeff laughed. "I've heard little Stevie Scott called many things, but never a psycho. Oh, he's salt of the earth, that one. I remember the day his cat climbed up to the top of old Miss Grey-son's oak tree. Stevie climbed up to rescue it, and he got stuck up there, too. His poor mother, at her wits end, had to call the fire department to get them both down."

"But that was—"

"Oh, and there was the time at the church Christmas pageant when Stevie was playing a sheep and thought that it would be really good for authenticity to eat the hay in the manager. He ended up choking on it and the young woman playing Mary had to use the Heimlich manoeuvre to save him. Oh, that was a good one."

"Thanks for that trip down memory lane, Uncle Jeff, but what am I going to do? I can't just stay out in the middle of nowhere with a guy I've never met before."

"Oh, you'll be just fine. He's a real nice guy. Goes to our church, belongs to the men's Bible study group. A true Christian through and through. He won't harm a hair on your head. And on the radio they're saying the storm should blow out some time tomorrow."

"Are you su—"

"See you then, Molly. Gotta go. Bye now."

Molly stared at her phone in disbelief. Her uncle had just told her to spend the night at the house of a strange guy in the middle of Timbuktu.

Whamp! Whamp! Molly's heart jumped into her throat. Someone was banging on her window.

Turning to the left, she nearly shrieked at the balaclava-clad face pressed to the glass.

"Molly?" It sounded like the male voice she had heard earlier on the phone.

She rolled the window down a crack. "Um… Hello again. Really, it wasn't necessary to come down. We can just wait the storm out here."

"Nonsense! I've got a nice warm fire going up at the house; it'll be much warmer for your little girl up there. Now bundle her up and I'll stick the tree on the sled behind the snowmobile."

"But she's not a kid—" Once again, though, he was gone before the words had even left her mouth.

Seeing no option, Molly stuck her keys in her purse, slung it around her neck, wrapped up Sadie in her blanket and picked her up, then climbed out of the truck.

Stevie had just finished tying the tree to the sled when Molly approached the snowmobile. Climbing on the snowmobile first,

Stevie reached for the bundle in Molly's arms. "Here, let me hold her while you climb on."

Molly reluctantly climbed on behind him. Reaching back, he carefully handed the bundle back to Molly. "Sure is a small kid. Good thing I didn't let you talk me into letting you stay out here; she'd have frozen."

Molly didn't even try to dissuade him this time.

Grasping Sadie tightly with one arm, she clung to Stevie with the other.

The snowmobile moved quickly through the storm, the strong wind tearing the breath right out of Molly, the biting snow stinging her face, she ducked her head down lower against Stevie's back. She was glad when the shadow of the house appeared ahead of them.

Opening the door of the house, Stevie gestured for Molly to enter while he retrieved the tree from the sled. She stepped into a brightly lit kitchen, which looked tidy except for a number of dusty cardboard boxes on the table and floor.

Stevie followed her in, leaning the snow-covered tree in a corner. Then he turned back into the closed in porch to remove his snow-covered clothes.

When he re-entered the kitchen, Molly's breath caught. She didn't know what she had been expecting "little Stevie Scott" to look like, but it sure wasn't the six feet of pure muscle standing before her. With dark brown curly hair and deep, chocolate brown eyes to match, he was a complete package in the looks department.

"Well, don't just stand there staring," he said. "Make yourself at home."

Molly felt her cheeks getting hot. She had indeed been staring. "Ah, thanks. This is very kind of you, Stevie."

He tipped his head back and roared in laughter. "Stevie? No one under the age of 60 has called me that in at least 15 years. Please call me Steve."

Molly's cheeks felt hotter. "I'm sorry, but that's how my Uncle Jeff referred to you."

The charming smile he gave her made her heart flip. "No damage. Now let's get that little one of yours unbundled before she melts in there."

Molly looked down. "Ah, here's the thing. Sadie isn't—"

Hearing her name, Sadie began to squirm until the blanket fell from her head, revealing a wet black nose in a brown furry face.

"—a kid."

Steve stared for a moment, then burst out laughing again. Molly liked the sound of his laughter. Wiping the tears from his eyes he said, "No wonder I thought that was the smallest kid I've come across in ages."

Molly relaxed. "No kids. It's just me and Sadie against the world."

She finished unwrapping Sadie and put the little dog on the floor, where Sadie promptly began sniffing the boxes.

"Do you need to let your family know where you're staying so they aren't worried when you don't make it home tonight?" Steve asked.

"I called Uncle Jeff from the truck, so he knows where I am. Sadie and I live alone so there are no roommates to wonder where we are. Or boyfriends," she added with a sigh. "I only moved here recently, so I haven't had much opportunity to make friends." Then, embarrassed that she'd said so much and anxious to change the topic Molly asked, "Just moving in?"

"No," Steve answered. "This is my grandparents' house. I've been staying here since the start of the school year when I took over the job of phys ed teacher at the high school in town. I was upstairs searching for my granny's boxes of Christmas decorations when you called. It's dark and cold up in the attic, so I thought I'd bring the last of the boxes down here to look through."

Well, that explains the breathlessness when he answered the phone. And the kick-butt physique.

"Now, where are my manners? You must be hungry. It's getting late." Steve opened the refrigerator.

Molly checked her watch. It was already seven, well past what she'd learned was the common suppertime in this rural area. "Really, I don't want to be a burden. It's kind enough of you to let us stay in the house."

"Don't be silly. I rarely have company, so it will be nice to have someone to eat dinner with for a change."

As Steve rifled through the fridge, Molly relaxed. It was clear that she wasn't in any danger here. *Lord, thank you for helping me find a safe place to stay during this storm.* She slipped out of her winter coat and hung it on the back of a chair, then left her boots near the door. She approached Steve. "Let me help, okay?"

"Fine with me," Steve said. "We've got mac 'n' cheese with hot dogs or frozen pizza. What's your pick?"

It was Molly's turn to laugh, "My, my, what gourmet choices. How about the pizza?"

"Sounds good to me," he said, pulling a pepperoni pizza from the freezer section of the fridge.

They sat in front of the living room fire to eat. After Steve said grace, which included a thank you for the dinner companions, which made Molly blush again, they dug into the pizza. Sadie got more than her fair share, as was evidenced by the streaks of tomato sauce on her nose.

When the meal was finished, the dishes had been placed in the dishwasher, and Sadie had had a much-needed potty break, Steve headed over to the corner where he'd dumped the Christmas tree and began cutting off the strings tied around the branches. "I know you're supposed to let trees stand for a day before decorating them, but this one isn't frozen and it looks as if the branches will fall okay. Would you like to help me set it up and decorate it tonight?"

Molly hesitated. She loved decorating of any kind. But... "Don't you want to wait and do that with your family, or your girlfriend?"

Steve laughed. "No girlfriend, and my family won't be able to join me for Christmas this year. Granny and Gramps are having a 'snow free' Christmas at the seniors' complex in Florida, where they moved last year. That's why I'm house sitting until they decide what to do with this place. And my parents are spending the holidays with my sister and her family in Alberta."

"That's too bad. Christmas is more fun with family around. But I'd be honoured to help. Do you know where the tree stand is?" Molly asked.

Steve found the tree stand in the third box he looked in, then set up the tree in the living room corner next to the fireplace.

Following Steve's directions, Molly found a pitcher in the cupboards, and brought water to fill the basin. Once that was done, they searched through the rest of the boxes to find the ones containing the decorations.

"Wow, these are the tidiest strings of lights I've ever seen," Molly said. "Ours are always tangled up in about a hundred knots, and it takes an hour to get them sorted."

Steve smiled. "Granny is a stickler about the lights. She hates wasted time and always says that taking the extra five minutes to wrap them on cardboard as they come off the tree saves hours the next year having to untangle them. She's right of course; she always is."

Pulling a shoe box out of a larger cardboard box, Molly laughed as she peeked inside. "Oh, these are cute little ornaments."

Steve groaned as he saw which "ornaments" she was referring to. "I can't believe Granny kept those all these years. My sister and I made them in Sunday school when we were little." Picking up a strange concoction of Popsicle sticks, glitter, and pompoms, he added, "*Very* little."

"I think they're sweet. Look, I think this one is supposed to be Santa's sleigh."

Steve grinned. "Actually, that's supposed to be the Baby Jesus in his manger."

"Oh. Well, it's still very creative and special. I'm going to hang it right here." Molly placed the ornament in the very centre of the front of the tree.

"Good grief, hide the thing in the back where no one will see it!" Steve reached for the ornament.

Molly smacked his hand away. "You wanted me to help; now don't undo my work. It looks perfect right where it is."

Steve laughed. "You're the boss."

Molly felt her cheeks getting hot again.

Once the last decoration was hung, Molly and Steve stood back and looked at their handiwork. "Okay, it looks really good," Steve said with a grin. "Even with the ornaments you put on the front."

"I think they make it special, don't you?"

  Hot Apple Cider with Cinnamon

"Yeah, you could be right."

Molly raised her hand to hide a yawn.

Steve looked at his watch. "I'm sorry. It's after midnight! I was having so much fun decorating the tree I had no idea it was so late."

"Don't worry about it. I've been having a good time, too. I love doing this kind of stuff. But I guess I am tired. I've been up since six." Molly yawned again.

"I'll go make up the guest room for you." Steve started toward the stairs.

"No, no!" Molly exclaimed. "Really, you've been more than gracious already. If you've got an extra pillow and blanket, I'll just crash on the couch here."

"Are you sure?"

"Of course. Sadie is already cozy in front of the fire." Molly pointed at the dog sleeping on her blanket in front of the fireplace.

"Okay then." Steve pulled a blanket and pillow out of the wooden chest in the corner and handed them to Molly. "Good night."

"Good night," Molly echoed.

"Thanks for helping with the tree."

"No problem. Thanks for dinner and a warm place to sleep."

"No problem," Steve echoed as he turned and headed upstairs.

Molly fell asleep watching the flames in the fireplace, glad that she'd let him talk her into coming up to the house rather than staying out in the truck. She'd had a wonderful evening and "little Stevie Scott" was definitely a very nice guy. She was so glad that God had led her to a new friend through the snowstorm.

In the morning, Molly woke to sunshine streaming in the window and hitting her in the face. She glanced at her watch. Nine! She'd slept in. She should have been at the garden centre an hour ago. Wait! Where was she? Oh, yeah, the storm, delivering the Christmas trees. And Steve.

Getting up, she walked into the kitchen where she could smell coffee brewing, nice and strong, just how she liked it. Sadie was sitting under the table eating what appeared to be a hot dog and looking pretty happy about it. After a quick trip to the washroom, Molly poured herself a cup of coffee and sat at the table. Just then the kitchen door opened and Steve came in, dressed in his snow-mobile suit and balaclava.

"Good morning! I hope you slept well," he said, pulling off the balaclava.

"I did, thanks. I see the storm is over. I guess I'd better call a tow truck," Molly replied.

"No need. I pulled your truck out with the tractor this morning after I blew out the laneway. And they're plowing the main road right now, so you're all set to go. No rush though," he added.

"You didn't need to do that," she said. Then she quickly added, "Thanks, though. I appreciate everything you've done for me and Sadie. It's been really great."

"I've had a great time, too." He smiled.

"I really should be going. I was supposed to be at work at eight. Although Uncle Jeff knows where I've been, he'll be worried if I'm not there soon." Molly stood and reached for her coat, still hanging on the chair where she'd left it the previous night.

As Molly and Sadie were going out the door, Molly turned and waved. "Bye. Thanks again."

"See you around." Steve waved back.

A few days later, as Molly was loading up the company truck for that day's deliveries, she heard Sadie give a cheerful little bark. Turning, Molly saw Steve crossing the parking lot, and her heart did a little flip.

He waved. "Hi!"

Molly smiled and waved back. "I'm surprised to see you here," she said when he came up beside her.

"I came to give you this," he said, handing her a white envelope.

Her heart dropped. The bill for his mailbox. She should have known he hadn't come just to see her.

"Aren't you going to open it?" he asked.

"Oh, sure." He likely wanted her to write him out a cheque so he could be on his way. She pulled off her mittens and slit open the envelope with her fingernail. Inside, instead of the invoice she'd expected, there was a brightly coloured piece of Christmas

  Hot Apple Cider with Cinnamon

stationary. Unfolding it, she realized it was an invitation to the holiday party for the high school staff. She looked up at Steve.

"I really enjoyed getting to know you the other night during the storm. I was wondering if you'd be my date for the party?" he asked with a smile.

Molly's heart did another little flip. "I'd love to go." She smiled back.

"Great!" He started to leave, but hesitated. "Will you be at church this Sunday with your aunt and uncle?"

"I'm planning on it."

Steve grinned. "Wonderful. See you then!"

Molly waved as he turned to leave. "See you!"

Thank you, Lord, for giving me a new friend. And even if he never becomes anything more than a friend, it will be enough.

Hot Apple Cider with Cinnamon

My Father's Tree

Nonfiction

Mario Dimain

It was December. Just two months away from my tenth birthday.

All across the islands of the Philippines, another birthday preparation was taking place. Christmas songs were being played on the radio. The birthday of the man on the cross was fast approaching. All of our neighbours in Quezon City were set for the season's festivity. The windows of their houses were adorned with star-shaped lanterns. A Christmas tree was sure to greet anyone who would enter their homes.

Our house looked empty and bare—completely lacking the Christmas spirit. I was so bothered by the lack of effort from my family to do something that I took it upon myself to bring the spirit of Christmas to our home.

My creative instinct led me to the young jackfruit tree growing in our backyard. There was no denying how valuable the tree was to my father, who had planted it four summers before. It was much shorter than I was then—barely a foot tall. I remember my father's confident voice saying, "When this little tree grows to be five times your height, it will bear fruit with thick prickly skin, containing thumb-size seeds covered with sweet and chewy flesh. Just like the ones your mom buys from the marketplace."

The tree had grown quite tall. But so far there'd been no fruit. And while my father had a good idea, I felt that I had a better vision. The upper half of the tree had a pointy, triangular shape that was ideal for a Christmas tree. Plus, because of its close proximity to the kitchen roof, its location couldn't be more perfect. Furthermore, standing next to it was a mature guava tree which could serve as my ladder to get to the roof.

It was crystal clear. The great opportunity was there for the taking.

Hot Apple Cider with Cinnamon

Without giving it another thought, I found my father's hatchet and climbed up the guava tree and onto the kitchen roof. I stood on the edge of the roof, the hatchet clenched in my right hand. The trunk of the jackfruit tree was now within striking distance. Without hesitation, I started chopping.

After I delivered the final blow, the upper half of the jackfruit tree went crashing to the ground. As it fell, it produced a whizzing sound that made me consider the grim consequences that might come next. I sensed trouble—big trouble.

Still holding the hatchet, I stood frozen, staring down at what was left of the tree. It was a mess. The unsettling sight caused me to visualize my father's disappointed face when he saw the tree. But still, deep inside, I was at peace with myself. There was a feeling of epiphany.

A voice came from below. "I am telling!" It was my older sister. The glow in her eyes didn't surprise me. She always found it amusing to see me in trouble.

Quickly she stepped back inside the house and ran to our mother to spill the beans.

I waited nervously. Any minute now, Mom would be coming out to whack me with her "dooms day" stick.

I heard footsteps rushing out and closed my eyes, anticipating the worse. But it wasn't Mom. It was my older sister again, with a devilish smile. "Mother is coming," she said with a tone of celebration.

But before Mom's fury could get to me, unknown to me, my dad came home. He'd been away for months on a military mission.

Having heard what I'd done from my mother and sister, he took charge.

My father seldom got mad, but it was scary when he did. With his military discipline as a soldier, he tended to be rigid in handling matters.

At those times, I needed very good answers to the dreaded questions he would throw at me.

His face was stern as he watched me slowly climb down from the kitchen roof. His words were concise and direct. "Explain yourself, son."

His commanding voice was so full of authority it made me stand up straight like a tin soldier. I gathered myself together and looked straight into his eyes. What could I say in my own defence?

Nervously, I replied, "We don't have a Christmas tree. All I wanted was to make one. I am truly sorry, Father."

My heart was racing so fast I could barely hear myself talking. When I finished speaking, I waited for my father to calculate the severity of punishment he was about to lay on me.

And then he looked away for a moment, and I realized his stern look had melted from his face, and, although he tried to hide it, there was a smile on his lips.

He came closer. He stroked my head and affectionately said, "Well done, my boy. Well done!"

My father then told me a great story about a little boy named George. He, too, got into trouble when he playfully chopped down his father's cherry tree. When his father asked who had done it, he told the truth. That boy grew up to be a brave general who won the battle against the British Empire and became the first president of the United States of America.

I'm no George Washington: I haven't attained greatness or fame. But I look back in fondness at that little boy whose strong desire to celebrate the birth of the man on the cross not only brought the spirit of Christmas to his home, but, in the process, won the approval of his strict father.

Looking back on that incident now, I believe that my father's approving words echoed what God would have said if He were to have spoken to me that day.

Even then, with my childlike faith, I somehow knew that God was smiling down on me and the angels were applauding.

God is our loving and forgiving Father in heaven. He is fair and He understands. As the Apostle Paul said in Romans 3:28 (NCV) "A person is made right with God through faith, not through obeying the law."

A Different Dad

Fiction

Bobbie Ann Cole

Mum clapped her hands in delight. "Oh, Teddy, it's just as I remember!"

I parked the rental car outside of what used to be our old New Brunswick homestead and bit my tongue. Mum was wrong. The house looked nothing like the ramshackle ruin I remembered growing up in. The trim home before us had butter siding and brown shutters, a heritage look. The original house had had peeling white paint and a lop-sided covered porch that had since disappeared. An orchard dripped rosy red apples where the old barn used to be. The lawn out front was green instead of strewn with rusting farm equipment amid islands of weeds. How I used to hate it when Dad took stuff apart on a whim and left it scattered across the yard, never to be put back together again.

I was surprised to find my knuckles white from clenching the steering wheel. Giving them a shake, I also shook my head. Why did this affect me so? Being ashamed of my Dad was something I'd gotten over a long time ago. I no longer cared. Nevertheless, I turned to Mum to set her straight. "Do you remember when Dad tried to take down the old barn out back?"

She giggled like a young girl. "It caved in on top of him."

"Yes," I said. "It was a miracle he didn't kill himself when he took it apart from the inside." The stupid man had sawn through the rotten wood of the support beams, then through the rotten wooden roof joists, while sitting on them. He had been almost through his third joist when the barn collapsed.

Mum turned to me and, with a smile, abruptly switched the subject. "He wrote me such letters about this place."

Sadly, Mum was losing her marbles, and this fantasy reminiscing was part of her decline. My father couldn't write. She knew that.

"You used to call him Dopey," I reminded her.

"Oh, son, that was affectionate."

I suppose it was. Mum never seemed disappointed in her husband, nor in the poor living he had eked out for the two of them and the six of us kids from haphazard crops, a pet cow, a lot of opportunist foraging and fishing, and a small army disability pension.

Born pretty much one after the other, we six little stair-steps had turned out just fine. Despite Dad's craziness, we were all well-adjusted and educated—one lawyer, two teachers, two nurses, and a celebrated musician.

The musician is me. Not the pop star kind. I'm first violin with the Royal Scottish Philharmonic Orchestra in Glasgow, Scotland.

As such, I like to invite famous guest conductors and singers to my condo for little post-performance soirées that include post-supper stories, told as we sit by the fire with our hands wrapped around our brandy glasses, warming the cognac.

My parents' wedding night is my party piece.

They had been given the loan of a cottage by a lake for their honeymoon. It was way more luxurious than they could have otherwise afforded, with a deck right above the water, fancy furnishings, and a lake view out of every window.

It was evening and the sun was streaming in as Mum, happy as could be, went to unpack in the bedroom. She thought Dad might follow her in. But after a while she realized he wasn't a very ardent bridegroom. She found him sitting on the living room couch, fast asleep. She didn't want to wake him right away. It had been a hectic day, and no doubt he was exhausted. However, after letting him sleep for an hour or two, she tried and failed to rouse him. Concerned, she picked up the phone and asked the operator to connect her to the local doctor.

"That's very common with bridegrooms," the doctor said, no doubt thinking that Dad had gotten blind drunk at his wedding. "Just leave him. He'll wake up, eventually."

Sniggers circulate among my dinner guests.

I pause at this moment, ahead of delivering my dramatic *coup de grâce.*

"He'd had a stroke."

An intake of breath. Dropped jaws.

Someone always protests, "But he must have been only a young man."

He was 25, recently returned to New Brunswick after active service in Europe. Mum was a war bride. They'd met in London, and fallen in love. Three months after he returned home, she came over from England to marry him.

At this point someone suggests that, since I was here to tell the story, things must perforce have worked out. How was that?

I tell them it was because the phone was on a party line, and a lady happened to listen to the call. I usually have to explain to my 21st-century listeners, unfamiliar with the term "party line," that this had nothing to do with festivities but was a telephone line shared by several houses, and quite common in those days.

This neighbour—a fortuitous Nosey Parker if ever there was one—who "happened" to overhear the call to the doctor, thought something didn't sound right. She showed up at the cottage and, seeing Dad's condition, took over, organizing an ambulance and getting him admitted to the local hospital, where they diagnosed the stroke.

He was then transferred to Montreal, where he spent six months recovering, while Mum lived with Grammy, AKA the "Dragon," back in New Brunswick. It must have been very hard for Mum, who was only 21, and thousands of miles from her family in England. Someone less dogged might have packed up and headed back.

Today was her 90th birthday, which was the main reason for my visit home. Her big party had been the week before, when all the rest of the family had shown up to take her to the Delta in Fredericton. Pressing engagements had prevented me from being here then. I was sure none of them had missed me.

This morning, I had asked her what she wanted to do to celebrate with me.

She said, "Go for a drive, out to the old homestead."

So, here we were, in nostalgia land.

My boredom must have been written across my face because, after a few minutes of half-finished reminiscences, Mum wheeled around, sharp as a 21-year-old, and told me, "They were good times, Teddy."

I glanced at my Rolex. We were expecting company that afternoon. "Yeah. Well, time is marching on. We'd better get back, Mum."

I turned around and headed toward Burtts Corner, the village Mum and Dad had moved to after they sold the farm, 20-odd years ago. Wisps of cloud shadows slid across the car's hood and were reflected in the broad St. John River alongside of us.

At two p.m., Pastor Garnet and two of Mum's ancient friends filled the little back room of her house for a celebration.

We had pink party hats and drank Earl Grey tea. I served ice cream cake from Dairy Queen. I entertained them with, "Happy Birthday" and "For She's a Jolly Good Fellow" on my violin.

Mum blew out the candles, a pink nine and a white zero. It was fun, I suppose, until Mum began to weep and moan.

"I miss my Dopey so," she said, over and over.

Soon after, everyone left.

"He's been dead 18 years," I said as I piled up the tea cups. "I'd have thought it was a relief not to have to worry about him any more. You never knew what he was going to get up to next."

"But I loved him," she told the hankie I leaned across to hand her. "You don't know anything about love."

"Touché," I said with sarcasm. I felt her remark was below the belt. I had a full and busy life, with little time for attachments.

Piling dishes in the kitchen sink, I could see, through the window, the overgrown oak that had taken Dad's life. The couple next door had complained about the big branch that blocked their bedroom view and Dad, nearly 78 years old, too proud to ask for help, and too penny-pinching to hire someone, had sat on the offending limb and sawed it off at the trunk. The barn fiasco clearly had taught him nothing.

How could she miss the man? He'd never done anything right!

That evening, Mum took to her bed. In the morning, when she wouldn't get up, I called in the doctor, who shook his head and said she needed round-the-clock care.

My older sister in Moncton, an hour and a half away, was the only one remotely near enough to do this. But she said she couldn't. Absolutely not. My other sister, in Edmonton, watched her grandkids after school every day and couldn't get away, or so she maintained.

I didn't even bother asking my brothers. They had always been jealous of my success and, since I was the only one of us all who'd never been stuck with a turn at geriatric babysitting so far, I was sure they'd reason that my stint was past due.

I phoned my orchestra's human resources department in Glasgow. They said they could wangle extra leave for me. There'd be no need to rush back, leastways not until rehearsals began for our China Tour. But that wouldn't be until January. This was September. Hopefully, Mum would be gone by then.

The shame I experienced following this evil thought was probably what led to the answer I gave Pastor Garnet when he said, at the end of his sickbed visit the following day, "See you in church Sunday, Ted?"

"Possibly."

I hadn't been to church in a very long time.

His sermon was about Jesus' words on the cross: "Father, forgive them for they know not what they do."

My dopey Dad was one of those who never knew what he was doing. I wasn't about to forget the time I'd shown up from school with a friend to find the furnace in pieces and him sitting in the middle of the living room, both him and the room sooty as a coal mine.

Though I felt like hitting him, all I did was get lippy to mask my humiliation. He just took that, too, which made me twice as mad. I shooed my friend outside while Dad looked on, bemused.

After that, I wanted any Dad but the one I had. I even envied my friend his boozing father.

"Bless those who persecute you; bless and do not curse," Pastor Garnet said. "Do not be proud, but be willing to associate with people of low position. Do not be conceited."

If Jesus could forgive his vile persecutors, I probably should forgive my benign Dad. After all, I was 60 years old. It was time.

Dear God, I prayed silently, *the resentment I feel for Dad is not good. Please help me forgive him.*

I felt more at peace after this. However, the good feeling left me when I came through the front door to hear Mum wailing, "I want to read Dopey's letters before I die."

I climbed up the stairs to her bedroom the way a condemned man might climb to the scaffold. "Where are they, Mum?" I said. I didn't think for a moment there were any letters.

Propped up in bed with pillows, she looked at me with eyes narrowed. "You don't believe me."

"Tell me where they are and I'll get them," I said.

She waved an arm. "They're here."

"Okay."

I tramped down two flights of stairs and made much of rummaging through the basement. "No luck," I said, sticking my head around the bedroom door half an hour later.

She made another vague gesture. "I tell you, they're here."

"I'll try the attic, shall I?"

Clambering about on all fours, I got dust all over my Diesel designer jeans and navy sports jacket. I returned, wiping cobwebs off the palms of my hands. "No luck there either, Mum."

The hand she lifted to beckon me shook so much that she had to grab hold of it with her other hand to support it. Her lips moved.

I bent to listen.

"If you'd only stop bobbing about like a jack-in-the box," she yelled, "and take some notice of what I've been telling you. The trunk!"

My eyes followed her gaze toward the corner of the bedroom where an old trunk had sat since they'd moved from the farm.

I removed the framed pictures and velvet cloth covering it. I lifted the lid, which creaked open, freeing an odour of moth balls. I rummaged through some cloths. The trunk was full of old curtains from the homestead. Whyever had she kept these?

At the bottom, I found a bundle wrapped in pink tissue paper, tied with a red ribbon. I tried to remain skeptical but I was beginning to wonder. Could there really be letters? I pulled back the tissue paper and saw a pile of blue airmail envelopes, addressed to Miss Dorothy Sparks, which was Mum's maiden name. The return address was Turner Farm, Douglas, New Brunswick. Well, I never!

"Here they are, Mum," I said, sweaty but triumphant. I placed them on her lap with all the gravitas of a Shakespearean actor and said, "I found them."

"Read them," she commanded.

I fetched my specs and sat on the bed. "Which one shall I read?"

"Any one."

I took the top letter out of its envelope and unfolded a sheet of thin, blue paper as flimsy as tissue. Dark lines from the folds were hatched across the copperplate script, faded to brown.

My Darling Dotty,

Well, the bank released the funding and the farm is mine. I mean ours. I feel so proud, my dear. I spent the weekend walking our land and planning what we'll plant.

Puzzled, I looked at Mum. This was a different dad from my dad. This one was granted a mortgage and bought a farm. This dad could write letters.

She was leaning back against the pillows, her look of anguish gone. She looked, well, serene.

I read on.

The soil here is wonderfully fertile. We'll have blueberries and corn, apples and vegetables. I already bought seeds and tomato plugs. In time, we'll have cows and hens.

I gulped, realizing that I was reading what might have been. "It sounds wonderful, Mum."

She nodded. "He worked so hard."

I noticed that my own finger trembled as I found my place again.

With a lick of paint, a few rolls of wallpaper and, of course, you, my dear, we'll be home. I can't wait to begin the life we've dreamed of.

Mum closed her eyes "Ah, Dopey." On her face was a big smile. And no wonder. *This* man was great.

"But he wasn't, was he?" I said, surprised to find myself annoyed by this discovery. "Dopey, I mean. He wasn't dopey when he wrote this letter."

"It was the stroke," she said. "He was different, after."

So this man had been hijacked on his wedding night and a changeling, my dad, had stepped into his body. A lump grew in my throat. My eyes prickled.

I took my mother's bony hands in mine. They were so cold. As I gently rubbed some life into them, I tried to speak, but the words took a long time coming. "What happened to you and Dad was... a terrible tragedy."

She sighed. "It was a blow I got used to, in time."

"I don't know why I never considered that he was different... before." I felt as if, my whole life, I'd kept an innocent man on death row.

"We had a good life, in spite of all," she said. "We were a happy family, weren't we?"

I thought about this. Happy? Well, maybe. "Yes," I said. "I guess we were."

And then I realized it was true. We *had* been happy. And I'd never known it until now. Yes, it could have been different, and better, if Dad hadn't had a stroke. Our house could have been like the one with the butter-coloured siding and the neat lawns. We could have all looked up to him.

It seemed as if my brothers and sisters had somehow come to terms with who he was. Mum, too, though what she had originally expected was *this* man, the one who wrote the letters. I was the only one who'd remained stuck in my resentment.

"How could you be so accepting of what had happened to him, to both of you?"

"You gotta have faith," she said.

"Faith?"

"Yes. Faith that everything comes out as it's meant to. I grew to love the man God gave me on my wedding night."

The thought of all the time I'd wasted on bitterness made my face crumple.

She patted my hand, still my Mum.

"Don't worry, Teddy," she said. "He forgave you."

My Mother's Gift

Nonfiction

Carol Ford

I step off the elevator. Tired and anxious, I make my way down the long hallway toward Palliative Care. What awaits me today?

Familiar hospital smells assault my nose—chicken soup on cold lunch trays standing outside the patients' rooms, the pungent odour of urine, and a nauseating combination of chemical vapours from the disinfectant used to clean the floors. In the beginning, the mixture was almost too much for me, but I'm used to it now.

I dislike this place, and I don't want to be here. I don't want *her* to be here, either—but what is the alternative? I can't bring her home to our small one-and-half storey house where I already have two-year-old and nine-month-old sons, can I? Sometimes the guilt overwhelms me, but guilt is something I've carried with me all my life, especially around my mother. Since I was little, she's known how to make me feel guilty, as if she were the puppeteer and I her puppet.

She's never let me forget that I'm an adopted child, and that I should be forever grateful for what she did for me. This has influenced both my thinking and my actions so much so that when I'm away from her, I tend to doubt myself and feel apprehensive.

If she thinks that I'm loosening those strings at all, the words, "After all I've done for you," will slip out. I then come back under her control with apologies, and I feel more guilt.

A few weeks ago, she began begging me to take her home. Her pleas left me crying outside her room in the hallway after each visit.

The last time it happened, a doctor saw me there and advised me to be firm, but kind. He suggested I tell her, "Mother, I have explained that I can't bring you home to my place, and if that is all we can discuss, I'll need to leave now."

As much as it pained me to say these words, I took his advice. She stopped asking me for what I couldn't provide.

Now, as I approach the nursing station, I spot her nurse talking to a young intern. While I wait at the counter, a code blue blares out over the PA system, startling all of us. The staff stops what they are doing and the young intern runs to the exit. My mother's nurse comes over to me.

"How is she today?" I ask.

"No real change."

"Does she seem comfortable?"

"Yes, she's been sleeping whenever I went into her room, but she's awake now and there's a visitor with her."

"Oh, I wonder who it is?"

As I proceed to her doorway, I plant a smile on my face to mask my worry. When I enter her room, the first thing I see is the back of a man's head. I round the end of the bed and recognize him. He's the young Guyanese minister from our church. I'm surprised to see him here. I'm also a little uneasy. My mother doesn't take well to those she calls "foreigners." However, today she looks happy and pleased.

"Carol, do you know Pastor Sukhraj?" she says.

"Yes, Mom, he's the associate pastor at our church."

"He came to pray and give me communion."

Pastor Sukhraj nods and smiles broadly. His bright white teeth contrast handsomely with his coffee-shaded skin.

Each breath my mother takes is a struggle for her at this point, and the skin on her cheek bones rises and falls in a measured pace. Wisps of grey hair spread out like a spider's web on the pillow.

I take the glass of water from the end table and help her manage a few sips through a bent straw. Her thin arms lay helplessly at her sides. *How much longer can she linger in this state?*

As I gently squeeze her cold hand in mine, I try to reassure her of my presence and love. She looks straight at me. And then something unexpected happens. "This is my beautiful daughter," she says aloud, presumably to Pastor Sukhraj. "She has been a

  Hot Apple Cider with Cinnamon

wonderful daughter to me. No one could have had a better daughter than Carol. I love her *so* much." Her eyes are beaming with pride as she utters these words.

I stand beside her bed, stunned. My throat constricts as I attempt to hold back my tears.

Of course, Pastor Sukhraj doesn't comprehend what just happened. He gives us both a warm grin and says his goodbyes.

A few days later, as I arrive home in my car, my husband meets me in our driveway.

I immediately know why.

Gently he says, "They just called from the hospital. Your mother died this afternoon at three-thirty."

Some years later, it's late in the evening and both boys are in bed. Michael, my youngest, is now 12 years old, but he still likes to have me read to him before he sleeps. This precious time will soon disappear, so I'm glad to hold on to it as long as possible.

After making myself a cup of tea, I settle into my reading chair and pick up *The Gift of the Blessing*.[1] It's a book that was recommended on the Christian radio station I listen to. It tells how you can give blessings to your spouse, friends, children, and parents. I'm enthralled. It begins with stories of a grown man and woman who are grieving their painful past. They have feelings of inadequacy caused by a lack of acceptance from their parents. The authors explain that what they missed was what they call "The Blessing."

The book goes on to describe how receiving The Blessing is not a new concept, but one that is modelled in the Bible. One such example is told in Genesis when Jacob called his 12 sons together and said, "Gather around so I can tell you what will happen to you in days to come."[2] He then blessed each one separately.

Elements of The Blessing described in the book include meaningful touch, words of blessing, an expression of high value in a child, a vision of a special future for them, and an active commitment to provide support.

I lay the book on my lap. I'm having an "Aha" moment. "She blessed me!" I say in wonder.

I'm euphoric. Yes, I did feel her touch during those last days! Yes, she did speak with pride regarding my worth as her daughter! Yes, my last memory is the love she felt for me!

Thank you, mother, for that last precious gift.

1. G. Smalley and J. Trent (1993) *The Gift of The Blessing* Nashville, Tennessee: Janet Thomas Books

2. Genesis 49:1, 28 (NIV)

Hot Apple Cider with Cinnamon

The Girl from the Other Side of the Tracks

Nonfiction

L. June Stevenson

When I was growing up in Eastern Ontario during the Second World War years and into the burgeoning 50s, it was understood that no one in my part of town associated with people who lived on the other side of the tracks.

There were two sets of tracks that carried the Canadian National and Canadian Pacific trains through the city on a regular basis. On *my* side of the tracks you'd find what I guess you'd call the middle class of people. On the *other* side of the tracks, the houses, or rather dwellings, left something to be desired. Some were constructed of various kinds of wood; some were plain with no porches; and inside the windows, straggly curtains hung haphazardly. The people who inhabited them had run-down vehicles, if they had any at all, and to me, they always managed to look dishevelled, as if they'd just crawled out of bed in yesterday's clothing.

My parents had a lot of rules regarding who I could spend time with. And I had been clearly told to stay away from people from the other side of the tracks. But then Lucy joined my class at school.

Girls usually wore blouses and skirts in those days, and Lucy fit right in. Her clothes were worn and threadbare, but they were clean and pressed. Her hair and nails looked clean too, not like those of the kids who came from the other side of the tracks, who usually looked unwashed and were often checked by the school nurse for lice.

Lucy also began to attend the same United Church Sunday school class I attended. And I liked her. So one day, ignoring my parents' rule about people from the other side of the tracks, I invited her home to play with me.

My parents liked her right away, too. Her bright smile and polite manners made it easy for my parents to agree to a follow-up visit that coming Saturday. I have to add that I never felt my parents were biased so much as careful. Anyway, they said I could ride my bicycle to her house and visit for an hour or so.

That visit was an eye opener for me in an unexpected way. At 13 years old I was just beginning to understand why parents got so uptight over so many seemingly innocuous things. I was also beginning to blossom in ways that men on the street who I didn't know appeared to notice.

Lucy's house lay not just beyond the tracks, but on the other side of the road beyond the tracks. Though small, it was presentable, and showed signs of care. Outside, Lucy's stepfather was renovating in his spare time, and building an addition, so everything was in a mess.

Inside, the house was messy, but clean. Lucy's mother was a petite woman with a permanently worried look on her face. As far as I knew, she spent all her time cooking, doing laundry, and picking up after Lucy and three more children under the age of 10.

Lucy seemed to like her stepfather. She told me that her own father had come home from the Second World War, unpacked, then repacked, and left her and her mother. They had never heard from him again.

Lucy told me she was embarrassed when she heard people whisper that her father had left because he'd found out his wife had been seen with other men while he was away. Afterward, when I told my mother, she explained that some women were lonely during the war and went out with men who were not their husbands.

That first Saturday I visited Lucy's house, we decided to get out of her mother's hair and visit Sadie, another girl in our class, who lived just up the street. Minutes later, I knew without a doubt that my parents would never have agreed to this visit had they known any of the things I learned during the time I spent at Sadie's house.

The building was a run-down shack between the tracks and the road, in a much more vulnerable position to the rumble and roar of the trains than Lucy's. In the dim light, I perceived that it was one large room composed of kitchen and living room, with curtained off areas to the side for bedrooms. The furniture was shabby and torn, and the smells were an odd mixture of urine, animal and human, spoiled meat, and what I later learned was stale whisky.

A half dozen younger children, whom I assumed were Sadie's brothers and sisters, were racing through the house.

Lucy and I were invited to sit.

Lucy was quick to pull out a kitchen chair. I was left to perch on the end of a rather lumpy, uneven sofa while Sadie sat on the other end. Wrong move. Her father quickly moved in between us. Sadie's father leered drunkenly at me and I shook my head to dissipate the smell of beer.

My father drank beer sometimes, but he never smelled like that at two o'clock in the afternoon. His hands didn't roam around indiscriminately either.

Since I was brought up to be polite to my elders, I managed to wriggle myself into a safer position and, as soon as possible, I reminded Lucy that we needed to leave. Did Sadie want to join us?

I never visited Sadie again, and I never did tell my parents what her place was like. That's just one of the little somethings I forgot to mention when asked, "So what did you do today?"

Lucy never said anything either. Perhaps she was used to similar circumstances, living where she did.

Lucy and I became fast friends, and each Saturday we'd cycle off into the countryside, hunting frogs for biology class, investigating rural cemeteries, or lying under a tree in a farmer's field with curious cows chewing their cuds nearby. When our bicycles weren't working, which was very often, we sat on the old couch in my porch or lay on the bed she shared with her sister, and acted like the teenagers we were: whispering, giggling, telling scary stories, or more seriously sharing the secrets that are so important to teenage girls. I loved to see Lucy laugh—her eyes twinkled. And when she smiled, the corners of her mouth crinkled. Lucy was quiet and often serious just like I was, and interested in other people. She was also sincere about her faith.

Along the side of Lucy's house, a half dozen sunflowers lifted their cheery heads to the sun. They were Lucy's favourite flower and she took responsibility for their care. In the fall, we would clean the seeds out, wash them, and put them in the oven on a greased pan to dry and crisp. Then, with her brothers and sister gathered around, we would sit on the grassy patch outside the house and munch on them, enjoying their nutty flavour.

Sunflowers became a symbol of our friendship, often a secret code we shared in our notes to each other.

Of course, boyfriends were the centre of our conversations, especially after we got into high school. Lucy had a crush on Timmy from the first day in Grade 9. Years later, she would still ask me how Timmy was, but he never reciprocated.

Lucy quit school in Grade 11 to work at a local five-and-dime store because she needed to help out at home. But she never gave up her dream of going to nursing school. She worked hard, saved some money, and finally was able to go into training at the Salvation Army Grace Hospital in Ottawa.

Her letters came infrequently to my boarding house near Toronto Teacher's College, where I was studying. They were hurried notes penned during night shift or on days off, but there was always a little sunflower drawn in the corner, coloured with a crayon if she had one. My notes to her were the same.

I wish I could say we were friends forever and both lived happily ever after. I guess we did, for a while. But then came the day when Lucy, heartbroken, phoned to say she'd met an air force guy who she thought was single but who turned out to have a wife back home. He'd returned to his wife after getting Lucy pregnant. She'd given up a lovely, healthy baby girl for adoption, and was heading west to put it all behind her.

A few months later, Lucy wrote to say she had a job in Alberta and was married.

Her letters (and mine as well) grew fewer and fewer. I had stayed in Toronto and was happy teaching. New friends had come on the scene.

Ten years went by and all I knew about Lucy was that she had two boys, her husband had committed suicide, and she had remarried. My last Christmas card, in 1975, came back. Someone had written on the envelope: "Moved. Address unknown."

Twenty-five years later, in 2000, I was making a business trip to Alberta. Since I'd be there for ten days, the local planners insisted in fitting in some R & R for me. "What do you want to do and see?" they asked.

"The Hoodoos, of course, and maybe the dinosaurs."

"Anyone you want to visit?"

Suddenly, I thought of Lucy. Could she be located? Was it even remotely possible that we might meet again?

They say truth is stranger than fiction. And so it was in that instance. One of the people planning my trip had United Church connections in the area where Lucy had last lived. Someone remembered that she'd gone to their church. The minister was contacted.

Yes, he remembered Lucy and her boys. There'd been some trouble in the family and she hadn't wanted to talk with him about it, so he'd suggested the local Presbyterian minister.

That minister not only remembered Lucy but knew where she was. Her second marriage had failed when her husband became abusive, and Lucy had moved some 50 miles away, later marrying a well-to-do business man.

On an early spring day, when the sun was trying hard to warm the earth, I finished my last meeting for a few days and stepped into the fresh air, where I was met by my faithful planner, Priscilla, who was grinning from ear to ear. Beside her stood an elegant, white-haired woman who looked vaguely familiar. Her eyes twinkled and her mouth crinkled at the corners. In her gloved hand was an artificial sunflower. Lucy!

The next few days were a breathless flurry of catching up. We sat up long into the nights, poring over photo albums, sharing adventures about which we laughed and cried, recalling long ago days of lost loves and strange events. We argued about whether it was butterscotch or caramel sundaes we loved so much.

Lucy's husband Glen was a kind, soft-spoken, gentle giant who doted on her. He left us alone to reminisce and quietly went around preparing meals and tidying up. Listening to Lucy's stories and seeing her happiness, I knew that Glen had been a bright light after a dark period in her life.

Then she told me about the past two years of her life. First of all, out of the blue, she'd received a letter from her real father, whom she'd never known. He was ill and wanted to have some closure over his past before he died. Lucy felt sorry for this man who'd never known his daughter, and since she'd long ago resigned herself to not knowing her father, she found she could handle seeing him without becoming overly emotional. It was nice to meet him, but it was too late for him to compensate for not being there for her.

Two months after meeting her birth father, Lucy's mother phoned from back east. She had been contacted by a daughter she'd given up for adoption during the war. A daughter Lucy hadn't known about. Now she understood why her father had left shortly after coming home, since the baby wasn't his.

Anyway, this girl wanted to learn about her family. Was Lucy up to meeting her? So there was her visit to see her mother and meet a half-sister she'd never imagined existed.

Could there possibly be any other surprises in store? A letter from the Children's Aid Society announced that Lucy's own daughter, given up so long ago, was searching for her parents.

It was a huge step for Lucy to reveal to her family that there was yet another member. Fortunately, her sons accepted their new sister just as they had accepted a new grandfather and an aunt. And her husband Glen was by her side all the way.

Sitting beside Lucy in her home, I shook my head in amazement at her stories, and gasped delightedly over the photos of her expanded family. The two of us agreed that the Lord works in mysterious ways.

How do you crowd years of loss and longing turned into joy and celebration into three days? Lucy and I did. We filled ourselves to the brim with life and all its idiosyncrasies.

And then it was time for me to get back to work.

A cloud crossed Lucy's face as she walked me to the waiting taxi. Glen took her arm and turned to me. "Lucy wants to tell you something," he said, "and she doesn't know how."

He turned to her with an encouraging look.

"It's been so wonderful." Tears filled Lucy's eyes. "In the past two years, my father found me; a sister came into my life; my daughter came back to me; and a long lost friend returned." She paused. "I'm sorry to say we will likely never meet again. I have cancer, and it's incurable."

I was dumbstruck. Three days to renew a wonderful companionship and share the past 25 years of our lives; three minutes to say goodbye forever.

Lucy pressed a tiny doll wearing a sunflower pattern into my hand. "Just remember what we had," she whispered, and squeezed my hand.

Two months later, a thick envelope arrived from Alberta. Inside was a cassette tape. With a sense of foreboding, I sat down to listen. Lucy's voice was strong and clear. She began, "If you are listening to this it means I am no longer here. I have gone to a better place."

The words faded and I was back home, crossing the tracks on my bicycle. Lucy was standing by the little white clapboard house, beneath the golden sunflowers, waving me over.

I knew a moment of gladness that in my youth I had been brave enough (or stubborn enough) to bend my parents' rules and regulations a little and get to know the new girl who lived on the other side of the tracks.

An Extraordinary Visit

Nonfiction

Ramona Furst

"Your destination is *what* country?" The high-pitched male voice was so loud I heard every word from where I was sitting next to my mother, who was holding the phone to her ear.

I saw her wince and move the phone away from her ear for a moment. Then she gave the travel agent an abbreviated geography lesson. "Before it became independent in 1960 the Central African Republic was a French colony called French Equatorial Africa. The most direct route would be to fly to Paris, France, and then to Bangui, the capital of the Central African Republic, or C-A-R."

She grinned at me and mouthed the words. "He's still looking for it."

Undeterred, my mother continued her one-sided conversation. "The CAR is in the middle of the continent of Africa. Well, not exactly in the middle. It's bordered by Chad to the north, the Sudan to the northeast, and South Sudan to the east. Then there's the Democratic Republic of the Congo and the Republic of the Congo to the south, and the country of Cameroon to the west."

Mom used hand gestures to ask me to look for paper and a pen.

While I jumped off the sofa, she kept talking to the phone, telling the travel agent about our upcoming trip. She was almost as excited as I was.

My parents had been missionaries in French Equatorial Africa for 12 years in the 1950s. I'd been born there. But when I was eight, my mother became very ill with encephalitis, and we had to return to the United States, where we were living at the time. Now, to celebrate my mother's 40th birthday, and my 13th, we were finally going back to visit the friends we'd left behind. Friends who were more like family.

With the travel arrangements finally in place, and notes about when to pick up the airline tickets written on the pad of paper I'd found, my mother thanked the agent for his help before hanging up.

She turned and gave me a hug, then brushed my long red hair away from my face. She said, "I've always so much wanted to go back and see our African friends. Especially Baba, Joni, Rebekah, and the rest of their family. I don't expect you remember, but for a long time after we returned to the US, you cried yourself to sleep because you missed them so much."

"I remember," I said.

"Yes." My mother nodded. "Well, we're going! But first you need to do your homework and study for your final exams. School will be finished in a few weeks. Then we both need to think about getting our hair cut. It's hot and humid in the CAR, and shorter hair will help keep us cool."

A few weeks later, visas in hand, my mother and I were in the New York airport waiting our turn to put our luggage on a conveyer belt. I wanted to pinch myself to make sure it was real. "I can't believe I'm on my way," I said. Then I prayed, "Please God, help us find Baba."

We settled in and the airplane took off for Paris.

I thought about the letters I'd written to the Central African Republic. I wondered if any of them had made it to their destination. In the past five years, we'd had no contact with Baba, who had been our cook, his wife Joni, or his daughter Rebekah, who'd been my best friend.

Once, when I asked my parents if I could telephone Rebekah, they said, "The drums used in villages are even more reliable than a trans-Atlantic phone call to Bangui. Neither Baba nor his wife knows how to read or write. The only way they can contact us is through other missionaries when they come back to the United States."

Just before I drifted off to sleep, I looked out the window at the dark night sky. Instead of my reflection, I saw a red-headed, pony-tailed girl, about six years old. She stood with her head tilted upward, intently watching an ebony-skinned man putting kindling into a wood burning stove. Both of them wore red aprons with white polka dots.

As I watched, the full lips on the man's scarred and tattooed face curved in a smile. He pulled a small stool from under the kitchen counter. The stool was made of zebrawood, characterized by long black stripes that look very much like a zebra's. He motioned to the young girl to come closer and helped her up on the stool. The red-haired girl was me, and the man was Baba.

I prayed again that somehow we would find Baba and his family.

I woke up hours later, thinking about Baba and Rebekah. When my parents went to Africa, they lived 200 miles northwest of the capital city of Bangui, in a small village called Bozoum. My father, who was trained as a linguist, had been asked to help translate the Bible and primers for boys and girls who were learning to read and write. Baba was my parents' cook, and since my mother had to look after my three-year-old sister, Baba was the one who helped my mother learn the local dialect, which was called Sango. Joni, Baba's wife, helped take care of my sister and introduced my mother to the women of the village.

A week before I was born, Joni and Baba had their first child. They named her Rebekah. From the time we could walk and talk, Rebekah and I were inseparable. When our parents tried to separate us, one of us would begin to cry.

There was no school for African children when I began to attend the one-room school house for the missionaries' children. At the end of each school day, Rebekah would be waiting for me near the school's large bell. Often she'd have two pieces of fresh sugar cane for us to suck on. We'd play and tell each other secrets in our own pidgin language (a combination of English and Sango) until Baba called for us to help him find eggs in the chicken coop.

I was also very close to Baba. Fortunately, my mother seemed to understand the connection I had for this gentle and kind man, because she never complained when I cried and said I wanted Baba to look after me.

It was Baba who explained to me one day, "Your mother is too sick to stay in Africa. You must go back to America." When I shook my head and said I couldn't leave, he said, "God will bring you both back someday."

Now that day was a reality.

We finally got to Paris, where I waited impatiently with my mother for the last leg of the journey to be over. I couldn't sleep because my mind was spinning in circles: "Where are you Baba? How are we going to find you, Rebekah, and the rest of your family?"

As we arrived on Central African soil, the bumpy landing on tarmac filled with pot holes launched butterflies in my stomach. I peered through the window and noticed brilliant terracotta red clay earth. This was nothing like the airports in Toronto and Paris!

Once the door of the airplane was opened, even before I began to walk out onto the landing strip toward a crumbling brick building with a metal roof, my blouse was stuck to my skin with perspiration.

Only a barbed-wire fence separated the small airfield from the brick building, a parking lot filled with trucks, and vendors selling their wares. Before my mother and I were ushered into the building by a uniformed officer, I noticed that chickens and goats had congregated around the strip of grass near the airplane we had just left.

Outside the airport, we tried to take in everything as we waited for a man who would drive us to the mission house in downtown Bangui. The area was crowded with people, trucks, and vendors.

Women wearing dresses and full-length skirts made from long pieces of brilliant, colourful cloth swayed gracefully through the crowd. On their heads they carried an assortment of items to sell. One woman carried firewood held neatly together by wire; another had a hobbled chicken sitting precariously on top of a bag of peanuts. I saw a young girl carrying small bananas with skins the colour of a Red Delicious apple. I remembered they were called monkey bananas.

Of course, our white complexions stood out against the sea of varying shades of black skin. A child giggled and pointed to my red hair. Soon, we were surrounded by children and adults, all fighting for our attention.

Since it had been five years since my mother or I had spoken Sango, our attempts to talk to them made our audience laugh.

Above the din of voices and cars honking their horns, I heard someone yell out our names, then saw a hand above the sea of faces waving and pointing toward a Land Rover. We walked toward the man and, as we shook hands, he said, "You must be Ruth and Ramona. I'm Ron." He looked at me and said, "I'm told you went to school with my brother. About the time your family left the CAR, I had already left for the United States to go to school. Let me get your things and then I'll take you and your mother to the mission station. You both must be exhausted. You can have something to eat and have a shower or go straight to bed."

On our way to our room in the guest house of the mission compound, we passed by the lounge. I noticed a citizen's band (CB) radio on a small desk. The short-wave radio can be operated by many people. Only one operator may transmit at a time, but other people can listen in on the conversation until it's their turn to talk.

"I wondered," I said to my host, "if CB radios were used now. But do you still use the jungle phone?"

Ron laughed. "Yes, word of mouth is still by far the best way to send messages up country to family and friends. When your mother notified us about your upcoming visit, we made sure to tell everyone both with the radio and with the drums."

I wondered if there was a chance that Baba and Rebekah might have heard the news that we were coming.

Birds singing in trees in the courtyard outside my bedroom window woke me up the next morning. As I pulled away the netting around the bed and got out of a cotton sheet made into a sleeping bag, I noticed my mother's empty bed.

  Hot Apple Cider with Cinnamon

Dressed and very hungry, I followed the smell of freshly made coffee and the sound of voices to the dining room. People I hadn't met the night before were already seated around a table. I soon found out some of the people were missionaries from the Sudan and Cameroon who were on their way home to Sweden, France, and the United States.

My mother waved me to a chair beside her. While I waited for my breakfast to arrive, a man in a uniform came in and walked toward us. He addressed my mother in English, speaking very slowly and carefully. "Mamma, there is someone outside who would like to speak to you. He came last night. We did not believe him, since you had just arrived from far away."

Conversation around the table stopped, and my mother and I looked at each other. With a nod, my mother pushed her chair away from the table and said, "I can't imagine who it might be, Ramona. Let's go see."

In the courtyard, an older man with ebony skin stood looking out of the gate toward the sidewalk and street, which were full of people and cars.

My mother politely coughed, and we watched him turn around.

His hair had begun to whiten above his forehead, but there was no mistaking his eyes, tattooed face, and beaming smile!

I ran forward, tears streaming down my face. Then I stopped, remembering my African manners. An adult must begin the conversation; staring is impolite; and you must first ask about family members who aren't present with you. I couldn't hug him, not right away. I wanted him to be proud of me.

Baba began to speak, and I heard the break in his voice.

He came over to my mother and said, "How is the family? Your husband? And your older daughter?"

"They are well. My husband is doing research in linguistics, in Paris, France, and Ramona's sister is with him learning French."

Mother suggested we find a bench and sit down while Baba told us his story.

We learned that shortly after our family had left the Central African Republic, the boarding school where many missionaries sent their children had been closed and a new one had been built in the western part of Central Africa. Baba and his wife and their six children had moved to the new mission station, called Yaloke, as head caretakers and cooks.

When Baba first heard from a missionary family about my mother's plans to come back to the Central African Republic with me, he asked his employers for an extended leave of absence so that he could find and take care of us.

"They asked me," Baba said, "'How will you know when you should leave, and how will you know how to find them?' I said, 'God will tell me when it is time to go and where to find them.'"

Baba had accepted rides from missionaries, travelled by foot, and finally boarded a bus into the city just a few hours before we arrived at the guest house! He had arrived at roughly the same time we did. And here he was sitting across from us.

Ron, our host, walked across the courtyard to where we sat and said, "Excuse me, but there's a truck heading for the mission-ary medical clinic in Yaloke." Ron turned to ask Baba in Sango, "Is that not where you are now the head cook for the boarding school?"

When Baba said it was, Ron said, "The driver says he has enough room for three passengers. If you'd like to go with him, he'll be here to pick you up in an hour or so."

Of course, we wanted to go to Yaloke.

"You'd better hurry," Ron said. "It's a ten-hour drive if you don't have a flat tire or get stuck in a pot hole."

When my mother frowned, Ron reassured her. "Don't worry. The roads right now are in good shape. The driver has spare tires in the truck in case of an emergency."

Baba's wife and their children, including my best friend Reb-ekah, were there to greet us as we drove into the mission compound.

Laughter filled the small kitchen of the guest house where my mother and I stayed throughout our two-month visit. Baba and my mother worked side by side cooking the meals, each with a red polka-dotted apron. I had one, too.

Rebekah and I spent each day helping her parents with work as well as helping in the medical clinic.

Shortly before we were to leave, I found my mother outside on the veranda crying. "Each day Baba has been here with us," she said, "he has refused to let me pay for the groceries. But they have so little income as it is."

In silence, we held each other's hand until I asked, "How do you repay such a costly gift of love?"

My mother leaned forward, hugged me, and whispered in my ear, "You can't."

We broke the rules of African etiquette the day my mother and I said goodbye to Baba and his family. We didn't hide our tears.

As I held Baba's hand one last time before I opened the door of the truck, he used my African nickname, *Goinynam*, which means "a person who loves people."

I turned, and as our eyes met, he said, "Our huts will be side by side in heaven."

Honey for a Woman's Heart

Nonfiction

Judi Peers

I'd been phoning the parents of the boys on my son's hockey team, checking to see who would need extra spots on the team bus. My husband was the coach; that automatically made me the manager.

One father referred the question to his wife. "Honey," he called, "do we need any more seats?"

Isn't that nice, I mused. *He calls her Honey.*

That same night, my husband and I painted the walls in our bedroom. I hadn't paid much attention to the name of the colour of paint we bought. The rich, golden hue had immediately captured my attention because it would set off the pine-planked floors and crisp white trim to perfection.

I left for church the following morning with a feeling of satisfied accomplishment.

Much to my surprise, I found a beautiful package of honey-lavender biscotti in my church mailbox. There was nothing to indicate who had put it there.

Who would have given me such a gift? Summoning up much-needed self-discipline, I refrained from nibbling and disturbing others during the sermon.

By the way, the sermon was delivered by a guest speaker, and he introduced his message with the question: "How far does a bee fly in order to make a pound of honey?" Suddenly, I recalled the name of the paint we had used the night before—*warm honey.*

After the sermon, which ended on yet another reference to honey, I was corralled by friends who'd been working in the Sunday school during the service. Ruth and Liz presented me with an intriguing glass jar, on top of which colourful floral fabric had been secured. "A gift," they announced, "for helping with the Easter celebration."

The beautiful material on the lid blended perfectly with the contents of the jar—rich, golden *honey*.

What on earth was going on? In the past, I'd noticed that whenever God wanted to send me a message, He'd put words or symbols before me over and over again, until I finally noticed. *What was He trying to tell me by the use of all this* honey? *Did He want me to do something?*

Later that morning, in the church parking lot, as I crammed my friend Margie's wheelchair into the trunk of my car, God gently, lovingly, spoke to me. "That's from me," He whispered. "I'm calling *you* Honey."

It was one of those magic moments in life when I felt a stab of joy so intense it brought to mind what Milton and C. S. Lewis refer to as "enormous bliss." I drove away from the church both encouraged and elated that the God of the universe had just called *me* Honey.

Several weeks later, while lying in bed, mind racing, fighting sleep, I pondered my "honey" experience. I finally decided I must have been crazy. God doesn't go around calling people *Honey*. As if He has time for that!

It was probably my overactive imagination. But, just in case, I prayed, *Lord… if you really did, could—would—you do it again? Tomorrow? Just so I know for sure.*

Early the next morning, there was a knock on the kitchen door. One of my six brothers stood on the front porch carrying a book that had been written by a friend of our family. It was a biographical account of his missionary experiences in South America.

As Gary and I sipped tea at the table, we quickly leafed through *Henry's Memories*. To my amazement, the word *honey* seemed to lift off several of the pages. Apparently, wild honey was a food staple for the Ayores, a violent, nomadic people who roamed the jungles of southeastern Bolivia and northwestern Paraguay.

That surely had to be a coincidence!

Later, while preparing to go to the gym, I scanned my bookshelves, searching for a small paperback to read to break the tedium of tramping on the treadmill. I chose *Singers of the New Song*, George A. Maloney's commentary on the Song of Solomon.

After I got the treadmill going, and placed my book on the reading rack, it fell open to page 81. Immediately, I adjusted the treadmill's speed, slowing it down in order to savour the words.

"Your lips distill wild honey" (Song of Solomon 4:11).

Maloney went on to explain, "Anyone who has fallen in love understands what the groom is saying with this phrase. Two in love resort to honey as a phrase of endearment, for they have found kisses as sweet as honey. Union is what God calls us to, both with Him and with our neighbour. To move toward such oneness is always a 'sweet,' like honey, experience."

I wasn't crazy. God really *had* called me Honey!

Back at home, energized by my workout and the fact that God had answered my prayer, I grabbed a trowel and a pair of gloves and headed for my back garden.

Spotting me, my neighbour shouted over the fence, "I'm dividing some of these huge hostas. My garden is jam-packed, but you've got space. Would you like one?"

We dug and dug and pulled and tugged. It was, indeed, a huge hosta.

As I lugged it back to my yard, my neighbour called out once more, "Would you like to know its name?"

I smiled. I had a pretty good idea what it might be.

"It's a Honeybells Hosta," she said.

Carefully, I positioned the plant by my front door, a constant reminder that the One who had divided the surging sea, the One whose Son had divided history, had called *me* Honey.

But God didn't stop there. He kept calling me Honey all week. Then, on Friday, it came to a halt, but not before one grand finale, one wildly delicious display of heavenly affection.

That afternoon, I was the guest speaker for the Young Author's Conference at St. Patrick's School in Peterborough. After a wonderful time with the children in the gym, I was directed to the library so I could view several posters the students had painted.

  Hot Apple Cider with Cinnamon

I did my best to focus on the posters and make gracious remarks, but when I saw the message for me on the back wall, I could hardly contain myself. Someone had written "Welcome Judi Peers" next to a slogan about reading.

My name and the word *honey* were side by side, and these three words were much larger than the others. So with my increasingly myopic vision, all I clearly saw when I entered the room was *Judi Peers Honey.*

Welcome   **Reading is a**

JUDI PEERS   **HONEY**

of a hobby

What an amazing God! What a romantic God! How wonderful that He, the God of the universe, would use a familiar term of endearment in pursuing intimacy with me, and put it in big, bold-faced print so I couldn't possibly miss it!

Holding back the deluge of tears that threatened, I quickly thanked everyone and made my way out of the library, retreating to the privacy of my car. Lingering behind the wheel for several moments, I wept with joy. Truly, this had been one of the most incredible weeks of my life. God had not only overwhelmed me with His love, He had shown that He delights in my love for Him. He had called *me* Honey!

Why I Went Away Sorrowful

Based on Mark 10:17–31

Violet Nesdoly

I was ready to catch His look
of admiration at my excellent taste
in robe and turban

ready for Him to make my day
with a healing, a quaintly wise teaching
or a Pharisee drubbing

ready to accept His gratitude
when I offered to support Him and His band
for a month or two

ready to defend myself
on whether or not I've kept
the finer points of the law

ready for swift congratulations
when I asked Him what more I need do
to inherit eternal life

but I was *not* ready
for His answer

*Go, sell whatever you have
give to the poor
and come, follow Me.*

Nor was I ready,
when I turned to leave

to see pure love
in His eyes.

Chapter Book

Fiction

Bobbi Junior

Carefully, meticulously, word by word, the child read the first sentence in Chapter One. She felt very grown up. This was her second chapter book. This time she wouldn't be counting how many pages she'd already read. This time she wouldn't be counting how many pictures were in the chapter. This time she would only read word after word after word of the 76 pages in the book. But really, she wasn't counting. And there were only two pictures in this chapter, as someone would know if they'd quickly flipped the pages, just to see.

Propped against the wall in the corner of the school washroom, knees tucked under her chin, the little girl closed her lunch box and leaned her head of unruly brown hair against the chipped, green tile. Releasing a breath of contentment, her eyes settled into their methodical journey.

"What do you think you're doing?"

The chapter book flew from her hands and her heart nearly flew from her chest. The book landed face down on the floor.

In her head, she heard the librarian's singsong voice. "Never lay a book on its face. The spine will be broken, the glue will crack, and pages will rain out like leaves in a storm."

Guilt and adrenalin swirled through her. Tentatively, the child peered up through thick glasses.

"I asked you a question. Lunchroom or playground is where you're to be. And yet here you are, reading a library book, in the washroom no less. What are you thinking?"

The teacher's words pelted the child. A heavy hand reached down and gripped her plump arm, tugging her almost off the floor. She tottered before finding her balance.

This was not a teacher who knew her. The woman was heavy boned and thick in girth. Big, and sort of like a dad. At the child's eye level pink ruffles with a brown stain by the button quivered over the teacher's protruding stomach. A black binder was tucked under a fleshy arm.

If the child could have found words, she would have said, "But my book! I was on page five." She wanted to peek to see how many pages had rained out like leaves, but didn't dare turn her head.

"Whose class are you in? What's your name? Come on, child. Speak to me."

Which question to answer? So many, so fast. The book, though. She was on page five.

"Is the bathroom floor where your family reads?"

"No." A tiny sound crept out. "Just me."

"Just you. Humph. Well, don't just stand there. Pick up that book."

The teacher let go of her arm and the child turned and bent.

No paper rain. A smidgen of relief. Perhaps she would still get to read page six.

The teacher stepped toward the child. "The principal will want to hear about this."

Involuntarily, the little girl's scuffed runners drew her back, bumping her against the wall.

The child felt teacher eyes weighing down on her head. Her own eyes locked onto the chapter book, now embraced to her chest. She waited, conscious of her breathing, conscious of her knees that weren't quite steady.

And then something happened. This big lady in pink ruffles put her back against the wall next to the child and slid down the tile to sit on the floor. The teacher sat on the floor.

"I see you're reading a chapter book."

The child nodded a tiny nod.

"What grade are you in?"

"Two," slipped from her lips.

"I have Grade 4s who I have to force to read chapter books. Are you reading this all by yourself?"

Another nod, not quite so tiny this time.

"In my experience—" the big woman intoned as she tugged her slacks down in a failed effort to cover bristled flesh above black ankle socks, "—children who read chapter books have a lot of words in their heads."

This wasn't a question, so the child remained silent.

"If there were words in your head that said the name your parents gave you, what would those words be?"

The child had to think around the twist for a minute before she got inside the question and figured out the answer.

She blinked. Twice.

"The name would be Marlie Fulton. Goranski."

"Marlie Fulton-Goranski," the teacher repeated. She paused for a moment, and then, "Would this Marlie be related to Elton Goranski in my Grade 4 class whose dad married Marlie's mom last month?"

Marlie tried to think of a way to deny this, but couldn't. She nodded again.

Both were quiet; the child standing and the teacher sitting, her grey head a little lower than the child's chin.

The teacher's head tilted to one side, but she continued to gaze across the washroom. "If Marlie were to write her own chapter book that told about her new family, what would the first sentence be?"

Thought prevailed over fear as Marlie considered the question. *What would it be?* After a moment she knew. "Marlie's mother didn't really ask Marlie what she thought about having a new family."

"Marlie's mother didn't *really* ask," the teacher echoed. "The reader of this story will want to know more about *really*."

The next sentence came faster. "Well, Marlie's mother told Marlie a new family would be good. But she didn't ask what Marlie thought."

Both were silent. Marlie waited.

"And now—" the teacher opened the binder sitting on her lap, "—you might need some paper to write or draw what Marlie thought, that her mother didn't ask about."

The teacher held up a lined yellow pad with her big man-hand. Marlie's fingers accepted it.

Now the teacher lifted her gaze to the child's, and Marlie let her eyes get caught.

"When you have something on paper, I would like to invite you to bring it to my classroom at lunch time. This could be the first chapter in your own chapter book. Will you share your story with me?"

Marlie looked at the chapter book from the library. Perhaps page six could wait for a bit. She watched as the teacher clambered up from the floor. The teacher turned back to the child, looking down from her great height, but not in a scary way now.

The child nodded. "I will."

Here, Mommy, This Is for You

Nonfiction

Ruth Waring

The sun radiated its August heat without mercy, causing rippling waves to seemingly bounce a victory dance as they hovered over the hot asphalt. Under the unusually desert-like conditions we'd had in Southern Ontario during the past few weeks, manicured green lawns had been replaced with a straw-like covering, and weeds thrived where the grass could not. Thistles roamed with a vengeance across the once-blooming gardens, and seemed to chant a song: "Death to the flowers and grass! Death to the flowers and grass!"

I sat limp, knees buckled, back bending forward under an ache that had taken hold of my entire body. Earlier in the day, as we emptied our house of all our belongings, my energy had been depleted.

With the knowledge that we still had to fill another house, I had caved, physically and emotionally.

I was now second-guessing our decision to move back to London, Ontario, after seven years of living on two and one-third acres in a small town less than half an hour away. The city had definite advantages: the convenience of a neighbourhood grocery store, a shorter drive to my new job, and an even shorter drive to a church we liked and the Christian school our children attended.

But now that our move was a reality, I was struggling with memories and longing to go back home to the country.

Our family consisted of me, my husband of 21 years, and our three children—two teenagers and a 10-year-old budding wannabe teen. Beyond the human element, a Siamese cat (lovingly named *Jay* after the Toronto Blue Jays) and two poodles (a mother and daughter in their senior years) completed our family picture. We'd all been very happy living in the country. But when a new job took me to the city on the weekdays, country living soon became a burden for everyone. For my sake, and for the sake of my children, the time had come to leave the place we loved and start again.

Now, as the heat made my headache worse, I sat looking at the mess in front of me. Half of our worldly possessions sat in a moving van that had been forced to straddle the sidewalk in front of our new home in order to accommodate passing traffic. The other half of our possessions, including tables, chairs, toys, pillows, and precious antiques—were spread over the driveway for the world to see what the new neighbours were bringing to the neighbourhood.

All I could do was sit and wait, and wait, imagining dollar signs in the moving van attendants' eyes as their normal-pay hours slipped into time and a half.

Where is the key to the house? Where is our lawyer? What have we done?

I turned to eye my husband, but he was busy socializing with friends who had come to help us, and all appeared unconcerned about the predicament we were in. Turning the inconvenience into a picnic, they stood in the shade of the red maple on the front lawn or sat and kibitzed on the front steps, toying with empty paper cups and indulging in the abundance of doughnuts someone had provided along with the coffee.

We were all in plain view of curious onlookers who passed by, and I couldn't help wondering, *Why didn't I notice how busy this street is before we bought this house?*

I shook my head and sank further into my dark mood.

All in all, I had two hours to contemplate the foolishness of our move before someone arrived with the coveted key, and the work of moving in began.

I busied myself, making sure the dogs and cat were safely locked in the bathroom with plenty of water, directing furniture and box placement in the house, and lifting boxes of dishes too heavy for me to lift.

While carrying some garden tools to the side of the garage, I paused, realizing suddenly how much my life was about to change.

On our acreage, I'd planted a half-acre vegetable garden each spring and reaped my success once the coons had decided to leave my garden alone. I'd discovered the value of canning tomatoes, peaches, pears, and pickles of various kinds. Of freezing strawberries for jam and elderberries, blueberries, and rhubarb for pies. How I had loved the fresh country air, the small-town Santa Claus parade, the Fall Fair, and the freedom my children had to roam the back acreage and build a tree house in the far corner. I'd even survived the smoke and dust from the tractor competitions and the aroma of my neighbour's annual fertilizer that fragranced our home, and, far too often, my laundry.

My children had helped with chores, chopping wood, feeding the dogs, and cutting the large expanse of grass. Sometimes under duress. I sighed woefully, remembering the complaining. But as I leaned the rakes and garden hoe against the garage wall, I knew in my heart that they had worked well together more often than not. *What will life be like in this new city house?*

My thoughts were interrupted by the arrival of my younger son.

Of my three children, he was the most charismatic—a sociable extrovert and an explorer. Wherever there were people to talk to, he would gravitate toward them. Wherever there was a place to be, he would go. True to form…

"Mommy! Mommy! Can I go down the street and check things out?"

Fighting the guilt of being relieved to have him out from underfoot, I nodded. "But stay within eyesight," I called after him, doubting he even heard me.

After what was probably 20 minutes, although my body screamed, "Two hours!" my 10-year-old reappeared, in desperate need of a quarter.

"A quarter? What on earth do you need a quarter for?" My tone matched my weariness, bordering on irritation. After all, there were beds to be set up and made, supper to be thought about, if not prepared, and bees to keep from flying in the open doors. I had no time for such trivial demands.

"There's a garage sale up the street and—"

I groaned.

"—there's something I just gotta have! It only costs a quarter. Pleeease?"

With reluctance, I searched for my purse and briskly placed a quarter in my son's outstretched hand.

He turned and, with untapped energy, ran back into his new world.

I turned and wearily walked back into my own.

Moments later, a little voice said, "Here, Mommy, this is for you."

I glanced down at the hands of my little people-person son and saw a four-inch cream-coloured statue of two small children hugging one another. Inscribed at their feet were words that read *It starts with 'L' ends with 'E' and in between are 'O' and 'V.*

He gave me a quick hug and then was gone again.

As I watched him race back to the garage sale, I suddenly knew without a doubt that the decision to move had been the right one, and I smiled.

That 25-cent garage sale purchase became precious to me. It was—and still is—a constant reminder that wherever we were, I had all I needed—my little boy's love.

 Hot Apple Cider with Cinnamon

A Small Pot of Nasturtiums

Nonfiction

Rose Seiler Scott

The doorbell rang. My 13-year-old daughter ran to greet her friend, who was coming over to spend time with her.

I had become acquainted with the girl's stepmom, Kate, when the girls attended the same elementary school, so she came to the door with her daughter to say hello to us.

Kate held out a miniature plastic pot, out of which sprang a stem with two tender leaves. "I've just been to the nursery, and these are for you," she said with a lilt. "Nasturtiums."

I'd dropped my daughter at their house on a number of occasions, and judging from the flowers adorning her front step and yard, had guessed that Kate was a gardener. My own attempts at gardening were often unsuccessful, and my physical limitations made keeping up an acre of property overwhelming at times. We'd opted for lower-maintenance shrubs and a small vegetable plot.

Accepting the unexpected gift, I was embarrassed to admit I couldn't even picture what a nasturtium flower looked like. "Thank you," I said, wondering if I could manage to keep the delicate plant alive. But I was determined to try.

Just as the nasturtiums were about to outgrow their two-inch pot, I transplanted them into a decorative wheelbarrow planter by the front door. That, in my mind, gave them the best hope of getting watered.

I waited.

At first, not much happened. A few times, due to my neglect, the plant nearly wilted, but before it expired completely I remembered to give it a drink. More leaves appeared and they grew a little larger.

Eventually, the planter was filled with roundish emerald leaves. A trace of white lines emanated like spokes from the centre of each leaf.

Then our family went away for a few days.

Upon returning, we unloaded the car and came up the sidewalk toward the front door.

I was stunned. "Look at that!" I said to my husband and daughter.

Orange flowers tumbled out of the container; a riot of florescent blooms trailed down the steps.

What a lovely surprise, reminding me of the cheerful, outgoing nature of my Irish friend who had given them to me.

In their outrageous brilliance, the abundance of those nasturtiums also made me think of God's outpouring of love toward us. He is more than I can ever ask for or imagine, especially when I feel overwhelmed or when my own efforts don't measure up. His love spills over; His grace is extravagant. I think of this every time I see nasturtiums!

Finding Shelter in the Storm

Nonfiction

Christiana Flanigan

That summer day started out with the same routine as every other day, with plenty of "to do" items and various places I needed to go. Once I retired, I'd honestly thought I'd have a great deal of free time to read and do other things I'd put off, but this tedious cycle of little chores seemed to be the norm. I also realized it took me longer to do normal tasks than it had when I was younger.

Plus, earlier that year, my daughter's world had come apart, and I felt distressed. There is truth in the saying that "a mother is only as happy as her unhappiest child." I couldn't seem to let go of that pain and sadness.

As evening approached after each busy, frustrating day, a feeling of being overwhelmed took over me. It was as if my life was falling to pieces.

Each time I returned to my home, I'd realize that my gardens were being neglected. Each time, I felt guilty, but nurturing my flowers and vegetables just didn't inspire me the way it had before.

I also no longer enjoyed the time set aside for playing my piano, which, in the past, I'd always looked forward to.

It had been a long time since I'd had a good night's sleep. In the middle of the night, I'd end up wide awake with my thoughts, turning small daily matters into out-of-proportion problems. Most mornings I awoke with a slight headache—just enough to take away any joy in planning activities.

After weeks of restless sleep and dissatisfaction with my life, depression-like symptoms had taken over. I didn't care about much of anything any more. In a way, I'd lost interest in my life. I lessened my time with neighbours and friends.

I did attend my grandsons' soccer and baseball games as often as I could, since seeing the boys made my heart feel lighter, but it wasn't enough. My depression grew deeper, and tears were abundant.

Being a private person, however, I didn't reach out for help. Instead, I kept my sadness bundled up inside, where it grew. Somewhere deep down in my soul, I knew I had to take control of my health, and that I was the only one who could make changes, but I was too lethargic to take action. And I was so good at hiding how I felt that even my husband didn't realize what was happening to me.

Something definitely has to change, I'd think. *I have to get off this continuous carousel ride while I still can.*

One day in late summer, I strode through my yard to the back of our lot to view my gardens. Of course, nothing had changed over the summer. Or rather, they had become even worse. They were in total disarray, with weeds towering over my struggling perennials. I shook my head. *How could I have let this happen to something I loved so much before?*

I sat on a tiny mound in one corner and pondered for what seemed like hours.

After a while my thoughts went back to a tiny, stone cottage, on a corner lot. It had well-kept gardens in the back yard, surrounded by a low, white lattice fence. The gardens flourished from spring to fall with a multitude of flowers in many colours, specific to the season. I had actually made it a point to drive by this house each time I went for groceries, just to have the chance to take a peek at the gardens.

The owner of the cottage, or as I had named her "the garden lady," tended her gardens constantly. Whenever I drove by the cottage, I'd see her pulling weeds, deadheading flowers, or watering thirsty plants. She wore a wide-brimmed straw hat with a large sunflower pinned to the side. So bright and cheery.

As if by instinct, she seemed to know when I was going by, and she'd give me a smile and a slight wave of her gloved hand.

I sensed peace and harmony in her tidy gardens.

I looked again at my own flowers and felt disappointment with myself for neglecting them. But in that moment, I also realized that I had been neglecting myself as well. My spiritual self, in particular, didn't appear to exist.

With a sigh, I did the one thing I should have done a long time ago, but had pushed aside. I prayed.

It felt a little uneasy and awkward at first. I guess I'd thought I could manage on my own and fix my problems without anyone's help—even without God's help.

Why, I asked myself, *turn to God last?* After all, wasn't it written, "Ask, and it shall be given you"[1]?

I sat silently on that tiny mound, deep in thought, pouring my anxieties and unhappiness out to God, with tears flowing freely down my cheeks. I didn't expect any miracles; I just needed to share my anxieties. And I knew, in my heart, that He would listen.

A soft breeze brought me out of my reverie. A warmth surrounded me, and I felt calm and at ease. Myriad colourful leaves flitted through the air, landing at my feet, forming a small carpet. Several squirrels scampered nearby, chasing each other in circles. Autumn, my most loved of all the seasons, had arrived and I hadn't noticed. I'd allowed my depression to take away my joy in appreciating the beauty that God had created all around me.

Once again, I surveyed my yard, but this time in a different sense. I wanted the serenity that the garden lady seemed to have. I wanted a special place to go where I could have alone time, pray, or meditate. I knew I didn't have to attend a church service to find that place. It was here in my own backyard.

I pictured a meditation garden on the same spot where I had felt God's presence—a place I could visit each day to clear away any muddled thoughts and savour the beauty in the simple things that were right in front of me. I drew a rough sketch, and the garden was born.

With my husband's help, I placed a bench in one corner, nestled between our maple and chestnut trees. An arbour served as an entrance to a little alcove, with flowering perennials and hostas on each side. Flagstones formed a path to the bench from the arbour. It was, for me, the ideal setting. Private and tranquil, so that I could hear my own thoughts.

During those autumn days of working on my meditation garden, I felt renewed strength and clarity of mind. My tears lessened, and I was able to get off that carousel.

Since then, several friends have sat with me, enjoying the beauty of my meditation garden. But the times I cherish most are those when I sit alone on my bench in the morning mist, kept dry by the canopy of leaves, totally at peace, savouring precious moments of silence.

1. Matthew 7:7 KJV

  Hot Apple Cider with Cinnamon

My True Love

Nonfiction

Maureen Fitzpatrick

Love encompasses many aspects of life—from God's love to our loving His world, which includes family, friends, pets, and the many ways people can interact with God's creation in artistic ways—dance, art, writing, and many more. While I love reading, if I had to choose only one kind of creative expression, it would be music.

Music is universal—it's played at christenings, birthdays, weddings, anniversaries, concerts, church services, and funerals. Music can be gospel, classical, jazz, country, rock-n-roll, calypso, love songs, and dance songs. Music has warmed the hearts of romantic souls throughout the ages and eased the sorrow of those who are sad.

Music is one of the ways God's love shines through to meet each individual's taste. Classical music stirs me more than anything else, especially when played on the piano. I once dreamed of becoming a concert pianist, but due to circumstances beyond my control that never materialized. I often wonder how my life would have turned out had I fulfilled my dream.

I appreciate Beethoven, Schubert, Liszt, Grieg, Tchaikovsky, and other composers. I enjoy a sonata, a concerto, a ballade, a rhapsody, and a waltz. But my favourite composer is Frederic Chopin, whose nocturnes and etudes warm my heart and make me feel near to God.[1]

The captivating tunes of music help to relieve my stress and melt any resentment or bitterness in my heart. My life hasn't been easy. My first love, my mother, died when I was only 15. My second love, my dad, died exactly three years after my mum. My marriage was abusive, and I had to get out and find a way to support myself and my children. Over the years, there have been other painful losses—my beloved cats, my favourite brother, friends... My children, whom I love, live far from me. But through it all, I know God is with me, and one of the ways He speaks to me is through music.

Music has lessened my hurts and disappointments, erased disturbing thoughts, and, at least for a while, eased the worries of everyday life. Music consoles, comforts, and transports me into an imaginary world where everyone is loving and kind; a world of beauty, peace, good health, joy, genuine laughter, order, harmony, and contentment. In music, everyone shares, so there is no need. There is no status symbol, racism, or terrorism. There is respect, understanding and co-operation, and thus no need for judge, jury, and executioner.

I know—that sounds like heaven on earth. Sometimes, music truly hypnotizes me into thinking such a wonderful world could actually exist.

And in those times I remind myself that we all have a choice, despite our circumstances, to make our own music—love in our hearts.

1. A few of my favourites:
   Nocturne in D Flat Major, op. 27 No. 2
   Nocturne in B Flat Minor, op. 9, No. 1
   Etude op. 10, No. 10 in A Flat Major
   Etude op. 25, No. 1 in A Flat Major

Not the Love I Was Looking For

Nonfiction

Laureen F. Guenther

When I was a young girl—six or seven years old—I had a large collection of dolls. I don't remember dressing them up or playing with their hair, although maybe I did. What I *do* remember is tucking them in beside me in my own narrow bed every night. I'd line them all up on my pillow, next to the wall so they wouldn't fall off.

I lay on the bed's outer edge—the *very* outer edge—even though my dad always warned me I'd fall out. "Put yourself next to the wall," he said, "with the dolls on the outside."

But I insisted I wouldn't fall out—and I was determined my precious dolls wouldn't either.

I remember the secure feeling I had as I lay there next to my dolls, imagining I was raising them, nurturing them, protecting them. One night, as I lay there treasuring that feeling, I decided, in my vivid imagination, that they were not all *my* children, because even then I knew they made a very large family. I fantasized that some of them were other people's children, and I was taking care of them. It made no difference to me. I watched over them all, no matter who their mother was.

I soon grew out of my fondness for dolls, and my treasured collection is long gone, who knows where. But I didn't grow out of my desire to nurture children.

I was barely 11 years old when I got my first babysitting job. I continued to babysit—caring for many, many children in many families—through the rest of elementary school, all through high school, and beyond. I enjoyed babysitting, and it was certainly nice to have the income.

I must have been relatively good at it, but I assumed that everyone finds it natural to care for children.

When I was 15, I volunteered to teach Sunday school. I offered because there was a need, not because I thought I had any teaching skills. I was assigned to a class of two- and three-year-olds, and I began to give my heart to teaching them. I hardly knew what I was doing, and some adults in the church even mocked my youthful efforts, but I discovered something that thrilled me: not only did I have a gift for teaching young children, but doing it filled me with joy!

Around the same time, long before it became trendy to adopt internationally, I began reading memoirs of couples who'd created large, adoptive families. I loved their stories of challenges and victories, and I was inspired to follow their example.

I developed a burning desire to provide a secure, loving, permanent family for children who had no family—older children, children with special needs, children in sibling groups, children who'd been hurt. I'd always assumed I'd marry a wonderful man and we'd give birth to a few children. Now I modified that dream— I'd marry a wonderful man, we might or might not give birth to a few children, and we'd make a home for a large number of children who would otherwise not have a home.

I dreamed of that. I longed for it. And I expected it to happen.

In the meantime, I earned a degree in Christian education, then another one in elementary education, and I began teaching Kindergarten to Grade 2 in a rural Saskatchewan school.

I was far from perfect, but I worked hard to be a good teacher, giving my students the knowledge and skills they needed, nurturing their emotional and social growth, and building their confidence by showing them they were loved.

Now, 20-plus years later, I've taught many children—in six communities, in two Canadian provinces, and in a beautiful, overcrowded nation on the other side of the world. I've taught children in public schools, private schools, and Christian schools. I've taught classes of children who were all as fair-skinned as I am, and classes that were so ethnically diverse I marvelled at all the ways God has made children beautiful.

I've taught young children, older children, children who were developing typically, children who had special needs, children who were loved and confident, and children who carried deep wells of sadness. They came from families who were struggling, families who were working hard but just making it, and families who were thriving in every way.

As I grew as a teacher, I also strengthened my ability to support my students' parents, building up their confidence as well.

I've also invested my skills and energy outside the classroom. That included every kind of children's ministry: Sunday school, children's church, mid-week clubs, Bible camps, vacation Bible schools, and special needs ministry. I started and led a leadership training program to train older children and youth to serve in children's ministries. I developed and led a ministry for families who had children with special needs. I've also trained adults and teens to minister to children, multiplying my skills by planting them in others. And I've tied all that experience together by writing curriculum for children's ministries.

I've built friendships with many, many children, some close to home and some in other parts of the world. I've invested in their parents, their families, and their teachers.

I've become "Auntie Reenie" to three nieces and two nephews. I've poured my life into each of them and into the lives of many more nephews- and nieces-by-affection.

God has given me an ever-widening circle of adult friends, spreading from next door to across Canada to around the globe. A few of those friends love me dearly, and they've proven they'd do (nearly) anything for me. They are truer and more devoted than I ever imagined friends could be. I count on their care, their affection, and their commitment.

And yes, along the way, I've met a few men I thought I might like to marry. But I'm glad and grateful I didn't marry any of them.

I haven't raised my own children, either by birth or by adoption. I did consider adopting on my own, but I realized that having the responsibility for children in my own home would redirect my focus from the children and adults already in my circles of nurture. So I threw myself even more fervently into building up those children and adults already around me.

I've given away a lot of love, and thanks to God's imagination and sweet goodness, I've received lots and lots of love in return.

The children and friends I've loved have poured love back into me. Their devotion and affection make my life rich and sweet. In truth, God has filled my life with love to overflowing. Not the love I was longing for. Not the love I was looking for. But a wonderful love nonetheless.

Although singleness and childlessness weren't in my plans, I've worked hard to be content, and usually I am. Most days I'm grateful, satisfied, even full of joy. With a full and honest heart, I can agree with what King David wrote in the Psalms: "The boundary lines have fallen for me in pleasant places; surely I have a delightful inheritance."[1]

That's most days. But it's not every day.

For me, there's a tension of contentment-versus-dissatisfaction that cycles through the months and the years. When I'm celebrating my singleness, I think of all the things I wouldn't have had if I'd been married—opportunities to pursue dual careers, diverse ministries, and far-reaching friendships; freedom to develop my own personality and character; flexibility to come and go as I wish.

But sometimes I don't like singleness so much. When I plan a holiday trip, and wish I weren't travelling alone yet again… When I attend yet another wedding of someone much younger than I… When I get together with my family at Christmas, and am reminded I'm still the only single adult in the house… When the entire world makes a fuss over Mother's Day but hasn't a single word for non-mothers who give their lives to other people's children… When my married friends circle their wagons so they can focus on their own families' needs…When a crisis occurs and I pour myself out for people I love, but they don't necessarily pour back into me, and I ask God in tears, "Who cares for Reenie?"

That's when I choose to believe that nearly all marriages are wonderful; that nearly all married women have their husbands' consistent, loving support. That nearly all husbands are kind and understanding and financially viable and supportive and committed and concerned, and that I'm the only one missing out on something that is every woman's right.

At those times, I feel alone and forgotten, like I'm the only one who hasn't found the love she was looking for. At those times I've found it easy to conclude there's a large and ungainly defect in me, visible to everyone but me. It's easy to feel that God doesn't really like me, or that He considers me of less value than all the women to whom He's given husbands and children. At those times, it's easy to resent others for the things that seem to come so easily to them. I may cry a few tears and engage in a solid bout of self-pity. It's easy at those times to minimize the value of the ones who care about me, just because they're not *the ones I wanted*. And sometimes I do.

For a long time I've known that He's promised to satisfy every longing, but it was only a theory. Recently, I've begun to take Him up on it. And I'm learning, to my amazement, that He does satisfy.

On those difficult-to-be-single days, I'm learning to turn to the One who loves me most faithfully, who loves me best. I can seek to be loved and satisfied by the eternal Lover who has loved everyone who'll ever walk this earth—whether they're single or married, listening or defiant, wrapped in human love or entirely alone.

I can turn to the One who has walked with me since the same year I lay in that tiny bed and guarded those precious dolls. The One who has tuned my heart to love Him, serve Him, and please Him, every single day, all these years.

It's not easy, but when I go through the work of telling Him how I feel…When I humble myself and ask Him to satisfy me… When I admit that His love isn't what I wanted, but I want Him to give it to me anyway… He does. He really does.

His love, the eternal love of God, isn't the love I was looking for. But it's the love I need, whatever my marital status. And it's wonderful!

1. Psalm 16:6.

Father's Arms

Nonfiction

Beverly G. DeWit

I look into the eyes of the woman who has filled our home with laughter. And I know that even though her life on this earth is ending, God's hand is on her now, just as it was on that fall day so many years ago when she was just a tiny girl.

Her father walked along the street in Velp, Netherlands on October 5, 1944 to visit his parents. For a while, he sat drinking a cup of strong coffee with them as they discussed the activity near the bridge at Arnhem. The bridge had become a point of interest for both sides in this war that grew more intolerable every day.

The wail of sirens broke the silence of the morning.

Fear gripping his heart, the man's hand went automatically to his chest. His wife and little daughter were at home alone.

His parents urged him to leave them and return home immediately.

His legs ran quickly, but his speed felt inadequate.

Behind him, many planes were flying overhead, dropping their bombs. The sky began to turn orange-red.

The adrenaline within him surged, and his strides quickened as he drew near his home. His hand grasped the doorknob. Hastily opening the door, he propelled himself forward into the dining room. He found his wife quietly sewing, as if not to panic their young daughter, Nelly, who was playing too near the window.

The sound of explosions grew closer, and the man grabbed hold of his wife and urged her to get down on the floor.

With one swoop of his arm, he picked up his daughter and tucked her under his body as he, too, bent toward the floor.

The next explosion forced the walls of the small duplex inward, and the blocks collapsed all around them.

Then there was silence.

Hot Apple Cider with Cinnamon

Outside, there was noise. Screams and cries as the neighbours scurried about trying desperately to remove the rubble, searching frantically—hoping, praying, that life could be found.

The air, full of dust, burned their eyes as they worked, and tears streamed down their faces as they realized it appeared to be hopeless.

Then a faint cry sent them scurrying to work even harder. Blocks were pulled away, and the still, lifeless body of the woman was uncovered.

Desperately they pulled away more dirt and blocks, and the man's back began to appear. His cold and lifeless body brought forth agonizing cries of grief.

As they moved his body, they found the little girl. She lay motionless in her father's arms, covered in blood. And then she stirred.

The neighbours took her to the hospital. The doctor washed her body carefully and discovered that the blood belonged to her father. All she had were a few little scratches.

Her father's brothers picked the orphan up to take her home to live with their parents.

However, circumstances forced their family to evacuate their home and flee to the south of Holland with only two handcarts of belongings. For ten days they walked, hiding in the ditches to avoid the bombing, and sleeping in barns.

Three months later, they returned home to find their house occupied by the Germans, who allowed them to stay in the cellar of their home. There was very little food during the cold winter.

On April 11, 1945 they were liberated, but life for Nelly was difficult in Holland.

At the age of 19, she met Gerrit DeWit, a trumpet player who, a short while later, announced that he had been recruited by the Canadian military band and would be leaving soon for Canada. She asked him to marry her.

From their union, three children were born. Her eldest son, Peter, planted churches in the province of Quebec for ten years before becoming a missionary in Thailand for 22 years and is currently serving in Paris, France. Her second son, Gerald (my husband), has done many mission trips around the world and is currently serving as senior pastor of Bethel Evangelical Missionary church in Lion's Head, Ontario, a popular tourist destination. Her daughter, Paula, has shared her gift of music with the city of Chilliwack, British Columbia for many years as a co-founder and conductor of the Chilliwack Symphony.

So much good would have been lost to this world if my mother-in-law's father hadn't rushed home that day to shelter his small daughter in the safety of his arms!

Hidden Treasures

Nonfiction

Heather Rae Rodin

The old cabin my grandfather built was situated in northern Ontario, resting on the shore of a peaceful bay, the front door not more than 30 feet from a sparkling, spring-fed lake. The cabin had served our family well for many years, but it had seen better days. Well, maybe not that much better. But now it really needed repairs.

The roof leaked so badly that every heavy rain meant there was an available indoor shower. Repurposed windows neither opened nor closed, and one of the two exterior doors was permanently jammed shut with old newspapers and foamy caulking. If ever we were curious about the comings and goings of our next-door neighbours, we only needed to open one of the kitchen cupboards. Second shelf down, three inches to the right, there was a knothole large enough to keep us informed. Of course, the hole also let in wind, rain, and snow.

The cabin was eventually passed on to my mom, who then passed it on to me. Soon after I was given the cottage, my husband, Gord, decided it was time to do some renovating.

Mom and I chose a rainy day to start cleaning out the kitchen cupboards, preparing them to be torn down. (I imagined I could see Gord waiting anxiously nearby with his sledgehammer.) Keeping an eye on the children working quietly at a craft, Mom and I chatted comfortably as we went through the rickety kitchen.

The cupboards were stacked with an assortment of discards from everyone's spring cleaning down through the years. I planned to dispose of the old dishes and line the new shelves with my latest fashionable acquisitions.

Among the eclectic collection of items we found in the cupboards were three dusty, old plates. They had obviously originated from different sets, but they shared a few things in common: each was terribly worn and was either chipped or cracked.

"Why on earth have we been saving these?" I picked them up and bent down to place them in the garbage box.

Mom moved quickly. "You know—" her sweet, gentle voice stopped me as she took the first plate from me "—this one belonged to my mother. It's from her good set, which she only used on special occasions. Our friends were always welcome in our home, and we really enjoyed having guests for dinner. With five siblings, it was a lot of fun around the dinner table. Maybe that's why we've stayed so close all these years." After a pensive pause, Mom set the plate in the "to save" pile.

She reached for the next plate I held, and a misty look shadowed her lovely face. "This one was from my grandmother's set. I recall us all going to visit Grandma and Grandpa for holidays and having these beautiful plates set before us." She chuckled softly. "It was so much fun to pile into the buckboard and cuddle under the bear rug, giggling with the excitement of seeing our grandparents. They didn't live very far away, but back then any travelling was a big deal. Grandpa owned the general store and always had a special treat ready for each of us. It was usually an orange, a peppermint stick, or a treasured nickel."

Her wistful smile lingered as she privately travelled back in time.

"Seeing this plate even brings back the mixture of smells in that wonderful old store. The wood stove in the middle of the room belting out its heat, bolts of fabric, sacks of flour and sugar, plugs of tobacco, and even the barrel brimming with pickles—a wonderland of delight to our curious minds." She put that plate in the "to save" pile also.

I stared down at the last plate in my hands. It reflected a beauty from days gone by, but a severe crack ran through it. Before Mom could reach for it, I handed it to her, suddenly anxious to hear its story.

"This set belonged to my Aunt Mary, an energetic, creative lady. She was an artist and had an eye for beauty. Everything in her home seemed beautiful to me. It was so different from the old farmhouse that sheltered us five rambunctious children, and I loved to go to her home and gaze at all the lovely things she had sitting about." Her voice had dropped to almost a whisper. "Why, this plate must be over a hundred years old." A soft sigh escaped her lips. "These dishes hold so many wonderful memories."

I remained quiet for a moment, looking at the old chipped and cracked plates, knowing they were no longer headed for disposal. As Mom had shared her stories, the battered plates had suddenly been transformed before my eyes. What I had thought deserving of a trip to the dump had been, to my mother, a refreshing waterfall of precious memories. The same flaws and marks that had annoyed me now made them beautiful.

I learned a valuable lesson that day. I witnessed useless clutter becoming beautiful treasures by seeing through someone else's eyes. My mother had shown me the loveliness that still remained amid the cracks and chips and dust.

Today those three plates are proudly displayed in a gilded rack on the wall of our nicely renovated cottage.

I love those old, beat-up dishes. Their worn beauty stirs a sense of belonging and renewal. Guests may wonder at their prominence, but for me they will remain a precious memory and a valuable reminder. When I look at them, I remember—not only a special time with my mom but also the heritage of my amazing family.

And I am reminded to look at others, as much as possible, through God's eyes, as glaring faults and failures are replaced by grace and mercy, and we find ourselves free to discover love in new and unexpected places.

Her Mother's Things

Vilma Blenman

She sits in spring morning light
Staring at her mother's things:
A museum memoir in her mother's garage
Displays on the driveway
Artifacts on a blue chenille bedspread on grass.
Garage sale bargain hunters saunter by
And I, her mother's friend, take change, make change
For the pretty, unwanted things
But all the while I want to hiss
"Don't haggle. These are her mother's things!"

Last night when we priced priceless things
She suddenly said out loud,
"When I was little, I loved playing with these bracelets
More than my toys. I remember Mom
Always taking them from me
And giving me play dough instead."
"Play dough is good," I said.

After a long silence while we worked, she said
"When I was ten, I loved dressing up in her clothes.
These silver heels hurled me headlong
Down the stairs one rainy day
And brought Mom hurtling from the kitchen with floury hands
Screaming, 'Dear God, have mercy! She's dead!'"
That's what she said, while I polished a silver teapot.

"At fourteen, I absolutely hated my mother's things," she said
I made fun of her fur collars, and begged her
'Take away your ugly blue bedspread.
My friends visit my room. Don't you want me to have friends?
Please mom, get a life. Let me have a life.'"

Hot Apple Cider with Cinnamon

At twenty-one, she barely saw her mother's things, she said
Backpacking in Paris was such a pleasant pastime
"Who was I with?" she asked out loud. "I'm not sure."
At thirty-four, she had a life, she said
What with the whisk-me-away wedding in Cancun
Their growing family and the company promoting her so often.

It was Thanksgiving, she said
When she last saw her mother's things
Saw her kids kissed below the same yellowy-orange wreath
Saw the corn-husk mat on the kitchen floor
Saw the table set with the white ceramic turkey platter
With the twenty tiny cornucopia carvings.
"I counted them all when I was four," she said.
And there was cranberry jelly on the Mikasa crystal dish.
And she rang the silver dinner bell
That still sat polished in the hutch.

"I'm keeping the bell, and the bracelets, of course,"
She said, showing me her left hand.
"Strange to think she and I both wore these
Both adored them. See how they catch light?
Mom and I, we both loved light. It's just that
Mom didn't love my choices, most of them anyway
Clothes, cars, companions, colours…
Still, I wasn't ready for the call this spring,"
She said, all in a rush, and then a hush
As we sat quietly after. The two of us. Last night.

Today when the cars stop coming by, she says,
"Just take what's left. Please.
For your church bazaar. Please.
Mom would love that. I'm sure she would."
So I walk to my car, carefully
Carrying her memory props in my hands
My heart held tightly in my chest while I wonder
What will my daughter do with her mother's things?

Not just the rings and the rose-pattern china and the down duvet...
Not that I have much of anything
For her to hold an estate auction at high noon.
But what will she do with the things I've said, or tried to say,
The things I've done, or not done well,
The things I've placed in her, before her?
The faith I found and fostered in her?
What will she do with her mother's things?

Hot Apple Cider with Cinnamon

A Flower for Mother's Day

Nonfiction

Linda Jonasson

I used to dread Mother's Day. I'd sit in church and wait for the flowers to be handed out to all the mothers at the end of the service. When someone offered me a carnation, I'd take it, my hands trembling, knowing I was accepting it under false pretenses. But I didn't want to go into a lengthy explanation.

It wasn't just Mother's Day that I found difficult. Every time an infant was baptized, I would pray that one day it would be my baby up at the baptismal font being sprinkled with water. But week after week, month after month, year after year, my arms remained empty.

Three times over a three-year period my husband, Rob, and I celebrated the news that I was pregnant and marked the due date on the calendar. Three times we suffered the devastating news that I had miscarried. I remember sitting beside Rob on the couch, tears streaming down my cheeks, protesting, "I wanted a baby. I wanted a baby. I wanted a baby."

It hurt to see other pregnant women. It hurt to see women pushing baby strollers down the street. It hurt to hear other people ask when we would start a family, as if my three miscarriages had never happened. There was an emptiness inside me that could only be filled by holding a baby in my arms.

Within a month of my last miscarriage, Rob and I decided to adopt a baby. A social worker paid us several visits as part of a home study, asking an endless list of personal questions about ourselves and parenting. We scrubbed our house from top to bottom for each visit. We prepared a profile to be shared with birth parents. We told everyone about our search for a baby. Then we put it in God's hands.

Everyone had told us to prepare for a long wait. A fellow teacher said that she and her husband had waited on an adoption list for ten years and still didn't have a baby. So we weren't expecting the call when it came. We had been on the adoption list for only seven months. It was December 1, 1998. Rob and I were sitting at the kitchen table. Rob had just finished decorating the Christmas tree. As he placed the last ornament on the tree, he said, "Christmas just isn't the same without children."

The phone rang. I answered it.

"Are you still interested in adopting a baby?" asked the social worker at Beginnings Adoption Agency.

"Yes!" I shouted, jumping several feet into the air.

Three days later, we drove to the Brantford Pregnancy Centre to meet the birthparents who had picked us from a choice of three couples' profiles. I had butterflies in my stomach. Rob tapped his foot. Sequestered in a small room waiting to meet the birth parents, who were in another small room, we felt like guests on the Jerry Springer Show.

Finally it was time. We opened the door and came face to face with a handsome teenage couple. The birthmother, Nicole, her belly round enough to be in her ninth month, wore pants and a beige peasant blouse with a pretty cross-stitch design. Her gentle smile warmed her face. She had that pregnancy glow. The birth father, Lance, a tall slender teenager wearing jeans and a T-shirt, stood by her side, gently holding her elbow.

Fortunately, one of the social workers had suggested we bring along a photo album to break the ice. So, after a brief introduction, I opened my photo album, and the words flowed out of my mouth: I described family picnics, weddings, and sleepovers with my two nieces. The four of us hit it off immediately. There was an instant connection and our nervousness subsided. Glancing at Rob, I could see he looked more at ease, too.

At the end of the visit, one of the social workers took a Polaroid picture of the four of us in front of the pregnancy centre Christmas tree. Moments later, when I held the photograph, I noticed an angel looking down at us from the top of the evergreen.

After a smooth first visit, I wondered if the second one would go as well. It felt like a second date to me. He liked me the first time, but would he still like me the second time around?

Rob and I met Nicole and Lance at a restaurant in Brantford. I can still picture the clothes we wore, the booth we sat at, the food we ate, the conversation we shared.

The waiter snapped our photo, saying that the birth mother and I could have passed for sisters. He knew how to flatter someone who, at 31, was already "over the hill."

Once again we enjoyed a great visit. It was as if we'd known each other forever.

Only three days later, the phone rang. It was Lance. Nicole had delivered a bouncing baby boy, weighing nine pounds and measuring 20 ½ inches long. The baby scored a perfect Apgar rating.

Rob and I felt both excited and confused. No one had told us what to do when the baby arrived. Should we introduce ourselves as the baby's parents? How long should we stay? What should we do?

We raced to the hospital and bounded up the steps two by two, stopping long enough at the gift shop to buy a white teddy bear with a blue vest.

We found the door to Nicole's room open, and there I had the privilege of holding Thomas Lance for the first time. It felt so good! I studied him closely. His hands were large and his fingers long, like his birth father's. His face was round and his cheeks chubby, like his birth mother's. His eyes were dark and his eyelashes long, like both birth parents'. It reassured us to see their traits in their baby, soon to be our baby.

The next day we returned to the hospital for a second visit. But this time, Nicole's hospital room door was closed. Should we return home? Had she changed her mind about placing her baby for adoption? We gently knocked on the door.

Lance poked his head out. "It's not a good time," he said, his voice breaking. I could see traces of tears on his cheeks.

But Nicole called from behind the curtain, "Is that Rob and Linda? Tell them to come in." I marvelled at how she had such a capacity for putting others first. That was the whole reason we were there; because the birth mother had put Thomas's needs first.

Our visit was pivotal. Taking a look at Nicole's flushed face, we could tell she had been crying, too. She had planned to be discharged from the hospital that evening without her baby, but the thought of what that meant had hit them both hard. We spent an hour reassuring them that we wanted them to be a part of Thomas's life. We fully intended to honour our gentlemen's agreement whereby they would visit Thomas twice a year.

That night, Nicole and Lance left the hospital, their arms empty.

Thomas stayed at a foster family's home for a short time because the adoption paperwork had not yet been completed.

The next 12 days were a flurry of activity: shopping at Sears for a crib, change table, stroller and car seat…wallpapering the baby's room…stocking up on bottles and formula, diapers and baby powder, sleepers and undershirts. I wanted everything to be perfect for our new baby.

We brought Thomas home three days before Christmas. When we picked him up from the foster family's home, he had a miniature baby-blue teddy bear that squeaked, a gift from his foster mom. Thomas was so small that the teddy bear covered a quarter of his body.

Holding Thomas again gave me an immense sense of relief. At the same time, though, I was shaking. My jitters could be attributed to the fact that I was a first-time mom, of course, but it was more than that. Nicole and Lance had chosen us to raise their child, not one of the 30 other couples on the adoption agency's list. I wanted to live up to their expectations. I so desperately didn't want to disappoint them.

On Christmas Eve, we bundled up Thomas in a red sweater that his birth mother had purchased, and took him to church with us. I remember sitting in the pew, my arms full, my heart bursting, gazing at the Nativity scene with Mary, Joseph, and baby Jesus. I looked at the baby in my arms and prayed that we would be the parents he deserved.

We drove two hours to my parents' house on Christmas Day. Before I could even say hello, my mom had taken Thomas, still in his car seat, placed him under the Christmas tree, and snapped a picture.

Although we had brought Thomas home, the waiting wasn't over yet. Ontario law states that the adoption cannot officially go ahead for at least three weeks after the birth parents sign a form to relinquish their parental rights. Would the birth parents change their minds during the grace period and take Thomas back?

However, between caring for a newborn and going to Christmas family functions, we were kept mercifully occupied. I felt a strange sense of peace. Finally, the waiting period ended. The birth parents had kept their promise! Thomas was officially ours.

That winter Brantford was blanketed in snow. I stayed inside, cozy and warm, content to cuddle with my new baby. He was my universe. When Thomas slept, I bent over his crib and listened to make sure he was still breathing. I treasured holding him in my arms as he guzzled down each bottle of milk. I remember his first word, "Daddy," at three months, his first tooth at six months.

The snow melted and the tulips bloomed. Mother's Day arrived. I sat in the pew at church. Once again, someone handed me a flower. This time, I accepted the carnation, wholeheartedly.

I dedicate this story to Thomas's birth parents, Nicole and Lance, who gave us the greatest gift of all, their baby boy.

Undeserving

Nonfiction

Patricia Anne Elford

I'd dealt with excessive bleeding for several years. In the spring of 1967 I was admitted to a Toronto hospital for what's referred to as a D&C. It's a fairly simple procedure women have to endure in which doctors clean up the lining of the uterus and diagnose problems. The bleeding had mysteriously stopped a couple of weeks before the operation date, but my doctor and I wanted to make sure nothing was wrong.

After I had been returned, groggy, to my bed in a ward with three other women, the doctor came to see me. His expression was grave as he pulled the curtains around us.

"I couldn't do the D&C. I've something to tell you."

Oh, no. I have cancer!

"You're about five months pregnant."

I lay there stunned. *Pregnant! A baby!*

It's strange how one's mind works. *That's why I suddenly started drinking powdered Coffee-Mate and warm water at recess time!*

Beginning a month after our wedding, I'd endured my husband, Gary's,[1] erratically abusive behaviour for four years. Some months ago, I'd decided to give our marriage one more year to become bearable. But since making that decision, I'd had to quit using the pill because of the bleeding. Contraception had become Gary's responsibility. And now Gary and I were going to have a baby.

When Gary visited the hospital, I made my "going-to-give-birth" announcement. His first response: "You're full of it!"

Feeling that I couldn't give up on our marriage now that we were having a baby, I continued to teach intermediate physical education and Grade 5/6 home room for the rest of the school year, cancelled my next year's teaching contract, and worked as an "office temp" during the summer months until the week before the baby's predicted birth date. Physically, I'd never felt better.

Kendrew was born in late September. I'd chosen an epidural over full anesthesia so I could be aware of everything but the final birth pains. In the delivery room mirror, I saw the top of his wet little head arriving. What could be more exciting than that?

When Gary arrived for his first hospital visit as a daddy, he commented, "Do you realize I'm missing the first day of duck-hunting season?" I think it was meant as a joke.

For the next two years, I persevered with my marriage. There were various reasons for this, but the main one was the negative stance of my church denomination toward divorce.

At one point, surrounded by couples, I participated solo in a church marriage counselling course. Gary had refused to accompany me. I earned the certificate, but despite my efforts, there was no change in the marriage.

Gary resented the Bible study group in which I was involved and, knowing nothing about the people involved, commented to me about their supposed "frigidity" and narrow views. Our own sexual relationship still existed, but was not as it once had been.

After a while, Gary stopped going to church with Kendrew and me.

During this time, the horror for me was that I was feeling increasingly vulnerable to the approaches of one man from a drama group I'd joined—a man who did attend a church. He treated me like an intelligent, desirable human being. I was susceptible because I longed for mutual love.

Then one day, I overheard Gary talking as he was changing Kendrew's diaper. "Mommy didn't paper that wall right, did she? She'll have to do better than that!"

Oh, Gary! You're already complaining about me to a one-year-old. What chance do I have? If we stay together, for the rest of his life, Kendrew will have to choose between us. He won't have the stability of parents agreeing on what's right. He'll hear you ridicule me, observe me being roughed up, and watch as you throw or break things. Eventually Kendrew won't respect either of us. I can never have a normal relationship with you or our son.

My God, I meant it when I said "until death do us part." Forgive me. I no longer believe it will be better for our child, or for me or Gary, for us to remain together. Rev. Williams had to rescue me from Gary's anger one Christmas in Ottawa. Things are no better here in Toronto. Nobody here knows what's going on, not even the police in the station across from our apartment building. I just can't report Gary to the police! Perhaps that bank teller suspects. I saw her looking at my lip and cheek last time I was there.

Gary, since you continue to buy things as if you're single, I can't even be a stay-at-home wife and mother. The credit card bills have to be met. You made no comment when I said I was applying for a teaching job to get us out of debt, yet when I was hired I had to face your wrath yet again. Nothing I do pleases you.

Despite Gary's initial reaction to the pregnancy, he was extremely proud of Kendrew, even wanting to pack up the diaper bag and take him along when he met with "the guys." Gary's face glowed when I pushed Kendrew in the stroller to meet him after work. Gary's physical aggressiveness seemed to be aimed only at me, though he also appeared to be extremely resentful of his mother, from whom I'd once believed I'd "rescued" him.

My thinking at the time was simple. *I have my faith, untrue to it as I seem to be right now, to help me through the severe pain of loss. Gary's parents will bail him out financially if necessary. Spiritually and emotionally, Gary would have nothing without Kendrew. Kendrew appears to be the only person Gary loves. Surely, if he's able to love Kendrew, then his heart can be opened to love someone else, someone who hadn't shared our miserable history. Please God, give him that, and keep Kendrew safe.*

When Gary and I legally separated, I had provisions written into the custody agreement that I felt would act as safeguards; but in a way, I gave Kendrew to Gary as if he were just a possession, a comfort toy.

I did this in spite of the fact that, earlier that month, in an apartment lined by "his" and "her" moving cartons, Kendrew and I celebrated his birthday alone. Gary "forgot" my birthday plans and arrived home late. I felt that was to punish me, not Kendrew. Only I would know the difference. Kendrew was too young to know what to expect.

On the last day of October, with the rent paid, we all moved out of the apartment. Gary took Kendrew, who had just turned two. I was then four-and-a-half months pregnant with our second child.

Some people thought it was because of my pregnancy that I let Gary have Kendrew.

The pediatrician chastised me soundly for doing so. "You're sacrificing your child for the sake of your husband!"

My mother was devastated.

I honestly thought I'd built enough protection into our separation agreement that if Gary didn't fulfill his part, I would be able to regain custody of Kendrew without much difficulty. However, my using the same lawyer Gary used, one found by Gary's father, was not a wise decision.

Most of the money we owed was as a result of Gary's spending, but I withdrew my retirement funds and evenly split the credit card payments so we could each begin debt free.

Because I could earn a decent income teaching, I sought no alimony. I asked for Kendrew's used baby clothes and toys for the child I was carrying. That request would be fulfilled once and only once, three years later, in the form of two large garbage bags plunked down in court where it could be seen publicly, on the day of the divorce proceedings. What I'd wanted most from Gary was not money, but his love.

I stayed in Toronto, but Gary moved back to Ottawa. I visited once a month—making a four-hour bus trip there and back. That became particularly challenging for me once my second son, Ian, was born. I was nursing him, so he had to come along.

Perhaps our visits together went too well. Gary forbade my having Kendrew stay overnight with me in my aunt's home, decreasing the precious time we actually had to only part of one day each month when visits weren't suddenly cancelled on some pretext.

Kendrew was actually living with a woman named Naomi, who was a loving caregiver. Naomi and her husband were always considerate to me.

She quit the caregiving job because she'd developed an ulcer from having to deal with Gary's undependability. He frequently showed up late for, or cancelled, his own times with Kendrew.

On the first night after I'd returned Kendrew to his new caregiver, Kendrew, still wearing his clothes, sobbed himself to sleep. I contacted Naomi to beg her to reconsider. She did. *Thank you, God.*

In divorce court, after the then-required three-year waiting period for non-adultery cases, I tried to regain custody of Kendrew.

The judge stated that I'd seemed to be well aware of what I was doing when making the original decision. "Both of your present prospective spouses appear to be better choices as parents than either of you two," he commented.

The judge then ruled that Kendrew, having already been in Gary's custody for three years, though not actually living with him, was to remain in his custody, along with that of Alena, the young, blonde schoolteacher Gary planned to marry.

I was devastated, but there was nothing more I could do.

I remarried shortly after the divorce was final—a wonderful man named James, with whom I'd connected through a series of "coincidences" after Gary and I separated. James was my true soulmate. I also inherited two daughters, one nine and one two and a half, left by his first wife two years earlier when she departed suddenly with another man. James and I later added another son.

Although I had Ian and my new family, I never for a moment forgot about my first child. But did he ever think of me? And if he did, was it with anger or longing?

  Hot Apple Cider with Cinnamon

How *could* Kendrew ever believe that I loved *him*? Kendrew couldn't know that just seeing a stranger's baby touch its mother's cheek could make me *feel* Kendrew's tiny hand on my own face. He couldn't know how often I'd prayed and cried and ached, particularly during the empty nights, endangering the health of the child I was then carrying. I loved Ian, my second son dearly, but no child can replace another. Did Kendrew know that?

Did Kendrew recall how we played pretend and sang action songs together, doing as much as we could, including a nap time curled up together because I was worn out? Did he still have *Then Kendrew Remembers*, the little picture book I made to try to ease him through all his earliest life changes?

Did Kendrew remember my taking him with me to church on a visit, leaving him my watch to wear as reassurance I'd be back to get him from the nursery after the service? So painful now to think that he might have believed I'd come back for the watch he was wearing but not necessarily for him.

Did Kendrew remember playing "Come Let's March along the Old Stone Wall?" or his aversion to the messiness of the finger-painting materials I'd brought along, the tea room game with the penny, Sparks Street Mall milkshakes, and the fun at the neighbourhood playground? Most of all, did he remember the hugs and giggles? Would Kendrew remember only that I cuddled him in one arm while I had another baby on my breast, if that?

Did Kendrew know that, after Gary remarried immediately following the divorce and moved out West, I sent cards, gifts, and notes for Kendrew's birthdays and Christmases, trying to let him know that he was loved without interfering with his new family situation? Not trusting Gary to give them to Kendrew, I sent copies of the notes to June, one of Gary's relatives whom I liked, asking that they be saved in case Kendrew wanted to know more about my feelings for him some day. Unfortunately, when that day came, although June could tell Kendrew *about* my notes, she'd misplaced them.

Did he know of the special love-link I felt to him? I once dreamed that little Kendrew, wearing a pale yellow jacket, had been approached by a child molester. Concerned, I wrote a note to

Gary's wife. She answered that Kendrew did, indeed, have such a jacket and that notice had just been sent out to area schools about a predator in their area.

When he was about seven, I felt sure Kendrew was seriously unwell. I sent a note enclosing a stamped return postcard, enquiring. Alena replied that, though he was now recovered, Kendrew had been ill for several days with a high fever.

For a while, Alena was kind enough to tell me about some of Kendrew's activities. She sent a few photos of him—a school picture and one with a horse. She refused to send his report cards, saying they were private.

But as Kendrew grew older, even though I sent communications only for birthdays and Christmas, attempting to reassure Gary by my lack of interference, there was no response, possibly because I'd refused Alena's request for adoption rights.

Once, our family went on a camping trip to B. C.

In Alberta, remembering how much Gary had liked camping, I found myself staring at young blond, blue-eyed boys passing by. *Could you be my son?*

When we stopped in Calgary to visit friends, I drove off on my own to try to find Kendrew's home with Gary and Alena—just to see it, perhaps secretly glimpse Kendrew.

Gary's continued negativity about giving me any access, despite the fact that I had the legal right to see Kendrew, meant it wasn't a matter of simply saying we'd be passing through and requesting a brief visit.

The phone book indicated the address was on a rural route. It was a Sunday, and I couldn't find anyone to tell me what area that route covered.

I'd hoped that our love-link would once more be effective and I'd somehow sense where he was, but all I learned was how very large and dusty Alberta ranches were, and how many of them had barking dogs. By sunset, I hadn't found the house.

Aware that Kendrew had been a Cub Scout, I sought the community campground I'd discovered they used. I took photos, or thought I did. Only later did I realize that, in my highly emotional state, I'd left the lens cap on.

In 1986, it finally happened—the day I'd both longed for and feared.

James had been moved to an Alberta pastorate. While we were still unpacking, the phone rang. It was Gary's younger brother, Tim, who'd been kind to me before, during, and after the ill-fated marriage. He was calling because his mother had asked him to find me.

My ex-mother-in-law and I didn't belong to a mutual admiration society, but I'd kept in touch periodically. I didn't want to deprive her of information about her younger grandson, Ian.

"Mom said to tell you that Kendrew is coming to stay with her and go to college in Ontario. Mom wants to know if you want to see Kendrew before he leaves Alberta. He's leaving in two days."

My heart jumped into my throat. *Do I want to see him? No doubt about it!* In a shaky voice, I said, "More to the point, does Kendrew want to see me?"

"Yes," said lovable go-between, Tim.

It was arranged that we would meet at the Calgary bus station where he'd be catching the bus to Ottawa.

All I could think about was that I hadn't seen him since he was five! *Will I recognize him? How will he know me?*

James drove me. At the terminal, I subtly pointed out a lanky teenager wearing a T-shirt bearing a tuxedo-and-bow-tie print. His shoulder-length, dark blond hair partially obscured his face.

"I think that's Kendrew," I mumbled out of the side of my mouth, spy style. "I just can't go up to him and ask, 'Are you my son?' There's no reason *you* should know how he looks. Will you please speak to him?"

James went up to him and soon motioned to me. He was, indeed, Kendrew!

My son! How we hugged, this tall, handsome 18-year-old and I. His sweet-smelling hair fell forward against my face. My heart melted. James, as planned, discreetly disappeared.

Kendrew, with his quiet western drawl, said, "I brought along a few pieces of my art and my writing. Would you like to see them?"

My heart soared. *He writes and is involved in art, just as I am! He wants to share that with me!* "Would I? Yes, please!"

Squatting by a blue locker, he dug into his duffle bag to produce carefully rolled-up art work samples and printed pages with stories he had written.

In an echoing bus terminal, scrunched down beside him, I admired his art work and read my son's excellent short story. *My boy has talent!*

Awkwardly, I suggested we go into the terminal restaurant. We sat on red plastic-upholstered benches, facing one another across a booth table, blue eyes reflecting blue eyes, staring and staring. My mascara-muddied tears dribbled as I tried to explain something that, in retrospect, I couldn't totally understand myself—why I'd given him to his father, a man with whom I, myself, couldn't live.

Then we held hands as we walked—something I knew I'd likely never do with my other sons when they were 18—but we were making up for years of missed physical contact. *It feels right! It feels wonderful!*

We walked and walked, talked and talked, and spoke of possibilities. We sat or strolled wherever the mood took us.

What was around us? I barely noticed. The sun was shining. Was there a sculpture on one park bench? I think so.

Back at the terminal, the hollow sound of a heedless stranger cruelly announced the end of our visit—Kendrew's bus was about to depart. A scramble for his baggage, one more crushing hug, and he was gone.

From then on, each time our family returned to Ontario during the summer holidays, we reconnected with Kendrew in Ottawa, going to places like an art gallery or museum and taking Kendrew to visit other family members eager to see him.

I had been concerned that his parents' difficult relationship might result in Kendrew's having difficulties. How could he trust a female when his parents had divorced and his own mother had deserted him? He had told me that during his teen years, he'd played the field, but hadn't dated much.

Our Calgary encounter and follow-up seemed to free him, and in Ottawa he began a steady relationship with Rachelle LeBlanc. How thrilled I was when he invited me to his apartment to meet her. When I came through the door, Rachelle threw her arms around me and cried out, "Oh, you're beautiful!" I wasn't, but I knew she was ready to appreciate me because of Kendrew. *Thank you, God!*

My father had died, last seeing his first grandson when Kendrew was five, but I was able to take Kendrew to visit my ecstatic mother, whose side of the family he most resembled. I was able to walk with him around my home town. "There's the swinging bridge. That's the shop where I bought wax candy lips, strawberry candies, and hit-tune lyric sheets. There's the corner restaurant. My high school's down there. Our beach is across town. See the railway bridge where your grandfather used to take me fishing."

I proudly introduced Kendrew to friends.

I was able to build new bridges and share portions of my life from which he had been excluded.

In February, 1990, as part of a Vancouver School of Theology spirituality course I was taking, I was at a silent retreat in a British Columbia monastery. I dreamed another of my few coloured dreams.

Gary was standing a few steps from me on some kind of platform, in what looked like a post office. He was smiling happily, a rare sight in my memory. "I'm fine." He said. "I have a new job."

Because of the vividness of the dream, I wrote a brief note to Kendrew, telling him about it and asking if all was well. Had I not been on that retreat, had I been operating on overdrive back in the piles of academic commitments, I would have delayed writing, perhaps not even have done it—it was, after all, just a dream.

Two weeks later, the phone rang. It was Gary's brother, Tim. On February 1, Gary had died suddenly in his home. He had indeed been job hunting again and was due to start a new position within a few days.

At the time Tim called, Kendrew had already returned home to Ottawa. Apparently Alena had told him to leave the house immediately after the funeral.

Tim's voice was clear. "I think Kendrew needs to hear from you."

I phoned Kendrew immediately. How glad I was I'd written earlier! Kendrew knew I still cared about his father. Though their personalities are quite different, his dad will always be a part of him.

In 1995, James and I were called to a church in an Ontario town, where we remained when we retired. Four of our grown children and all of our grandchildren live in this province.

Kendrew, however, is in Vancouver. He and Rachelle, accompanied by their beloved cat, went to B. C. to plant trees, fell in love with the province, and stayed there. Having lived there for a time, I understand that.

Kendrew had warned me of their plans. Still, it was a shock to hear his by-then-familiar voice sing out on the answering machine, "We are away, away, away!"

Kendrew's painting is now of a more practical nature. As my father and my maternal grandfather once did, Kendrew earns his main income by interior painting.

He's still writing—for charities and social justice organizations—while optimistically creating scripts for the burgeoning Vancouver film industry. We continue to be in touch, by phone calls and computer, though not physically. Maybe, someday soon, we'll be able to afford the trip to hug again.

I am so blessed. There were many times I believed my oldest son could never possibly want to meet me, never mind love me. Yet, he does.

I can only think it's because of God's love-link. I frequently thank God that my son was able to forgive my apparent betrayal of his baby trust. I'm so happy to be Kendrew's loved old mom.

1. All names have been changed

  Hot Apple Cider with Cinnamon

From Heartache to Heart Restored

Nonfiction

Sally Meadows

Fifteen years after graduating with my Master of Science, I was nervous about returning to university to get a degree in education. While earning my first two degrees, I had been a single woman with few responsibilities. Now I was married and raising two boys. Furthermore, I was functioning as a single parent half the time while my husband worked alternating weeks at a northern Saskatchewan mine. Could I juggle it all? Would I be able to keep up good grades? Would I fit in, despite being a mature student?

As it turned out, my initial fears were all for naught—I had the time of my life and graduated at the top of my class. Despite mixed feelings about working in a classroom setting, I had great fun and success as a substitute teacher that first year after graduation. I set my sights on having my own classroom, and was delighted to be offered a job in a private school for the coming year.

However, despite the small size of my class, I soon discovered that the work load was extraordinary. I had to find ways to meet the needs of children with significant diagnosed challenges, those with hidden disabilities, those who were academically gifted, as well as those of average ability.

Although all of my students had strengths I enthusiastically built upon, I was ill-equipped to play what I felt were the dual concurrent roles of both a special needs teacher and a regular classroom teacher. This would have been a challenge for any educator, let alone a novice. Further, I found it difficult to balance work demands with family commitments, as well as my own need for rest and relaxation.

By the February break of my second year at the school, I could no longer ignore how much stress I was under. When I met with my family doctor, she confirmed that my health was being compromised, and we agreed that my best recourse was to resign immediately.

Packing up my things at school that weekend, I felt devastated that I wouldn't have a chance to say a proper goodbye to my students. I also felt that I was a failure for not being able to work through the pressure. But after a month of rest, alone time with God, and the healing power of long walks, I felt well enough to start looking for other employment opportunities. I applied for a couple of interesting education-related jobs, remembering that God had whispered to me during my first year of teaching that He had plans for me that went beyond the regular classroom.

Six weeks after I'd resigned from my teaching position, I was relaxing in my sunny front room when a dull ache started in my abdominal area. I initially dismissed it, and went out for my morning walk. But by the time I reached the top of my street, I could barely walk. With the pain growing steadily, by early afternoon I'd decided I needed to see a doctor.

The medical clinic ruled out appendicitis and arranged for me to have an ultrasound. I was diagnosed with a baseball-sized growth on my womb and referred to a gynecological specialist.

As I waited two weeks for the appointment to discuss my prognosis with the surgeon, the pain continued to ebb and flow. I hoped that the growth could be taken care of without radical measures.

We were only a few minutes into our conversation when I realized that the specialist and I were diametrically opposed as to how to resolve my health issues. While she mechanically rattled off the surgical options, she completely missed how emotionally distraught I was about having to have surgery. Despite my attempts to articulate my concerns, by the end of my appointment, the doctor insisted that there was only one option: I must have a hysterectomy.

I was devastated. Although I was approaching the end of my childbearing years, I hadn't given up hope that we might add a little girl to our family of two boys. This operation would end that dream with a finality that was heartbreaking for me. Although I considered going for a second opinion, I left the doctor's office resigned to the fact that there was no other option.

As I waited for the surgery, I cried many tears, mourning the loss of what I longed for and would never have. I wondered if the growth had been caused by the stress I'd been under while teaching, or if it had already existed and, as it progressed, had gradually reduced my overall health and my ability to manage the challenging classroom.

Inexplicably, I also developed a fear that I would die on the operating table. My life became a series of "lasts"—last time I'd celebrate my children's birthdays, last time I'd talk with my mother, last time my husband would hold me. I put my financial affairs in order, spent as much precious time as I could with my family, and prepared my heart for eternity. When the time came for the surgery, I felt at peace, ready to leave this earth for my forever home.

As I slowly drifted back to consciousness after the operation, I felt neither joy nor sorrow. Still groggy, I was wheeled to a private room, where my husband was waiting. Only through God's infinite grace and mercy did I remain composed as my husband told me the shocking news—I had been misdiagnosed. The tumour was actually on one of my ovaries, not my uterus. But because I had agreed to a hysterectomy, the surgeon had removed both my ailing ovary and the uterus anyway.

I cannot stand injustice, and my normal reaction would have been anger and outrage. But, somehow, I calmly accepted what had happened. After coming face to face with my own mortality before the surgery, I had a measure of peace that truly surpassed all understanding. So when the surgeon dropped by after my operation to check up on me, I had forgiveness in my heart. My priority now was to recover from surgery and move on with my life.

A couple of hours before I was scheduled to leave the hospital, my husband called to let me know that one of the organizations I had applied to before finding out about the tumour had left a message saying that they wanted to interview me.

I phoned them back right away. The position seemed a perfect fit for my strengths and passions: the director of a university outreach program providing real-world, hands-on experiences in the sciences for disadvantaged youth. Further, it would give me the opportunity to redeem myself as an educator.

I explained that I had just had surgery and asked if they could delay the interview. They were willing to delay for one week, but no longer. Even though I felt better than I'd have believed possible, I knew in my heart that what I needed most right now was time to heal. So I thanked them for their offer, and let my dream job go.

Those weeks recuperating at home were a sweet time of rest, prayer, and quiet reflection. One morning I had a vision of a light coming down from heaven and healing me completely: physically and emotionally. God poured out His love over me, and I felt very close to Him.

During this time, I received with tears of joy a lovely package of hand written get-well notes from my former students. Further, a treasured colleague from the school dropped by and assured me that I had indeed made a difference in the lives of my students. It was a word of encouragement I needed to hear.

By the end of the six weeks, I was fully healed in all ways, just as God had promised.

Seven weeks after my surgery, I was thrilled to get a letter from the organization whose interview I had turned down: could I please drop by and see them? To my delight, that meeting resulted in the creation of a new position, tailor-made for me, even better than the one for which I had originally applied.

Just weeks into my new job, a friend returned to her home in Africa for a year to fulfill work obligations, leaving her two oldest children behind in Canada with their dad. We invited her husband and the two kids over as often as we could.

I had always had a special bond with her daughter, and while my friend was away, I had the blessing of spending time with her, shopping, going to the movies, and just hanging out. I even taught her to sew, just as my mother had taught me.

As I watched her blossom into a beautiful young woman, I thanked God for the opportunity to experience, if only for a short time, what it felt like to have a daughter.

I am amazed at how gracious God was to me during this difficult season of my life. Instead of letting me become bitter and angry over the wrong diagnosis and unnecessary hysterectomy, God gave me peace and forgiveness.

  Hot Apple Cider with Cinnamon

Instead of allowing me to wallow in grief that I would never be able to have the little girl I longed for, God gave me the opportunity to grow a lovely relationship with a young woman I cared about.

Instead of leaving me heartbroken that I left the teaching profession, He gave me a career that allowed me to influence many more students than I ever could have as a classroom teacher.

I've lived the truth that what may appear to be devastating circumstances can turn into a blessing. I'm eternally grateful that even in the midst of this time of heartache, my heart was already on its way to being fully restored.

A Touch of Sun

Nonfiction

Angelina Fast-Vlaar

I've decided that the kitchen in our new cottage needs to be yellow. Sunshiny yellow.

In an effort to downsize, we've bought a smaller, more convenient house a few blocks away. We've lovingly dubbed the new house "the cottage," and our soon-to-be-sold large home "the castle." We have a few months between closing dates, which gives us the chance to move at leisure.

In the mornings, I playfully say to my husband, Joe, "Where shall we have coffee today, Hon? At the castle or in the cottage?" I'm glad when his answer is the latter because I'm praying for him to adjust to the coming move.

For some reason, I vividly remember the kitchen of the farmhouse where I lived some decades ago when my children were young. The sun poured in through the window above the sink, drenching the yellow gingham wallpaper in morning light. Yellow, the happy colour, created a warm welcome in that kitchen. And so, today, I hunt for yellow paint. Once more we need the warmth of sunshine in our lives.

The paint store offers, among other tantalizing tastes and aromas, Vanilla Milkshake, Butter Cream, Lemon Slice, and Touch of Sun. I choose one shade for the walls, a lighter one for the cupboards.

My sister and a friend come to help. Armed with rollers, brushes, drop-cloths, and pans of paint, we fill the room with laughter as we spread sunshine on the walls. My granddaughter Jaden, who is six, is staying with us today. When we arrived, she claimed the front bedroom as "my room" and has been playing quietly with her favourite doll and some colouring books. But after a while, she enters the kitchen.

"Can I help paint?" she asks, her blue eyes searching mine.

After thinking it over for moment, I smile and say, "Of course, you may."

I pour a small amount of paint into a plastic yogourt container and, brush in hand, she happily begins to spread the yellow sunshine on a small patch of wall.

Just then, Joe enters the kitchen.

Before I left him this morning, I suggested he might walk over to the cottage later. I'm glad to see he's done so, but my heart plummets when I see his face. He looks so lost.

For a split second I see him as he was when we built the addition to the "castle." Tall, strong, in charge, he showed up at the building site every day to make sure the plans were followed to a T, to see that every nail was hammered in place. I remember his hearty laugh as he proudly showed my mom the skeletons of added rooms and the grand staircase.

Now he asks if there's anything for him to do, but his voice is harsh, almost rude. I notice the shocked look on my sister's face. I realize she's never experienced Joe like this. She, along with everyone else, has always known Joe as the gentlest of gentlemen. And that's the Joe I've always known, too. But advancing dementia has changed his personality as well as limiting his abilities. The well-known twinkle in his stunning blue eyes is now absent much of the time.

I've learned to soothe him when he's angry or upset, so now I gently say, "Would you like to help fasten the new handles to the cupboard doors?"

"Sure." His voice is flat.

A row of cupboard doors are lined up along the dining room wall like soldiers standing at attention. I painted them yesterday and they're nice and dry. I take one of the doors, place it on the covered dining room table, and show Joe how each handle's two prongs fit into two small holes in the door. Then, taking two wing nuts, I show him how to fasten them on the prongs and tighten them to hold the handles in place.

"Okay," he says.

"Have fun," I say, kissing his cheek lightly. I leave him and go back to the kitchen to continue painting.

After a while I lay down my roller and enter the dining room to see how Joe is doing.

"Is this right?" he asks as he shows me the door he's been working on.

The handle is on the inside of the door.

We unscrew it, place it on the right side, and I help him fasten it in place before going back to painting.

But I'm concerned, so after a few more moments, I check on his progress again. This time, one end of the handle with the prong is sticking out at the edge of the door.

Jaden enters the dining room behind me, scopes out the scene, and asks, "Nana, can I do this?"

Her eyes hold mine.

"Yes, of course, you can help," I answer.

I begin to explain, but she quips, "Yes, I know how to do it."

Joe's face darkens, tightens.

I tense, knowing how close to the surface his frustration lodges. I go to him and stroke his back. Pointing to the cupboard drawers standing upright in a row on the other side of the dining room floor, I say, "These drawers all need a knob. Let's work on that."

I place a drawer on the table. "Look," I say, "the knob's prong fits through this hole and we fasten it on the inside with a little wing nut."

His face lights up. "All right," he says.

Jaden glances my way as she places a door, handle neatly in place, back against the wall. We exchange a knowing smile. I return to Touch of Sun.

My ears are tuned to sounds in the dining room, and when I hear Joe's deep sigh of frustration, I take a peek. I see two heads close together—one grey, one blonde—bent over the table, concentrating, whispering.

I hear Jaden's kind, soft voice, "Look, Grandpa. It goes like this—the knob goes on the outside of the drawer. See?"

Joe takes the knob. His hands tremble slightly but he manages to fit the prong into the small hole.

Jaden holds out her hand with a wing nut resting on it.

Joe takes it and tightens the knob in place.

"That's right, Grandpa," she whispers.

They exchange a smile.

I shake my head and ask myself, *Where did this child absorb her amazing capacity for empathy?*

In my mind, time skips back and I see Joe and Jaden together four years earlier.

I am sitting on the front porch. Joe is planting pansies in the half-barrel by the road of our house. He has two in, and is about to plant the third.

Jaden, who is two and a half, runs across our lawn toward her grandpa. "Can I do this, Grandpa?" she asks.

"Yes, of course you can help." Joe kneels down so he is at eye level with her, and smiles. "First we need to dig a hole with this little spade. Then we drop the flower into the hole with the roots hanging down. Finally, we cover the roots with dirt and pat it tightly around the plant."

"I can do that!" Jaden squeals as her small hands take the spade. She giggles as she tosses up soil.

Joe encourages her until the hole is deep enough. "Okay, now take a plant," he says.

Jaden reaches for a small pansy plant.

"Hold it carefully," Joe says gently.

Their two heads close together—one grey, one wispy blonde—they fill the barrel with happy, yellow pansies.

And now, I watch the child teach her grandpa, using the same gentle tone, and realize how profound an influence on her young life Joe has had.

After a moment, my hands begin to shake with the realization that Joe is now unable to process what a six-year-old can readily understand.

Some say that our journey with Alzheimer's or dementia is much like a long train ride with no fixed route and no estimated time of arrival. Along the route there are many stops, and with

each stop, something is lost. I can attest to this. I also know that with each loss, the caregiver experiences the typical emotions of grief.

As I return to my new kitchen, I'm struggling to keep my tears at bay. But as I find myself surrounded by a glowing, sunshiny yellow, my spirits lift, and I send up a quick prayer. "God, please send a touch of Your Son to also warm this kitchen during the uncertain days ahead."

Hot Apple Cider with Cinnamon

Real Love

Historical Fiction[1]

Kelsey Greye

Maria Klassen fiddled with the edge of the pale green curtain as she looked out the parlour window. Her eyes rested, unseeing, on the street leading to the edge of town. She tried to ignore the harsh sound of her mother barking orders at her younger sisters in the kitchen.

She wished she could turn off her mother's voice as easily as one could turn off a phonograph. Not that she had ever seen a phonograph in the small, Mennonite community of Schoenfield, Saskatchewan, but the description in the Eaton's catalogue she had surreptitiously perused at her Uncle Henry's house in Swift Current made it sound easy. Even though such devices were commonplace elsewhere in this spring of 1937, in her rural Saskatchewan cloistered community, they were forbidden.

"Are you listening to me, Maria? I want to know if it's true that George Rempel has been paying court to you. Lydia says he told her he intends to marry you!"

Maria sighed, turning from the window to face her mother. Sarah Klassen's lips were pursed in a frown as she scrutinized her 16-year-old daughter's face.

Maria studied her mother's face in return. A temperament prone to disappointment and fretfulness had carved dour lines into what her father had told her was once the loveliest face in the area. Maria knew from looking in the single mirror in the house that she'd inherited her mother's large brown eyes and thick, dark hair, but otherwise, she both looked and acted more like her father. He was generally a quiet man but could be blunt and forceful when he felt he had something important to say.

Maria thought that too seldom happened but knew it was likely due to his wife's quick temper and sharp tongue. With her mother, Maria had long ago decided that there was no purpose in saying what she really meant. The older woman rarely listened to anyone's opinions and it wasn't worth the energy or emotion to engage with her unless absolutely necessary. Unfortunately, this was one of those moments.

"I don't care what George Rempel told Lydia," Maria said. "I've never given him a reason to think I would accept him, and as for paying me court—" she gave a snort of disgust "—if you call attempting to kiss me and paw at me in the barn during the last outing with the young people 'paying court,' then I guess that's true."

"Oh, come now—" her mother's tone turned wheedling. "You can't expect a man to behave properly when he is so enamoured with you. It is a compliment that he wished to kiss you! And you know how wealthy his family is. With your father unable to work due to his frequent illnesses, we can't afford to turn down his proposal."

"He was looking for more than a kiss, Mother," said Maria flatly, "and I sincerely hope that he'll look elsewhere for favours now that I've made my feelings on the subject quite clear."

Her mother frowned. "What do you mean? What did you say to him?"

Maria smiled, satisfaction filling her at the memory of her response to George's advances. "I grabbed Father's handsaw from the hook on the barn wall and told George if he came one step closer, I'd use it to lop off whichever body part was closest. He thought I was joking until I went for his arm. I nearly got him, too, but he was a bit too quick." She shrugged. "I did manage to slit open his shirt sleeve, though."

"Oh, Maria!" Her mother's anguished wail filled the room. "What am I going to do with you? If you had wounded George, you could be put out of the community for violence! What were you thinking? Will you never stop bringing shame on our family?" Wringing her hands, she strode from the room, slamming the door behind her.

The thumping of her mother's heavy footsteps on the stairs to the second floor bedrooms was as much a relief to Maria as was her departure. When Sarah retreated to her room in a rage, she seldom emerged before the following morning, giving her family a

  Hot Apple Cider with Cinnamon

much-needed break from the constant reminder of her disappointment in them.

Sighing again, Maria turned her gaze back to the window. She really hadn't intended to hurt him, but she'd been certain that George wouldn't leave her alone if she didn't do something to protect herself. So what should she have done? It seemed that she never did the right thing, at least not according to her family and the rest of the community. Every time she saw other girls pairing up and marrying, she wondered if she would ever find the kind of love she prayed for. She just didn't see how it was possible with anyone she'd grown up with. None of the men her age seemed to want to know her for herself. They were only interested in her looks or in finding someone to clean and cook for them. That was hardly the love she dreamed of.

Sometimes, when the pastor spoke at church about God, she almost believed that He saw her exactly as she was, and loved her anyway. Unfortunately, her encounters with family and townspeople during the rest of the week made her doubt it. *Father in heaven, if you are truly there and you do love me, would you please send me just one person who could love me like You do?*

She touched her forehead to the cool glass, fighting the tears rising in her eyes. Looking out to the countryside visible from their house on the edge of the community, she traced her fingertips down the road that led into town. She stopped the motion abruptly as her index finger nearly covered a dark form that was approaching in the distance. Tears forgotten in her curiosity, she took a step back from the window so as not to be seen, and watched as the figure grew steadily larger and clearer. It was a man with a pack on his back. His features were indistinct, but she could see he had straight shoulders and the loose, long-legged stride of a young man.

Oh, Father, she prayed with a catch in her breath, *could this be him?*

Since strangers were rare in their community, Maria learned in no time that the young man's name was Abe Friesen, and that he'd found a job working for Ernest Jansen.

Maria was hoping that Abe would come to church on Sunday so she could get a closer look and find out more about him. But she had a chance to see him again even sooner.

That Thursday there was a sewing bee at the Jansens' house, and Maria and her mother went. Maria saw Abe, very briefly, and from a distance. She also learned a few more things about him.

As they sat sewing in the front room, Martha Jansen glanced out the window and noticed her husband's new hired man returning to the barn for a drink of water. "That new man Ernest hired is a sly one, I think. Hardly a word, he says, no matter how friendly we are. I don't trust these silent types; I never know what they're thinking."

"Maybe he's just shy," Mabel Giesbrecht, whose reserved manner often garnered spiteful comments about her pride from the other ladies, offered. "Being quiet doesn't mean he has something to hide."

Martha snorted, clearly unconvinced.

Maria smiled down at her sewing. A quiet man sounded very nice to someone used to frequent tongue-lashings from her mother. She began to anticipate seeing him on Sunday even more than before.

When Maria saw him across the church on Sunday morning, seated with the other men, she had a few moments to study his face, and she felt her stomach flutter. His clear blue eyes were kind and his smile gentle. She strained to hear his voice over the chatter of the other people, but he spoke too softly for her to make out any words. Hope rose inside her that perhaps this quiet young man really was the one God had chosen to answer her prayer for love.

That hope was crushed four hours later when she walked into the church basement for the young people's gathering and saw him standing in a dim corner with Agnes Rempel, George's younger sister, clinging to his arm.

Maria felt foolish as she recalled the special attention she'd paid to her appearance, carefully smoothing her dark brown hair into glossy waves and making certain every line of her plain, dark gown lay right. She'd bemoaned the lack of bright colour in her

Hot Apple Cider with Cinnamon

apparel much more vehemently than usual. Thank heaven she hadn't given in to the impulse to pick a couple of the small spring violets she'd seen as she walked to the church and dress her hair with them. That would have made her humiliation complete.

"Maria, aren't you having fun?" Maria's cousin, Lydia, who was a year younger, tugged at her arm. As usual, Lydia was out of breath from trying to fit too many words in too short a time. "Doesn't George look handsome tonight? And see—" she pointed, heedless of the attention she drew "—he's watching you again. How romantic!"

"Hush, Lydia." Maria frowned at the younger girl, feeling an embarrassed flush working its way up her neck. "You're making a spectacle of yourself, and of me. I've told you before, I'm not interested in George and I never will be."

"Well, I don't see why not." Lydia's brown eyes widened in genuine confusion. "He's rich and so good-looking. What more do you want?"

"Never mind, Lydia." Maria's own dark gaze softened as she patted her cousin's hand. "I'm not in a sociable mood this afternoon. I should have stayed home. Ignore me."

Taking her at her word, Lydia flitted off to giggle with a group of girls closer to her own age while Maria lingered in the corner of the church basement, sipping her punch. She really wasn't feeling sociable, she admitted, but not because of George. Her eyes turned to the strange young man who was standing across the room from her.

"You look as beautiful as always, Maria." George had sidled up to her and now he reached out to touch her hair.

She jerked away, folding her arms across her chest as she glared at him. "I wish you'd stop saying things like that," she whispered fiercely. "I've told you that it makes me uncomfortable."

"You'll come around yet, my girl," he insisted, trying to take hold of her arm.

She moved further away, closer to the centre of the room.

"You just need to lose your uppity ways and that'll happen soon enough, once we're married. You're fortunate I like high spirits, or I'd have taken my attentions elsewhere long ago."

"Please do. George Rempel, I told you I don't want to marry you and I never will. Now leave me alone!" She'd started out whispering, but she'd almost shouted the last sentence, forgetting where she was in the heat of the moment. Silence fell over the church basement. Tears sprang to Maria's eyes as she felt her face turning crimson. She whirled around, pushing past her shocked companions as she fought her way to the stairs.

She was rushing out the door into the cool, spring afternoon when a gentle hand grasped her arm. She stopped, refusing to raise her gaze, too embarrassed to speak to whoever had come after her.

"Let me walk you home, Miss Klassen," said a low, quiet voice. "I wouldn't consider myself any kind of man if I didn't make sure you got there safe. After what you said to George downstairs, he's got to be feeling a mite angry. I'd hate for him to take it out on you by doing something foolish."

Shocked by the kind words spoken by the strange voice, Maria lifted her eyes to find Abe Friesen's gentle blue ones resting on her face. There was no judgment in them; nothing but genuine concern etched on his features.

Somehow, she found a few words. "Thank you. I would appreciate that."

He took her arm and fell into step beside her. After walking a half-block in silence, he asked, "May I call you Maria?"

"You may." Her voice was breathless with nerves and something else she couldn't quite define.

"Well, Maria, I'm sorry that you had such a troublesome encounter this afternoon. I was having a bit of difficulty myself, and when you spoke up, I thought perhaps we could escape together. I'm awfully glad you were willing to allow me to see you home."

She stopped and stared at him. "*You* were having difficulty?"

He stopped also, and looked down at his feet. "The thing is, I didn't quite know how to get myself away from Miss Rempel without hurting her feelings. She clings like the leeches in the pond out behind my grandfather's house. Those things will just hang on forever."

Maria giggled at the image and found herself meeting his gaze again.

  Hot Apple Cider with Cinnamon

"I thought," she said slowly, "that you were enjoying her company. You didn't seem to be too upset that she was hanging on so tightly to your arm."

"I didn't want to embarrass her by telling her to let go in front of so many people, but I'm afraid—" he coloured slightly "—that I also knew it probably wouldn't do any good."

"How could you know that? You've only been in town a week."

"It's been an eventful week." His blush deepened and they walked on in silence for a moment before he cleared his throat. "Do I have your word that this won't go any further than between you and me?"

"Of course," she promised.

"Well, you remember the sewing bee at the Jansen's house? Well, when you ladies were all getting ready to leave, I was working in the barn. I heard a sound behind me. I turned around and there was Agnes, just standing there watching me mucking out stalls. I said hello and then went back to work, feeling pretty uncomfortable." His colour rose again. "I thought she'd leave, but a few seconds later, I heard her skirts rustling and realized she was coming closer, and then I felt a hand somewhere no woman's hand had a right to be, if you follow me."

"What?" Maria was aghast. "She didn't! I knew George had trouble keeping his hands to himself, but his sister, too? What did you do?"

"I did just like Joseph in the Bible did when Potiphar's wife got too interested in him. I ran out of the barn for all I was worth, headed into the field, and hid there until everyone was gone."

"Oh, my." She squeezed his arm gently. "What a horrible experience! But you handled it in the best way possible, in my opinion."

"I'm glad you think so," he said, relief crossing his face. "I'd hate for that to stop you from allowing me to call on you."

"You want to call on me?"

He looked away and coughed. "Well, you see, when I came in the house and saw all of you ladies at the sewing bee, I noticed you in particular with your big dark eyes and soft hair. I asked Mrs. Jansen, and she said you weren't married or engaged to anyone.

And I thought that maybe—" he coughed again, avoiding her gaze "—well, maybe you were the reason God brought me to this town."

"Oh," Maria said.

He rushed on, as if he'd planned what to say. "See, my pa's always told me I'm no good, even though I took care of my brothers and sisters from when I was ten years old, because of his drinking. A few years back, he got married again, and his new wife didn't have any use for me either. I hated to leave my brothers and sisters with them, but my stepmother told me I wasn't welcome in their house any more. I've been working these past three years on my own, and I'll tell you, I feel pretty lonely sometimes. I told God that if He would bring me a good woman who loved Him and would love me, I'd love her as much like God does as I could. When I saw you, I felt He'd answered that prayer."

Maria studied Abe's face with wide eyes. How incredible that his prayer should so closely echo her own. She smiled shyly and felt her heart bump as he smiled back.

"You will allow me to call on you, won't you? Of course, I'll ask your father first. I want to do things right."

"I will. My father won't have a problem with your paying court to me, although—" she shuddered, "—my mother will probably make both our lives a misery whenever she can. She has her heart set on my marrying George Rempel."

"Well," Abe said determinedly as they turned in the gate to her house, "she'll just have to get used to it."

Sarah Klassen never did get used to Abe. From the day she met him to the day Maria married him two years later, she never ceased reminding her daughter that Abe was the son of a drunk, without family, money, or the potential for either. She was certain that apples never fell far from the tree and that Maria was throwing her life away by choosing him over George.

Maria's father, Jacob, was a man of weak body and few words, and was often overruled by his wife, but on this issue he refused to give in. He gave his blessing to Maria and Abe, and bore his wife's wrath with the patience of a saint. Maria thought it was possible

  Hot Apple Cider with Cinnamon

that he was trying to prevent her from enduring the same kind of loveless marriage he and Sarah were caught in. Whatever the reason, she was grateful for his support, which continued even after she shocked the community by eloping with Abe in a gown of royal blue adorned with a sparkling rhinestone brooch Abe gave her as a wedding present.

In the nearly 70 years that followed, the prayer that Maria had prayed as she stood by the window on that day so long ago often came to mind. She'd asked God to send her someone who would love her the way He did, and what an answer she'd received! It was evident in her husband's kindness to her, in his provision for their children, and in the increasing grace he extended to others as they grew older. She offered that same love back to her husband and children, and then to their grandchildren and great-grandchildren.

It was, thought Maria, as she lay, breathing laboured, in a hospital room watching the light fade to dark, *a real love.* And it was a love that had enabled her to find an unanticipated measure of comfort when her husband went to be with His Lord four short years earlier. Deeper than she'd dreamed possible, more steadfast than she could have imagined, Abe's love had been a constant reminder of the greatest, most surprising love she'd ever received—that of God Himself.

Jesus, she prayed as her eyes closed for the last time on this earth, *thank You for answering my prayer so long ago, and for answering my every prayer. Now I'm coming home to Your love. I'm finally coming home to You and to my Abe.*

1. Based on a true story

Love Uncovered

Nonfiction

Ruth Smith Meyer

We watched her stomp up the slight incline to the Seniors Activity Centre as well as she could with one lame leg. Her long legs and height emphasized her disability. Her grey hair pulled tightly from her face was twisted in a firm bun at the nape of her neck. Her scowl encompassed every feature of her face. Her cane whacked the cement with each step as she barked, "I am here, but I'm not going to enchoy myself." Joanna glared at us, daring us to refute her. "Only because of my family am I here. To them I will prove it vill not vork."

We weren't totally surprised at her attitude. When our director had made a home-visit to discuss her coming, Joanna made it quite clear she had no interest in attending our program. She said she didn't speak English well enough and nobody would understand her. She had consented to try it out only after her family pled with her and promised that her neighbour, who also spoke German, would attend with her.

"You don't have to enjoy it if you don't want to—" I smiled "—but we're glad you're here anyway. I, for one, am going to enjoy getting to know you."

"Hmph!" she grumbled in disbelief as though she thought I was lying to try to win her over.

Our day proceeded with morning coffee, an easy craft, a short reading, and lots of conversation. Joanna took part in the craft and listened closely to the reading, but her friend did most of the talking, making sure Joanna understood what we said.

As she left, I asked, "So what did you think of the day, Joanna?"

"Oh, I might try it one more day, but more than that I won't promise you!"

She swatted her hand in the air as if to scatter any attempt to soften her statement.

Our program, which was open three days a week, was for elderly people who were either living by themselves or with family but who were isolated from community activities because of lessening abilities. Most of them no longer drove, so they were brought by volunteer drivers.

Some clients came every day we were open, but many came only one or two days a week. While there, they were given a full-course hot meal and had access to tub baths as well as foot and hair care. The programming attempted to keep the participants' interest alive and growing as we introduced them to the wider world and new activities they could still manage. It was evident that just being with others in the same stage of life was reassuring to those who came.

Joanna finally agreed to give it a try one day a week.

"How are you today?" I asked her each time she came.

"No good!" she'd mutter, scrunching her eyebrows as if to give weight to her words.

But one week, she surprised us. "I'd say 'No good,' but you won't believe me anyway, so I might as well say, 'Good!'" She grinned.

One morning, as we visited over coffee, she complained, "It's so hard to say things in English when you have not the right words. Even if you do, they come not out right."

"I know what you mean," I told her. "Just this morning, when my daughter asked which blouse she should wear, I told her '*Es macht mich nix aus*.'" I saw Joanna's eyebrows rise as her eyes widened in surprise, but I just continued. "I told her that, literally translated, what I said means 'It makes me nothing out,' but that doesn't make any sense in English. What I meant is that it doesn't matter to me."

"You know German?" Joanna sputtered.

"My first language was a German dialect," I told her. "I've forgotten a lot, but that is probably the reason the German words you occasionally use don't confuse me. I understand most of them."

Before that day, Joanna had been coming on Thursdays for several months. The next week, she phoned on Tuesday morning.

"Could your driver come and get me this morning too? I sat here watching my family work all day yesterday and feeling sorry for myself because I manage no more to do much physical labour. I might as well be at the day centre, where I have something else to think about." From then on, she came twice a week, and, little by little, in conversational times or when we had "memory lane" topics, we found out more about her life and the difficulties she had endured.

Born and raised in Germany, she'd married in her mid-thirties. She and her husband Heinrich had only a few months together before the German army called Heinrich into service. One day she said, "I was left to look after both of our elderly parents and two family farms. Most of the time, I lived on Heinrich's farm with his parents.

"I had a difficult time at the birth of our first daughter. It left me with the permanent limp you see. Of course, that added further to the complications in my life.

"Heinrich was allowed to come home for a few months after Gerda's birth. When he left, I found out I was pregnant again. This time there was no leave or home visit when our son was born.

"Soon after, Heinrich was captured by the Russians when the German army was retreating from the Russian front.

"For many years, I knew not if Heinrich was alive or dead. I kept on looking after both farms through the war years. When bombs destroyed the house on Heinrich's farm, we all moved in with my parents."

Another time, she told some of us what happened after the Second World War ended. "Quite a while after the war was over, I received a letter from a far northern Russian camp," she told us. "They said Heinrich was to be released. It gave the date just a few weeks distant for his arrival home. After the long years of alternating between hope and fear, I was elated, yet I could hardly believe that it could really be true."

Joanna shook her head at the memory. "The morning he was to arrive, I dressed in the best I had and got the children ready to meet their father for the first time in their memory. I felt strange, for I'd known him only briefly before marriage, then had such a

  Hot Apple Cider with Cinnamon

short time with him followed by his long absence. I fluctuated between joy, anticipation, and uncertainty.

"The hours ticked by. No Heinrich. Lunch time came and went." We could see the desperation and confusion still in Joanna's eyes at the remembrance.

"I thought perhaps he would still come in time for the evening meal. We waited past the usual hour, but still no Heinrich. The children got sleepy, so I put them to bed; but I waited until way past my bedtime. Yet Heinrich did not come or even send a message. *Was this all a hoax?* I wondered.

"I was so sad! I took down my hair, braided it, changed into my nightgown, and went to bed." Joanna paused and stared pensively into space. "Through the day I'd stayed in control because it still seemed so unreal. But the tears came in the darkness, along with a flood of disappointment and self-pity. I went to sleep crying."

In the morning, Joanna and her parents came to the conclusion that the letter must have been a sick joke. She was glad his parents were no longer living to experience the renewed disappointment.

Her mother took pity on her grieving daughter. "Why don't you go visit your aunt for a few days? We'll manage here with the children, and it will give you something else to think about." It seemed to Joanna that it would be no better than staying at home to grieve, but she felt so numb and let down that she consented.

Three days later, there was a knock at her aunt's door. "Would you get that, Joanna?" her aunt asked as she stirred the pot of soup on the stove.

As Joanna moved toward the door, there was a second knock. A very loud one. She opened the door to find out who would be so rude and impatient. Shock pulsed through her whole body at the sight of the figure on the step. Conflict, defence, and disbelief battled within her.

"Can you believe it?" she asked us. "I slammed the door shut in my husband's face and ran to my bedroom and banged that door shut, too. 'No, no, it can't be!' I said as I threw myself on the bed and burst into tears. 'I can't let myself believe it again!'"

Voices from the adjoining room floated through the door into her consciousness. Then she heard a gentle rap at the door.

"Joanna, my beloved, can I come in?"

"Yes," she answered, rubbing her eyes free of tears while shame reddened her cheeks. "It was a thinner and older-looking man than I remembered, but it was Heinrich."

Sadness filled her voice. "It was difficult to start all over again. He had spent long years working in the camps with guards ready to whip anyone who faltered because of weakness, so our family had to quickly learn not to make any sudden moves. It was as if he had been mentally programmed to protect himself at the slightest movement. Even while we slept, my brushing against him could result in a sudden slap because of the rats that had threatened to gnaw him in his sleep. He was a much different man from the one I married. And, yes, I was different too, for I'd had years to be independent."

Wanting a place of their own, Heinrich cleaned out the remaining building on his farm—a pig pen—and changed it into a place for them to live while he dug out the remaining debris from the war so he could farm once more. Another son was born to them.

Another day she told us that after the war life became unbearable for Heinrich. East Germany had been placed under Russian rule, and when he remembered what the communists had done to him in Russia, he found it impossible to be content to live under them.

Heinrich and Joanna decided to attempt escape to West Germany and then try to get to Canada and start over. Much planning had to be done. Joanna and the children could get permission to travel by train to visit a relative in West Germany, but Heinrich, a former soldier and captive of the Russian army, would not be given such freedom. He would have to find an escape route and travel on foot by night.

After such a long separation, Joanna's inner being groaned with fear at the thought of his being captured once more. However, she could plainly see that staying in a communist country was, for Heinrich, like living with a phantom of past terror. For his sake and that of her children, she consented to the plans.

"In case they would say something that would put us all into danger, we only told the children we were going to visit our family. We told them their father wouldn't be coming with us."

Hot Apple Cider with Cinnamon

"I had never even unpacked our wedding gifts because I was waiting for a place of our own. It hurt to leave them all behind. I searched for a few treasures I could pack in my suitcase that would bring no suspicion if our bags were searched. I chose a tablecloth and a crocheted doily, and packed them with only enough clothes that would be a believable amount for the three-week visit we proclaimed we were going to make. Gerda and Cornelius were old enough to carry suitcases, but having to carry Willy while walking with a cane restricted what I was able to take.

"We said our goodbyes to my parents and to Heinrich at the train station, and boarded for the journey." Joanna wiped a tear. "I didn't know if I would ever see Heinrich again.

"As we neared the border, I got really nervous. What if the officials became suspicious? I looked through my papers and quietly recited the answers I would give to their possible questions. When the train slowed down, I whispered to the children to be quiet and let me do the talking." A grin spread across Joanna's face. "As the official came through the car, I was afraid he would be able to see my heart beating with big thumpity-thumps." She hit herself on her chest in demonstration. "He seemed satisfied with my answers, though! He moved on to the others behind us and I took a deep breath.

"We waited for two terrifying weeks before Heinrich finally appeared at my relative's home in West Germany. A guide had led him across the dangerous guarded border, dodging the rotating flood lights, and then through the woods to safety.

"We began immediately to work on papers and plans to go to Canada, but it was a year before we were ready to sail, and by that time little Helena had joined our family, so we needed one more ticket."

We were all interested the day Joanna told us about their early life in Canada. "Even though Heinrich sighed in relief to be in a free land, our troubles weren't over when we arrived in Canada," she told us. "When we finally got our farm, the house was so old and in such poor condition it was hardly fit to live in. There were mice and rats in the house, and the first winter the snow blew in around the windows. Since the farm had to come first, I plugged all the holes I could and we managed for quite a few years until we built a new house.

"Neither of us knew much English, but the children soon learned in school, and Heinrich was out in the community more than me because he had to get things for the farm. He usually took my grocery lists and bought the household needs, too, because I hated trying to make myself understood in the stores. That is why my English is so poor now yet.

"My older children had some memories of the old country, but our youngest was all Canadian. She didn't want to learn anything about our home country. She scolded me when I tried to teach her some of our ways. 'Mom, we're in Canada now!' she reminded me over and over. I was often dismayed with some of the things she wanted to do—things that were so different from the way I was brought up—and that just made her more determined to do things her way." Joanna's eyes clouded with sadness. "I think Helena still is ashamed of me with my old country ways."

Many times Joanna would say, "I've never told anyone this before, but…"

The staff and clients at the day centre seemed to be a sounding board for her, and although complaints still made up a lot of her conversation, we could see that sharing her stories was having a therapeutic influence on her.

The subtle changes in Joanna gave me another idea.

About a year after she started coming, when Mother's Day came along, I planned a surprise for the women who attended the program. I contacted members of all the women's families and asked them to write a letter or find a poem to describe their mother, and tell us why she deserved to be *Mother of the Year*. As the responses came in, my co-workers and I chose a specific award for each of our women, and made up certificates like *Most Charming* or *Most Loving Mother of the Year*. Both of Joanna's daughters sent lovely letters, but because I knew of the conflict between Joanna and her younger daughter, when I read Helena's response, my heart was especially touched.

On the Friday before Mother's Day, we set up a beautifully decorated chair upon which the recipients of the awards could sit in turn. When it was Joanna's turn, she fussed about being the centre of attention, but nevertheless, she came and sat on the special chair. I handed her a rose and the certificate for *Most Courageous Mother of the Year*. First I read Gerda's letter, then I began to read Helena's.

She listened intently to the first few paragraphs, but then turned and interrupted me with a hint of anger, as though she felt I had gone too far this time. "Are those your words?" She demanded.

"No, they are your daughter Helena's words."

I went on with my reading again, but soon she looked over her glasses at me. "Are you sure those are Helena's words and not yours?"

"Joanna, what I am reading is word for word what Helena wrote."

Through the rest of the letter, Joanna listened, shaking her head from side to side.

Helena had expressed her great admiration and appreciation for her parents, who had left all that was familiar to them to come to a new country so their children could have a better life. She related how her mother had suffered through difficult years on the farm, living in a ramshackle house without complaint. She commended her for the hard work she did, helping on the farm, gardening, and caring for her children's needs, and for making do when she had to. She acknowledged how difficult it must have been for her mother not to be able to communicate with her neighbours because she'd been too busy to have an opportunity to learn English. She closed by admitting to the conflict she and her mother had often experienced, but expressing her deep love and gratitude all the same.

At the end, Joanna, in awe and wonder, whispered, "I don't believe it. I don't believe it."

We went on with the rest of the senior women, each getting her turn. You could almost feel a tangible pulse of warmth growing stronger with each reading. At the end of the day, as they all prepared to leave, Joanna came over to me, placed a hand on each of my shoulders, and looked me straight in the eyes.

"Ruth, today you gave me the best gift anyone could ever have given me. You have no idea how much it means to me. I had no inkling that Helena had any appreciation for me, much less love.

Thank you, thank you, from the bottom of my heart." Then in a gesture unfamiliar to her, she drew me to her and gave me a hug.

I hadn't realized the awesome impact that activity would have on the participants. Nor did I expect to observe lasting, visible effects. But in the weeks ahead, we saw a transformed Joanna. When on arrival, we asked her, "How are you today?" her answer was always, "Good! Good!" Her beaming face confirmed the truth of her words. No longer were there complaints about her family, but affirmation of their kindness and goodness. There was an ease about her that was contagious. Her astute observations about the rest of the clients and her concern about their needs were a delight to behold. She became one of the most positive influences of our day centre family. Her expressions of thankfulness were a strength and encouragement to us all.

The glow of my own gratification for carrying out that Mother's Day program lasted for a long time. But the most amazing realization for me was that the love that blossomed forth from Joanna had been there all along, buried so deeply under layers of conflict and misunderstanding that no one, including Joanna herself, knew it was there.

It may have helped that the sharing didn't need to be face to face, because that would have felt awkward and unfamiliar to both mother and daughter. In any case, because her daughter had the courage to bare her soul and write down her honest emotions, Joanna's generous heart was freed from its captivity, liberating her many good qualities and allowing her to make a difference in other lives. Love does that!

Hot Apple Cider with Cinnamon

Old Ladies' Perfume

Nonfiction

Glynis M. Belec

"I was thinking of getting Blue Grass perfume for the girls for Christmas this year," Mom said. The "girls" were her granddaughters—my daughter and five nieces. "The sets are on special," Mom added.

"No!" I said without thinking. "Blue Grass is an old ladies' perfume!" I immediately wished I hadn't blurted that out so quickly.

Mom, usually quick as a whip, frowned and fell silent for a split second.

I shut my eyes. I knew that Blue Grass was her favourite fragrance. So I'd just managed to insult her twice in one go. Not only had my thoughtless words berated her choice in perfume, but I'd called her "old" in a derogatory way. I knew my words had to have stung.

As I tried to think of a way to backtrack, I was relieved to see that familiar faint twinkle in Mom's eyes.

"Cheeky Cat," she said. "So, what do *you* think the girls would like?"

I apologized and she told me to forget it.

Her granddaughters didn't get Blue Grass perfume that Christmas, and I never did forget.

Neither did Mom.

In fact, my *faux pas* became a standing joke. Sometimes when I was visiting her, she'd ask me to get her "old ladies' perfume" from the dresser for her. If someone else complimented her or her fragrance when I was around, she'd say, loudly enough so I could hear, "Thanks. It's my old ladies' perfume."

The thing is, by the time I was in my twenties and she was in her fifties, I really did think of her as an "old lady."

Mom's grey hair was a definite indicator of age, or so I thought at the time. And then there were all those creases on her face. She called them "laugh lines," but I had noticed that those "laugh lines" didn't exactly disappear when the joke was over.

"You're as young as you feel!" That was Mom's mantra, and although some physical challenges prevented her from actually chasing her grandchildren around the yard, her perspicacious personality remained, and she didn't miss a thing. Quick-witted and fun-loving, Mom always had a snappy comeback.

"You just wait," Mom would say with that lovely, familiar twinkle in her eye. "Your time will come, and you'll realize how young I really am right now."

I don't remember my response, but it likely consisted of rolling eyes and a smart-alecky comment.

And then my time came.

I can't believe how wrong I was. Fifty isn't old at all!

Another thing I've realized is that, even at my age, I'm still my mom's daughter, and I'm grateful to have had such a good mom. I'll never forget her or the life lessons she taught me along the way.

When I was growing up, I never tired of listening to her stories. She relayed some heartwarming and sometimes shocking times from her stint in the military during the Second World War. She served in signals and as a telephone operator in the Auxiliary Territorial Service (ATS) during the war, and later worked as a nurse in the Voluntary Aid Department (VAD). Her compassionate heart helped many, and she continued her nursing career after the war.

Mom loved poetry and could recite many by memory, including *The Highwayman* by Alfred Noyes and *Song of Hiawatha* by Henry Wadsworth Longfellow. She also loved to write poetry and even tackled some short stories, although she never made an attempt to publish anything.

I knew that Mom had actually been a bit of a free spirit in her younger years, but she always clung tightly to what she believed and wasn't overly concerned about how others perceived her. Her motto was "To thine own self be true."

  Hot Apple Cider with Cinnamon

Mom knew she wasn't perfect, and she made no apology for that. "Everybody's a little daft, when you stop to think about it," she said on more than a few occasions. She taught me to focus less on my weaknesses and more on my strengths.

Honesty, reliability, and a brilliant sense of humour propelled her. Her forthright nature landed her in hot water sometimes, but it also made her many friends.

Mom liked a good debate—and really, really liked to win. She ruffled a few feathers over the years with her feisty British bulldog stubbornness, but she had a heart of gold, and those she befriended, she befriended for life.

Mom believed in God. I remember her teaching me how to pray when I was a little girl. But she also abhorred hypocrisy. I didn't find out the reason for us not attending church regularly until I was an adult. Mom shared how she had been sexually abused by her own grandfather, who was an "upstanding" elder in the church she attended at the time. Though she never actually told me that was the reason we never attended church, I could see how the abuse by someone who should have protected her would have influenced her perception of the church, and why hypocrisy infuriated her.

I'll always be thankful to Mom for planting that tiny seed within by teaching me to pray. That led to my discovering God.

I'll also always be thankful to her for showing me how to be strong and teaching me to stand up for what I believe.

Mom and I shared many precious moments and some wonderful laughs over the years, and I was honoured when she asked my input on certain matters. It didn't mean she was going to take my advice, but the fact that she asked was the honour.

Mom always had a quick response or a story to share, usually a humorous one. I remember the "surgery story" well. Mom was going in for abdominal surgery. Apparently she'd taken a black marker and drawn arrows and a happy face on her legs and abdomen to direct the surgeon!

That was my mom; a funny girl to the end. Was it any wonder that she crossed into heaven with a smile on her face?

Mom passed away in her 81st year. I miss her terribly and still often think of that time when I hurt her feelings. The Christmas after Mom died, I bought three bottles of Blue Grass perfume: one for each of my sisters and one for me.

Oh, and one more thing. A little while ago when I was spritzing on a squirt of my Blue Grass perfume, my 30-something daughter happened to be in the room.

"Want a squirt?" I asked.

Guess what she said?

Hot Apple Cider with Cinnamon

Notes from a Sacred Journey

Nonfiction

Bill Bonikowsky

My wife of 45 years died last fall. We knew it was coming—she had cancer—but nothing can prepare you for that journey. You can read books about it. You can search for words to comfort others on this road. But until you walk it yourself, it is impossible to plumb the depths of that word, *grief.*

I was a bit of a romantic as a teenager. I didn't date much, because the girl I would have dated wasn't interested.

In the fall, I would walk down our street, Water Street, thinking about Joy and humming one of my favourite tunes—"Autumn Leaves," sung by Frank Sinatra. I'd start by singing the first lines, then drift into humming mode since I didn't know the lyrics that followed.

Somehow I timed it so that, by the time I reached the glorious stand of maple trees at the schoolyard, I could switch from humming to singing the only other line I knew, which talked about how much he missed his girl when autumn leaves began to fall. I sang with pretty deep emotion, because I really did like that girl I was not yet dating, and the lyrics mirrored my emotions.

Last fall, I stood in that same patch of trees. They were glorious in their autumn splendour. I couldn't help thinking of "my song." Of how the girl I had once longed for more than 50 years ago had become my wife.

This autumn God called her home.

As I watched the leaves fall, those words from "my song" stirred my heart with renewed emotion, and likely will for the remaining autumns of my life.

"The girl" was Joy McCallum. We met in church in Guelph, Ontario. Born in Belfast, Northern Ireland, she had immigrated with her family when she was about nine.

This dark-haired girl with hazel eyes and a mischievous smile gradually drew my attention away from Pastor Boyd's sermons.

Every Easter, Joy would arrive at church with a perky new hat. I still remember the white one that accentuated her black curls. I was too young to know what to do with the growing attraction I felt toward her.

When I was 14 and Joy was 13, the two of us were helping out with vacation Bible school, so I saw her every day. By mid-week, I'd summoned up the courage to ask her on a date. Leaping out of my comfort zone, I invited her to go roller skating with another couple. She said she would have to ask her mother.

On the last day of VBS, making sure I was within earshot and paying attention—how could I *not* be paying attention?—Joy took her girlfriend aside and, casting a glance in my direction, told her, "I'm going roller skating on Saturday." Simple words, but such a profound impact on my young heart!

My enduring memory from that double date is watching Joy fall on her rear, and standing there wondering if you're supposed to pick a girl up, and if so, how to do it.

Our love story took a hiatus after that first date. Throughout my teen years, I pined over that Irish lass while she frolicked with her girlfriends. Occasionally I would screw up the courage to ask her out, and would hear her disheartening response, "Heather and I are doing something that night."

As Joy explained later, "I knew you liked me. You weren't a challenge."

At the end of my first year at college, everything changed. Joy wondered if we could have a talk.

When I agreed, she asked a question that turned my world upside-down: "Where do I stand on your list?"

I was dumbfounded. Pausing a moment to corral my thoughts, I blurted out the half-truth, "Pretty near the top."

Truth is, I didn't have a list. Or if I did, hers was the only name on it.

That happened in the spring of 1967. We were engaged by Christmas that year, and we married in 1969.

In the ensuing years Joy stood by my side as I completed Bible college and seminary. She followed me as we stepped out in faith, moving across the country to Vancouver, BC, where we ministered with Youth for Christ for 27 years. She then supported me through two and a half years as a pastor and over 11 years of service with Alpha Ministries Canada.

During those years, we had three boys: Mark, Tim, and Jonathan.

In 1998, Joy endured a serious encounter with breast cancer, but she survived to witness three weddings and the births of nine grandchildren.

In all that time, I never contemplated life without her.

And then the cancer returned.

As I reflect on the 18-plus months since the day the doctors told us the cancer was back, I can see that Joy's journey toward the hospice was a process of letting go in stages.

As a lady who loved to walk, it was hard for her to have that ability decline to where she was confined to bed. Once able to buzz about doing household chores and happily preparing dinner for guests, the simplest tasks gradually began to exhaust her.

Once able to crawl on the floor with the grandkids, she now had a hard time even holding and hugging them.

It got so that even driving in the car or sitting in church became too much for her to bear. The wheelchair obtained from the Red Cross as a means for me to take her on her familiar walks was borrowed too late. It sat unused until I returned it.

Then came the day when Joy was alarmed to discover that she was too weak to lift her legs in the bed.

But the one constant (and a nurse commented on it at least once a day) was Joy's smile. Her trademark smile still lit her face no matter what else was missing.

I've heard that eagles have a unique method for helping their young leave the nest. When it's time for them to try their wings, the parents begin to remove the material that gives the nest a soft, comfortable lining. As the nest becomes more and more uncomfortable for the eaglets, they become less reluctant to leave it.

As Joy experienced the mounting loss of things she once enjoyed, the prospect of leaving this "nest" became more attractive to her. And the things that could never be taken away, like her relationship with Jesus, became more precious.

The Apostle Paul put it this way: "Yes, all the things I once thought were so important are gone from my life. Compared to the high privilege of knowing Christ Jesus as my Master, firsthand, everything I once thought I had going for me is insignificant." (Philippians 3:8, *The Message*)

It was Sunday evening, September 28, 2014. As I started to write, I didn't know this was to be Joy's last evening on earth.

I wanted to write about a profound moment Joy and I had just shared. As I finished, my finger grazed some link on the side of my iPad. Immediately, a new screen began to open, and I desperately tried to recover what I had just written. It was gone.

At that moment the nurse came in. She looked at Joy, then startled me with words for which I was unprepared: "I think she's gone."

I was sitting right beside Joy, but I was unaware she had slipped away.

I have replayed that moment over and over, trying to push aside regrets that in that precious moment when her faith became sight, I was fiddling with an electronic gadget!

I can't get that moment back, but I will try to re-create the words that described the time leading up to it. I call it "The Lost Post."

Joy was especially restless tonight. Most of what she was saying was unintelligible, but she was quite vocal. Several times, I went to her side only to have her say, "Go. Go. Go away."

I went back to my desk feeling a bit sad and wondering why she was saying that.

Once more she called out. This time, when I went to her, she reached out toward me, and took both of my hands in hers.

We couldn't carry on a conversation at that point, but I began to do something that comes as naturally as breathing to me. I began to sing. "Fairest Lord Jesus," "I Dreamed of That City Called Glory," "How Great Thou Art," "This World is Not My Home."

At first, I didn't know if she was listening, or was able to comprehend the words. Then I began to notice something. In the midst of the unintelligible sounds she was making, I began to recognize words that I was singing. And when I finished a song, she would stop too, as if waiting for the next one to begin. She was singing with me!

I ventured further, and started to sing Christmas carols. "O Come, O Come Emmanuel," "O Little Town of Bethlehem," "Silent Night." Singing carols that early in the year would have bothered her in an earlier time, but tonight was different. I could tell she was engaging with the music and the words.

Those moments together, holding hands, singing on the threshold of glory, will be a cherished memory. A sacred concert.

That is roughly what I was trying to capture on the iPad that night. As I wrote, I was conscious of Joy settling and getting quieter. As I saw my words suddenly disappear, and scrambled to find them, the nurse came in. Joy had had the last word.

Jennifer and Sarah had done the hard part—going through Joy's clothes. But two and a half weeks later, the neatly packed bags labelled "for MCC" (Mennonite Central Committee Thrift Store) still lay in the guest bedroom where the girls had placed them.

With a heavy heart, I decided I had to take them in. I moved decisively, quickly loading them into the car and driving straight to the Thrift Store.

I got a bin from the store and wheeled it out to the car.

There were some pretty ratty-looking cushions and other donated things in the bottom of it. Something within urged me to impress upon the staff that the things I was loading into the bin were special.

"My wife just died," I blurted out, "and there are some really good clothes and shoes in these bags."

"I'm so sorry," I heard as I wheeled the bin to the corner.

And then I was out the door.

I made it to the car before dissolving in tears.

I knew they were just clothes, but I couldn't shake the sense of loss I felt in leaving behind another part of Joy.

Between tissues, I prayed. I thanked God that Joy was now clothed in robes of white (although I suspect other colours and styles are available up there). And I prayed that God would help get Joy's earthly clothes into the hands of the people who really need them.

As I drove away, I felt as if something had been removed from my chest, leaving a hollow space filled with a tender ache.

While I completed my other errands, I wore my sunglasses and listened to a beautiful worship CD. And, as always, I felt God clothing my inner being with His love.

Grief washes over you like an incoming tide—except with the tide, you know when to expect it.

On another of my "good days," when I was feeling strong and positive, I decided, "This is a good time to take back all of Joy's unused medications. I should be able to keep a stiff upper lip today."

I walked up to the counter, smiled, and said, "This time I'm giving the drugs to you."

The girl behind the counter looked quizzically at me, then at the arsenal of meds I had laid on the counter. I explained that we had just filled a lot of these prescriptions in August but that, three days later, Joy had ended up back in the hospital in palliative care.

As I explained, my throat began to tighten. When I shared that Joy had passed away, the tears began to come.

I managed to hold it together while we finished blacking out Joy's name and Rx number on the bottles, but I was glad when I could retreat to the safety of my car.

I tried to analyze why, when I felt so strong, a few words could open the floodgates again. I think it was more than the fact that I was giving away one more thing that had belonged to Joy.

On Wednesday, August 27, 2014, Joy had been released from a 10-day stay in the hospital. Her symptoms were now reasonably under control. We'd picked up new prescriptions to add to the current ones and bravely set off for home.

That night I sat at the kitchen table, happy to have her home but a little nervous. I stared at all the medications, hoping I could keep everything straight.

Very soon Joy's nausea resulted in the loss of both food and pills, and her pain was difficult to control.

Friday, August 29, The Red Cross delivered a hospital bed that we set up in the family room because Joy was having difficulty with the stairs to our bedroom. But the new bed wasn't comfortable enough for Joy to spend the night on, so we did one more journey up our stairs, with me half-carrying her. Joy struggled all that night, trying to get comfortable and deal with the pain. By 6 a.m. her pain was unbearable, and I called for an ambulance.

Up until this time, Joy's focus had been to fight this battle at home, and we'd struggled to keep up with treatments and medications to make that happen. Now there was a great release in Joy's mind. She talked with me about making this the last trip to the hospital and looking for hospice care. While we both shed some tears, that decision brought release. By the time we arrived at the hospital, Joy had peace.

I still have the text I sent to our kids from the ER: "Hi, family. Here is where we're at. We called the ambulance early this morning because Mom could no longer stand the pain. Joy has made a decision that she is totally at peace with. It was confirmed in a chat she had with the paramedic in the ambulance, and just a few minutes ago with the ER doctor.

"Mom feels that home is no longer the best option. Mom wants to go to a hospice. The doctor just came in and told us that a bed is available on the palliative floor right now. Mom is getting some fluids as well as pain and nausea medication by IV, then she will be moved. Will keep in touch. Love from us both."

Within a couple of hours, Joy was back in the same bed she had left on Wednesday. The same kind nurse greeted us. That was the beginning of the end.

I came home that night knowing that—barring a miracle—Joy would not be in our home again. But it gave me much comfort to see her looking forward to her eternal home.

It had been difficult news for the kids to hear, but we had wonderful, deep, heart-stirring visits with all the kids and grandkids. You could almost hear them growing.

Now that I've taken time to relive this, it has become clear why the tears came at the pharmacy. Those medications represented that one, final, brave battle for Joy and me to keep things the way they'd been.

An outside observer might say that we lost and the cancer won. But there's something powerful about the phrase, "Death is swallowed up in victory" (1 Corinthians 15:54).

Joy's painful struggle was only the blink of an eye in comparison to the eternal happiness she is experiencing now. She doesn't need any medication—she is pain-free, her sorrow ended. And in killing Joy, the cancer actually set her free and killed itself.

Tears will come again when I recall what Joy endured. But my spirit will always be filled with gratitude at the grace of our Saviour in preparing a place for her in His house. Apparently, He's working on mine now, and He'll have a place for you as well, if you desire.

A friend embraced me after a meeting at church one night and said something like, "Oh Bill. How are you doing? It will be so hard for you tomorrow!"

I did a quick survey of my memory banks to see what it was I should be aware of "tomorrow." Coming up blank, I asked, "What's tomorrow?"

"It's Joy's birthday!"

After that, I had similar questions from my children, daughters-in-law, and friends about how I was handling Joy's birthday. But the funny thing is, when the question was first posed to me, I wasn't yet conscious of the significance of November 24! And all day I've been asking myself why.

Part of the reason might be that not a day goes by when I *don't* think about Joy. In that regard, tomorrow is the same as today. I look at her picture on my bedside table when I get up in the morning and again when I go to bed at night. A birthdate could neither add to my love nor diminish my sadness at her loss.

But it is very significant to me that family and friends are remembering that today is Joy's birthday. It confirms the special place she held in all of our hearts. And it makes me wonder if they celebrate birthdays in heaven, where time is no longer relevant.

I did find a birthday present—a photo our niece Sarah Chaudhery sent us, taken at her wedding. Awkwardly, with big smiles, we were "dancing" at her wedding reception.

Joy sometimes mentioned that we should take dance lessons. We never did. But we did have a little shuffle together at weddings. And in her last month, when I had to put my hands under her arms and lift her from the bed, we would stand face to face for a few moments and pretend we were dancing.

On the night that Joy slipped into eternity while I was distracted, a friend suggested that when I wasn't looking, Joy's First Love took her hand and brought her home.

There, she'll be able to dance!

Christmas was Joy's favourite time of year. She loved to get the decorations up early.

Joy specialized on the indoor decorations, and I invested hours on the outside, much to our neighbours' delight. Garlands laced with lights adorned the garage door, the front door, and the bow windows at the front of our home. Small white lights, carefully placed, brought the shrubs to life.

I always seemed to pick the coldest days to do it.

When the last strand was up I would bring my frozen fingers into the house and announce that the lights were done. Joy would slip on a big coat, slide her feet into my slippers, and shuffle out onto the street. I can still see the reflection of the lights in her eyes, and her smile of approval.

The house was quiet this Christmas, except for the whisper of memories that greeted me at every turn.

It's harder when grief finds you alone, so I decided to embrace Christmas, immersing myself in its activities and accepting the emotions as they came. I put up the lights and garland outside, knowing Joy would not be there to admire them. The tree went up, sparkling with its silver, gold, and red accents. The other decorations were tenderly put in their place. Then I invited my neighbours for an open house. Joy and I had often talked about doing that, and I told my guests it was an expression of her heart too. They absolutely loved it.

December 24 was a full day.

A two-hour visit with a friend of Joy's who, because of physical disabilities, is confined to her apartment. I brought her some Christmas goodies as Joy used to at Christmas.

Two more hours on the road to complete two more errands.

A 5:30 Christmas Eve service at our church, followed by a visit with my son Mark and Jodi and the kids in Tsawwassen.

A quick nip across the border to pick up a package in Point Roberts.

And then... The road leading back into Canada from the border crossing runs right past Boundary Bay Cemetery, where Joy was laid to rest. I slowed as I came to the entrance and was surprised to find the gate open. The back section of the cemetery was lit by a floodlight, so I ventured in.

A light, cold breeze was blowing as I stood at Joy's graveside. I always get a bit choked up at this point, but I said a few words to her on this Christmas Eve. I searched my heart and my mind as I did this. Why would I "talk to her" when I know that the real Joy isn't there beneath the cold mound of gravel still covering the grave? I guess it's solely for my benefit. There's a kind of physical connection at this place. So I talked to her.

Then I looked up and talked to my Father about taking good care of my girl, and if possible, letting her know I love her. I noted how brightly the stars were shining, and I took solace in the thought that she was somewhere far beyond these stars that shone on the place of her burial.

As I made my way home, I felt my heart being stretched once again. I looked forward to coming home and curling up with my thoughts.

But one of those thoughts led me in a different direction.

I recalled a church in the area that used to have an 11 p.m. Christmas Eve service. Joy and I used to go, and even took her mom and sister Yvonne with us one year. A quick search on Google confirmed that Peace Portal Alliance Church was indeed having a late service, so I headed back on the road one more time.

The service was beautiful. I fought back tears for the first ten minutes and then entered into the celebration of the Christmas story.

The evening ended with their pastor of worship, Phil Vanderveen, singing one of the most beautiful performances of "O Holy Night" that I have heard. I was struck by the opening words: "O holy night, the stars are brightly shining."

It occurred to me that the stars that had caught my attention at the cemetery were the same stars that shone on the night Jesus our Saviour was born. The One Who created those stars lay as a baby, entering our human condition so that we could one day be freed from it.

Because of Jesus, that cemetery holds no claim on Joy Bonikowsky (McCallum, if they use maiden names in heaven). I can go there and visit her grave. I can talk to her if it helps me. But she is hearing other voices now, including The Voice of her King, who exchanged a throne for the manger.

Mother, Go Gently

L. June Stevenson

Mother, go gently into sleep,
That final sleep.
Pale and silent, you lie enclosed in a cotton-cloud cocoon
Of drugs and coma.
Already far beyond the sights and sounds of life.

I will watch through the night with you—
Your hand in mine.
A scene we've often shared,

Then it was your strength and comfort flowing into
   my fevered child-body
Through hours of measles, flu, and chicken pox.
But now my hand the stronger one, yours thin and fragile.

Our roles reversed now: I the mother, you the child.
Would that my love could renew your dying cells
And return yesteryear's bloom to your cheeks.
Did you always believe that my tomorrows would bring health?
Or did you sometimes fear, as I fear now, the end is near?

Go gently, mother, into sleep,
I'll dream away the night with you
Recalling countless examples of your motherhood
From my treasure box of life:
Picnics in the park and valentine cakes.
Christmases beyond imagining,
Pink candy floss hours of fantasy and fun,
And my growing, always onward, to womanhood
As if it were the most natural thing in the world,
With your loving example there to guide me.

And still you show the way, teaching how to move from this
world to the next
Gracefully—a lesson I would delay if I could.
I cry as you must have cried when I was born,
Anguish mingled with ecstasy.
I relinquish you reluctantly only because I must
I know your time has come, and I am helpless in life's ceaseless
flow.

Trembling, I encircle your frail frame,
Grown smaller now than mine.
Remembering…
And smiling
As I weep.

Go gently, mother.
Sleep.

The Eye of the Beholder

Fiction

Wendy Dewar Hughes

First, take an orange from the fridge. Set it on the cutting board. Get a knife.

But the knives are all dull. David used to keep them sharp, but since he's been gone, they've become dull, just like everything else.

Everything always comes back to that. David's being gone.

Ever since the night when David got up to go to the bathroom and never came back to bed, everything has been different.

Maggie found him before first light, right after the neighbour's car wakened her and she rolled over to snuggle against David's back. Only he wasn't there.

Press the knife to the side of the orange and saw back and forth until it breaks through the skin.

Maggie has to talk herself through even the simplest tasks. Otherwise she knows she'd simply forget why she was standing in the kitchen until she realized she had an orange in one hand and a knife in the other. The moment she discovered David's cold body lying on the bathroom floor in the semi-dark, her mind ceased to work properly.

"I really must sharpen these knives," she mutters, pressing harder. The blade slips off the stubborn orange rind and slashes her finger. A deep red bubble of blood appears, growing in size until it slides onto the cutting board and makes a little splat. She watches it, almost transfixed.

That's when the telephone rings.

Grabbing a tissue from the box next to the refrigerator, she presses it to the cut and picks up the phone.

"Hi, Cara," Maggie says, holding the phone with her shoulder while she checks the tissue, surprised to see a quarter-sized red splotch on it already. "You'll have to hang on a minute. I'm bleeding."

  Hot Apple Cider with Cinnamon

She hears her daughter squeal as she puts down the phone and runs to the bathroom to hunt for gauze and tape. After hastily bandaging the cut, she catches sight of her reflection in the mirror. Ever since David's death, eighty-seven days before, it's as if a stranger has taken her place in the glass.

After the ambulance came and took away his body, after the funeral, after the well-wishers and sympathizers went home, after her two daughters went back to the city and their respective lives, she'd been left alone to deal with the crushing mountain of grief that threatened to bury her. It had hung over her heart every day since then, like an avalanche about to let go and suffocate her.

Nothing seems important any more. She's almost stopped eating. She just grabs whatever is handy when she thinks she ought to have something. An apple. Some cookies. Chocolate. Now and then she rouses herself enough to heat a meal from the ones the ladies from the church brought to stock her freezer. Otherwise, she might slowly starve.

"I'm back," Maggie says, picking up the phone and pushing a lank strand of hair away from her face. It occurs to her she hasn't had it cut since the day before David's funeral. She's not even sure when she washed it last. She'd always been conscientious about her appearance because it made David proud, but what does it matter how she looks now?

With David gone, what's the point of anything?

"Mom, what happened? Are you all right?" She can hear alarm in Cara's voice.

"Don't panic. I just cut my finger trying to slice an orange for breakfast. What's up?"

"Thank goodness, you're all right," Cara says. Then excitement takes over from her relief. "Mom, my company is sending me to Montreal for a conference in three weeks. Do you want to come with me?"

Maggie has always wanted to see Montreal—but with David.

Now she does a quick mental calculation. It's a five-hour flight from Vancouver. Packing, getting to the airport, finding a hotel, finding her way around a strange city—it all just seems like too much.

"Oh, that's lovely, dear," Maggie says, "but you don't want me to come with you."

"Mom, you've hardly been out of the house since Dad died. Please come. We'll go a day or two before the conference to look around, and then while I'm at the meetings you can explore or shop or sightsee. We'll have the evenings together to try different restaurants. We can stay a couple of days after the conference, too."

They talk about it for a few more minutes and Maggie allows Cara to convince her to take the trip. She doesn't have the heart to quash Cara's excitement about her first big business trip in her new public relations job. Or maybe it's more that she doesn't have the energy to make a decision and simply lets Cara do it for her.

After hanging up, Maggie uses a different knife to cut the orange, eats it, and then decides to have a shower. Standing before the bathroom mirror, she takes a long look at the woman in the baggy cotton pyjamas with reading glasses hanging from a string around her neck. Streaks of dull grey thread through the lifeless brown hair that hangs to her shoulders. New lines have appeared around her eyes, and folds pull down the corners of her mouth. She knows she hasn't smiled in many weeks, and she looks it. Still, she can't muster the energy to care.

"God," she says out loud, "what's happening to me? With David gone, I can't think of a reason to live. You must have something for me, but look at me. I'm only forty-nine but I look like I'm sixty. I know you love me, and you know I don't care much about what I look like right now, but if there is any beauty left in me, can you please show me?"

With a deep sigh, she turns away from the sad woman in the mirror and steps into the shower. Talking with God about whatever was going on in her life, from the important to the trivial, has been a constant in Maggie's life since she was a young girl, but since David's death she hasn't wanted to talk to anyone, including Him. And God doesn't seem to be listening anyway.

The few weeks until the trip to Montreal drag by for Maggie, but Cara's excitement is contagious. Her daughter has scoured the internet for things to do there: museums and other historical buildings to visit and special events taking place while they'll be in the city. Cara's list of activities after her conference is over includes seeing old Montreal, visiting the Notre-Dame Basilica, and taking in a tour up Mont Royal. Maggie has no idea what she will do while Cara is busy but decides to think about that when she gets there.

The flight lands after dark, and the shuttle drops them off at their hotel, a lovely suite establishment on a quiet street lined with shops and restaurants. They check in, but since they're on west coast time, Maggie and Cara go in search of dinner.

The night air holds the crisp chill of autumn as they stroll along the street, and Maggie takes Cara's arm in hers. Though she came on this trip mainly to please Cara, Maggie is surprised to feel a quiver of excitement about being in this strange city. Suddenly the prospect of spending nearly a week on vacation here fills her with a sense of anticipation she hasn't felt for a very long time.

"Look at that," Cara says, stopping in front of a salon with an elegant black-and-white sign swinging over the door. Translating into English with her high school French, she smiles. "They have a special on cuts and colours this week. And it says they welcome drop-ins. I could use a new 'do.' Let's stop by in the morning and see if they can fit us in. What do you say?"

"Oh, I don't know—" Maggie begins. Then she remembers the reflection she's been seeing in her mirror each day. A new hairdo might make her feel better. "All right," she says. "If they have space, we could do it tomorrow and start the week off right."

The next morning, because their bodies are still on west coast time, they sleep later than they had planned, but after a quick, late breakfast at the hotel they put on their jackets and walk down the street to the salon. A woman looks up and smiles when they come through the door. She appears to be in her early fifties and her hair, worn long and loose, shines like polished teak. Another beautician, a young woman with pale pink hair, is busy wiping down the salon's chairs.

"I want the older woman's colour," Maggie whispers to Cara.

In her best French, Cara says to the attendant, "Would you have time today for the two of us to have your cut-and-colour special?"

"*Bonjour, mesdames,*" the woman says before switching to accented English. "Actually, you've picked the perfect day. We've only just started opening on Mondays, and our regular clients haven't caught on yet, so we can fit you in right now, if you like."

Later, when offered a deal on makeup and eyelash extensions while having their nails done, Maggie and Cara giggle like girl-friends and agree.

Four hours after they entered the salon, as her stomach begins to growl for lunch, Maggie is sitting in the stylist's chair gazing at her reflection in the mirror. She looks like a different woman from the one who walked into the salon earlier.

With the new makeup and those long eyelashes, she can't decide if she looks glamorous or ridiculous, but she feels better than she has in weeks. No, months. She can't help but wonder what David would have thought of her new look. She smiles at her reflection and tosses her chestnut hair. *I think you'd love it, David.*

After lunch at an Ethiopian restaurant on the same street, Maggie and Cara check out the shops. Cara buys three sweaters and a huge salmon-coloured pashmina scarf that she tosses around her shoulders. With Cara's encouragement, Maggie buys a new fall jacket in a subdued leopard print and a pair of tall leather boots, shiny black with low heels. Cara talks her into buying a pair of red skinny jeans to wear with them. All of it feels so out of character for Maggie that it's as if she's someone else watching herself go through the motions.

In the morning Cara rises early to the sound of her travel alarm and is up and gone to her conference before Maggie fully awakens.

Now that Maggie is on her own in a strange city, she's at a bit of a loss for what to do. On her way to the breakfast café in the hotel, she passes a rack with cards and brochures about local attractions; she picks up a few and reads them while she has her morning coffee and toast. She decides to see the city by the sim-plest method—she'll buy a ticket on a hop-on-hop-off bus tour. Afterward, she can choose what she wants to see again.

  Hot Apple Cider with Cinnamon

Maggie checks herself in the mirror before heading out for the bus tour. She has to admit the eyelash extensions, by some miracle, still look pretty amazing. Her hair has gone from drab brown streaked with grey to a vibrant shade of mahogany highlighted with glints of gold. The stylist layered it so it has lift and bounce. "Is this really you?" Maggie says to the woman in the mirror. She turns her head from side to side.

As she slips on her new jacket she sighs and, without realizing it, talks to God for the first time in weeks. "This is all fine, Father," she says as she puts on a touch of pink lipstick, "but in the end, what does it matter? Does anybody really care what I look like?"

Taking the city bus downtown to the Information Centre, also known as Centre Infotouriste de Montreal, Maggie finds a seat near the front of the bus. Wrapping her arms around her purse, she slides over next to the window and looks out.

The tour takes two hours if you stay on the bus, but since the ticket is good for two days, she decides to explore Notre-Dame Basilica in Old Montreal. As imposing on the outside as any of the cathedrals Maggie visited in Europe years before, the interior stuns her with its grandeur and beauty. The brilliant colours, the stained glass, the exquisitely carved woodwork, the mosaics, and even the hushed sounds of the visitors nearly take her breath away.

Slipping into a pew away from the crowds, Maggie gazes up at the beams of light streaming through the stained-glass windows. She thinks of David and how much he would have appreciated the beauty of this place. He always noticed the loveliness in everything—especially in her.

Reaching up to run her fingers through her newly styled hair, Maggie shrugs. Would anyone ever see beauty in her again? She doubts it.

The next day Maggie sleeps late. She doesn't even hear Cara leave. After her shower she sits on her bed with the mid-morning sun slanting into the room and flips through a city guidebook she picked up at the Information Centre. Montreal has many different and interesting districts she's always wanted to visit, and she now has all day to discover some of them. Cara has a banquet to attend in the evening, so she won't be back until late.

By the time Maggie reaches Boulevard St. Laurent, the street is buzzing with pedestrians. Outdoor cafés with chairs and small tables spilling onto the sidewalks dot the street. Heads are bent over cups of coffee and cell phones as bright orange and yellow leaves rattle down the street ahead of a light breeze, and mass in drifts against the curbs.

Maggie tugs her collar up under her chin and ducks into a nearby shop. A rack of multi-coloured scarves stands next to the door and she's about to choose a soft brown one to go with her coat when the sales clerk comes over.

"You don't want that one," the smiling woman says. "It's too dull. You need this one." She whips out a brilliant cobalt scarf and hands it to Maggie. "It will look fabulous with your hair."

Maggie allows herself to be talked into buying the blue scarf. *Blue, brown, what's the difference?* She flips the scarf around her neck and folds the ends in at the collar of her coat, then makes her way down the street. After picking up a pair of earrings to take home to her other daughter, Janine, she stops outside the jewellery shop to tuck them into her purse.

"I love that colour on you. It brings out your beauty," says a young woman who passes her without stopping, indicating the scarf. Surprised, Maggie comes to a stop and answers with an automatic "Thank-you" as she watches the woman disappear down the street.

By now it's after one o'clock, and she can smell something tantalizing drifting from a nearby deli. Choosing the only free table outside, she drops onto a chair near the street and sets her purse down at her feet. A few minutes later, a young waiter comes toward her, weaving between the crowded tables. "*Bonjour, Madame. A beautiful day and a beautiful lady.*" With a flourish, he hands Maggie a menu. "May I bring you something to drink?"

Taken aback by his flamboyance, Maggie orders a mineral water. Later, as she eats a bagel with cream cheese and a salad, she watches the people passing by on the street. Hurrying, talking, laughing, strolling, they flow by in a steady stream. A young mother walks slowly past, pushing a stroller holding a small boy who locks eyes with Maggie and doesn't let go until he can no longer turn his head far enough.

By three o'clock, Maggie's throbbing feet tell her she has walked a long way and she'll need to figure out how to get a bus back to the hotel. However, when she turns a corner into a side street, she can't resist stepping into a tiny kitchen shop with colourful displays of pottery and ceramics from Italy and Portugal in the window. As she wanders through the shop, admiring the dishes and coordinating table linens, she's so captivated by the wares she forgets the pain in her feet for a few minutes.

One style in particular catches her attention. On a deep blue background, the artist used delicate brush strokes to fashion tiny white flowers with pale green curling vines and heart-shaped leaves. Even after touring the store three times examining all the designs, she feels drawn back to this pattern. David's favourite colour was blue; he would have loved this. Not only that, but Maggie loves it. She finally chooses a pitcher and a bowl to take home and put on display in her kitchen. These will be her souvenirs of this trip.

Carrying the heavy bag containing her new ceramic pieces, she steps out into the October sunshine and sees a bus stop bench across the road. Looking both ways, she crosses the quiet street and sinks onto the empty bench, slipping her heels out of her loafers to ease the pain in her toes. The schedule she pulls from her purse indicates the bus won't be along for another twenty minutes. She's just missed it.

Oh well, she thinks, settling in for a relaxing wait in the oblique afternoon sun. She decides this would be a good time to peruse the visitor's guide for places to visit tomorrow.

The peaceful side street has few people coming and going, so Maggie is startled when a man stops a couple of metres from where she's sitting and stands looking at her. She glances up at him and frowns. He looks to be around her age and is wearing grey dress pants and a black leather jacket. His black hair has been combed back from his high forehead, revealing dark, intense eyes.

"I am so sorry," he says, placing a flat hand to his heart. "I did not mean to surprise you, Madame, but you look so beautiful sitting there." His accent sounds eastern European. "I am so sorry, so sorry. I am not meaning anything by it, but I am an artist, and when I saw you sitting there…" He hesitates and draws in a deep breath. "You look so beautiful, so beautiful."

He edges around her with his back toward the street, not taking his eyes from her. "I know beauty when I see it, Madame," he says, "and you look so very beautiful. I had to tell you." With that, he turns, strides to the street corner, and disappears from sight.

Stunned, Maggie stares after him for a long while, processing what just happened. Perfect strangers have never in her life told her she was beautiful, or even that she was pretty. David was the only person in her life who ever saw her that way.

So why had this happened to her today? First the young woman, then the waiter and the staring child, and now this man. Was it because of her new clothes, the hairdo, and the lashes? She shook her head. No, she' had looked just as good in the past, when David was alive, and no one had ever called her beautiful then. No one except David.

Then why today?

Her heart quickens.

Only God could know how much she has missed hearing those words from David. Only God could know that hearing those words from strangers would be exactly what she needs to make her frozen heart want to beat again.

Suddenly, she can feel God's love enfolding her in a long embrace.

After several minutes, Maggie sees the bus approaching. As she wipes away her tears, she gets to her feet. Smiling to herself, she thinks, *Beauty is in the eye of the beholder, and, truly, the beholder is God.*

Champ!

Nonfiction

David Kitz

"Do you think this one will make it?"

"No." My sister Edith shook her head in glum resignation.

As we gazed down at the shivering, whimpering pup, the prospects for his survival beyond a year were anything but promising. You see, in the space of five years we had gone through a string of canine disasters.

Five years earlier, our dog Collie—yes, he was a collie—had passed on after a long life of service on the farm. All subsequent dogs were inevitably compared with Collie. For the Kitz family, he represented the gold standard in dogs.

The next dog was Pubby, a fiercely loyal black spaniel that met his grim fate when he was hit by a car.

Next on the list, Topsy, an excellent cow-herder, was in a terrible accident with a snowplough.

A young lab, Sandy, though lovable, turned out to be completely useless as a farm dog—dumb as a stump.

Our latest dog, Buddy, proved to be even worse than Sandy. He chased chickens, and when he caught them, he killed them. Naturally, my mother would have none of this. Buddy's term as a farm dog was abruptly cut short.

Now all six Kitz children were staring at a scrawny brown pup of uncertain pedigree. After these five disasters, we were almost afraid to become attached—hesitant to open ourselves to love yet another dog and face more disappointment.

But a whimpering pup has a way of tugging at your heart strings. He spent much of his first week curled up on an old towel in a cardboard box in the basement. One by one, each of the six Kitz children ventured downstairs to comfort the timid, whining puppy. My memory is that during this time I adopted him and he became my dog. Dale, my younger brother, disputes this. In retrospect, I guess that, despite our initial misgivings, we all claimed him as our own. Or he claimed us.

We named him Champ. I believe I was the one to come up with that name, but this too is open to dispute. It was a rather bold name for a dog that didn't look much like a champion. Even when he reached adult size, he was still scrawny, fine-boned, and barely knee-high. Did he weigh 25 pounds? Possibly not.

His hair and ears were a silky brown, lovely for stroking, but the rest of his short body fur had an odd grizzled appearance, a mix of various shades of brown, black, and white.

What breed was he? I have no idea. I have never since seen a dog like him. Some odd mix, I guess. The Champ breed.

On the Kitz farm, every animal needed to prove its worth, and that included dogs.

Farms in Saskatchewan are big, and at 1,120 acres, our farm was no exception. In addition to fields of wheat, barley, and oats, my dad had 80 head of cattle. We had a dairy herd and a beef herd on separate pastures about a mile apart. The dairy cows were brought to the barn for milking twice daily.

Nothing is more frustrating than having to tramp across 160 acres after an ornery cow. Believe me, I know, having done it more than a few times. A good cattle dog will do this chore for you and save you much time and trouble.

Champ took to cow herding like a duck to water. He loved instilling the fear of God into thousand-pound steers. He would get behind them and then bark and nip at their hocks (ankles) to get them to move. Doing this just right requires a good deal of precision and agility. Precision, because ideally the dog bite should be hard enough to cause pain, but insufficient to pierce the skin. Agility, because the startled bovine kicks back reflexively and the dog needs to move fast and in the right direction. I've seen a kick from a cow send a slow-moving dog flying through the air.

Champ seemed to instinctively know what to do. With lightning speed, he applied just enough jaw pressure to get the desired result, and then he got out of the way. In a matter of seconds, he could turn a cantankerous ton of live beef into a spectacle of meek compliance. He demanded respect, and knew exactly how to get it.

Cows aren't dumb creatures. Usually, it took only one encounter with Champ to establish who was boss. After that, the mere sight of the dog brought obedient submission.

With Champ as helper, rounding up the herd and moving it to a new location became much easier. A single command from one of the Kitz children— "Sic 'em!"—and Champ did all the work.

Champ seemed to have an innate intelligence—much more than the average dog. But he had two other strong character traits as well.

First, he was incredibly eager to please his human masters. In fact, nothing delighted him more. If we were happy with him, his tail wagged with such enthusiasm that his entire hindquarters joined in the rhythm. A simple pat on the head after a job well done was enough to send him into spasms of pure joy.

Second, he hated being reprimanded. When a voice was raised in correction, he was totally crushed. His head would drop. He would tuck his tail tightly between his legs and slink away with the most mournful look on his honest face. With quick, woebegone glances, his eyes would plead, *"I didn't mean to! I'm sorry! So sorry!"* With his intelligence, his eagerness to please, and his strong desire to avoid a mistake, obedience training was a cinch.

Furthermore, Champ was a dog with a conscience. If he transgressed some established rule, like coming onto the porch without permission, he would skitter away in a state of cowering humility. Not once did he find himself on the receiving end of any form of corporal punishment from me. It wasn't needed. He learned to watch your eyes and the expression on your face. If you were happy, he was beyond happy. In my later life as a teacher, when a student was caught red-handed in some infraction, I would long to see half the contrition shown by my dog Champ.

At command, Champ showed his aggressive side when herding cattle, but in truth he was a soft-hearted mush pot. Nothing brought out this characteristic more fully than the birth of a farm animal. When my dad rose in the early morning to check on the cattle, he'd know immediately if a calf had been born during the night. As Dad stepped out the door of the house, Champ would greet him in a state of total ecstasy. He'd hustle dad over to the barn where he would stand over the newborn with a doggish grin as if to say, *"Look, what happened here! Isn't it wonderful?"*

Champ took it upon himself to be the guardian of any newborn animals. The cows, for the most part, understood his intentions and put up with his hovering enthusiasm. But Champ was equally enthused about newborn piglets, kittens, or chicks, and his guardian instinct would immediately kick in.

However, despite his valiant efforts, Champ's intentions were sometimes misunderstood. This led to a farmyard standoff I'll never forget. One afternoon, our bantam hen sauntered over to the house to display her clutch of freshly hatched chicks. When he saw this brood of fluffballs, Champ went into paroxysms of ecstasy. He ran in circles, wagging his tail, and barked his joyous greeting for all to hear.

The poor hen had no idea what to make of this crazy dog. Sensing a threat, she hastily gathered her chicks under her wings.

Champ reacted in shock. Clearly, this hen had swallowed these chicks whole. This could only mean one thing. He had to rescue them. He lowered his head and barked angrily at the hen.

This only confirmed the hen's worst fears, and she went into a full defensive posture. No chick would escape from beneath her wings while this vicious beast was about.

Meanwhile, the humans on the scene were doubled over in laughter.

Eventually, someone restrained Champ, and the hen allowed the chicks to resume their roaming.

In due time, the dog and hen arrived at peace terms. There was plenty of skepticism on both sides, but from that day on, an uneasy truce prevailed.

Little did I suspect that one day I would be in need of Champ's watchful protection.

During our summer vacations, my younger brother Dale and I loved to tramp about the wooded pasture land that surrounded our farm home. The summer I was 11 we found a secluded spot in the far corner of the pasture, where we chopped down a few saplings and set up a makeshift tent. Champ always tagged along on these excursions.

  Hot Apple Cider with Cinnamon

One day, while Dale and I were relaxing by our tent, Champ began barking frantically. He ran in tight circles around us. Every hair on his back stood erect. To us, he seemed totally panicked.

We looked about to see what had set the dog into such an astonishing frenzy, but could see nothing. But his urgent alarm grew even more intense. The dog was completely beside himself with fear, running in circles around us. Each frantic bark seemed to urge us to get out of there.

I picked up the axe, and together the three of us ran for our lives. What we were running from Dale and I could only guess. Was it some large wild animal? A malicious human intruder? I had never seen my dog react this way to anything or anyone before.

We reported this event to our parents, who listened with interest but could offer no further insight except to say that we were wise to heed Champ's warning and leave.

We were spooked by this, and for two weeks we didn't return to our favourite spot.

Finally we took courage, and on a sunny summer afternoon, we set out for our secluded campsite once again. Of course Champ tagged along with us.

All went well until we were near our destination. As we emerged into an open grassy area, Champ suddenly went ballistic. But this time I clearly saw the cause of his alarm. A short distance ahead of us, a huge tawny cat—a cougar—reared up and bounded off into the woods, with Champ in hot pursuit! Dale and I froze in our tracks, shaken to the core.

Wisely, Champ's pursuit was brief. He returned after the cougar entered the woods. But now we knew what was out there. On the earlier occasion, only our faithful dog stood between us and that powerful predator. Without Champ's fierce protection, two prairie boys may well have become a meal for a hungry cougar.

A week later, after the morning milking, Champ and I were leading the cows back to the pasture when I spotted the waist-high cougar standing on the driveway leading to the machine shed. Completely fearless, Champ was off like a shot! Again, the cougar fled—and this time it didn't return.

For me, these cougar encounters became the stuff of legend.

You see, up to this point, no one in recent years had ever reported seeing a cougar in Saskatchewan. During my childhood, cougars were commonly called mountain lions, because their range had been reduced to the Rocky Mountains. When I spoke of this experience to friends at school, they scoffed at me in disbelief.

Even my parents were doubtful. They never saw the big cat, although my dad saw Champ's reaction to the second sighting from a distance.

After a while, I learned to keep my mouth shut about this matter. But I knew what I had witnessed.

Twenty years later, a cougar was hit and killed on a roadway about 30 miles from our farm. After that news report, I spoke openly about my childhood experience with the cougar. The evidence of the big cat's presence was now irrefutable.

Unfortunately, in recent years, cougar attacks on humans have become increasingly common. Each time I hear of such reports, I think of Champ. I owe 50 years of my life to that skinny, whimpering pup in a cardboard box.

As for me, I grew up and moved to Edmonton for university. I married and settled there.

My younger brother took over the farm. Every time I returned home, my dear four-legged friend would greet me. He'd rest his head on my knee and I would stroke his silky head.

Of course, each year he was getting older. On one of those summer trips it was clear his health was failing. He knew it. We all knew it. It was so hard to leave that last time.

Jesus said, "No one has greater love than this—that one lays down his life for his friends" (John 15:13 NET).

The first one to demonstrate that kind of love to me was a champion—my fearless, four-legged Champ.

My Legacy

Nonfiction

Brian C. Austin

Mom's been gone for years, but Dad lived to be almost 94. Just recently Dad's estate was settled, and a large cheque went into my bank account. While I appreciate that a great deal, the cheque isn't the legacy I celebrate. It did, however, get me thinking of the legacy I want to leave.

I was born in 1954, the second youngest of seven kids, five boys and two girls. We lived with Mom and Dad on a mixed farm in central Alberta. We had a good, but not-quite-perfect, home. We weren't model kids and my parents weren't flawless parents. But over the years I've seen enough of family dynamics to realize that we children were privileged and blessed in a measure almost unparalleled on this globe.

With a large family, a big garden, and the farm raising beef and dairy cattle, pigs, chickens, grain, and hay, Mom, like so many mothers of the time, had more than a full-time job at home. Giving birth to seven kids over a 13-year period also meant she'd have had huge challenges trying to work outside the home even if she'd wished to.

I have many memories of Mom holding a book in one hand whenever a task could be done with the other. She loved jobs like churning cream into butter, because she could read a chapter or two without guilt. When her work needed two hands, she often sang.

She was a small but sturdy woman with a huge love for life. She was my biggest encourager. I still looked up to her when I stood head and shoulders taller. Even in the many times when I frustrated her, she somehow always communicated deep respect and unconditional love.

Mom and Dad both delighted in getting their fingers in the soil. The vegetable garden, bigger than a double town lot, received careful and consistent attention. They also lovingly tended multiple flower beds. Looking back, I don't know when either of them found time.

Dad was a good farmer. Between the farm and the garden, we ate simple but excellent meals. Unfortunately, the income from our farm never quite paid all the bills, so Dad also operated a road grader and smoothed gravel roads during most of my childhood. He typically worked on the road for 12 to 14 hours, six days a week, and then tried to do a day's work on the farm. He was usually gone long before I got out of bed in the mornings. My older brothers carried much of the farm load.

During the winter, if the weather required, Dad plowed snow seven days a week. Somehow, even within that schedule, we almost always made it to church twice on Sundays and took part in midweek cottage prayer meetings. We also had consistent family devotions around the supper table, reading from a Bible story book in my younger years, and then from the King James Bible, before kneeling at our chairs to pray.

There was a short interlude before I reached my teens when Dad left the road grader and worked at a garden centre. My memory of that time is him coming home full of joy and vigour, often with some new, exotic plant. Mom and Dad would then work together at something they both loved—preparing more flower beds. Dad worked shorter hours during this time, and I assume his take-home pay was much less, so I think it only lasted a single season.

Dad also took great pride in his work on the grader. Many people claimed that they could feel the difference in the roads as soon as they crossed into his district. But with the long hours, he would come home many, many nights with either of two lines: "Oh, Elsie, I've come home to die" or "I'm tired into the middle of next week."

Even in his eighties Dad would still break into a jog if he needed to go for a tool while working at some project. There was a sense of urgency, almost drivenness, about him—always with more work than could possibly be done. That intensity would almost disappear when he was digging in a flower bed.

As a kid, I didn't understand the need for the long hours Dad worked. As the youngest of the five boys, I came in for my share of chores—carrying pails of water to the pigs, gathering eggs, getting in the way as I "helped" milk the cows—but I spent many hours playing in a sandpit while the other four ran the farm machinery. Because of that, I missed the training and mentoring that Dad somehow squeezed in for the older boys. So when I did eventually end up on the seat of the tractor, I managed to smash more equipment than all the others together.

I have no memory of Dad even once *speaking* his love to me in the first 40 years of my life. I had a desperate, though unrecognized hunger to *hear* the words. Like many men of that generation, Dad had no language for my needs. On the other hand, he had very effective language for communicating his exasperation at my skill at destroying farm equipment. You can probably understand why he became terribly frustrated with me, and why I came to dread his being at home.

It took me more than 40 years to begin to grasp that Dad's love actually did reach as far as me. I slowly learned how rare he was among dads, how deeply committed he was to Mom, and how much he sacrificed for his family.

I realize now how often we wounded each other. For years, because I felt that nothing I did was ever good enough for him, I became increasingly bitter and even intentionally cruel to him. I knew his hot buttons and used them ruthlessly.

The older I became, the more I realized how similar we were in a number of ways. I inherited many of his character traits. As a result, it was far easier to fight the faults I saw in him than to acknowledge those faults in myself. I have also discovered I am privileged with a few of his strengths as well.

Slowly, with time and distance, I began to see him as a man of integrity, and I began to see love in his actions—a love that he never knew how to put into words. I even realized, with a sense of wonder, that he was worthy of my deepest respect. Most amazing of all, I discovered that I loved him intensely.

A man shouldn't be in his mid-fifties before he begins to understand his father, but I'm so thankful that in the later years of his life I was able to find ways to tell Dad I respected and loved him. I couldn't take back the angry words I'd spoken earlier, but as we celebrated his life at his funeral, and as I stood by his grave, I had no regrets over words left unspoken. Before that day, we had spoken words of love. We had forgiven each other. We had exchanged hugs—genuine, body-crushing hugs, not the rigid, duty-bound kind.

Having parents who loved God, each other, and their kids— that's a legacy worthy of celebration. That's the standard I aim for, the bar I've set for myself, and that I long to model for my children and grandchildren.

Thanks, Dad!

Doris Fleming

If I found the right words,
Though few would I need,
I'd plough a sweet garden
And plant them as seed.

A story would grow up
To make people glad,
A story of good things
I saw in my Dad.

I'd tell of his humming
And making up rhymes,
Of riddles and teasing
And acting out mimes.

Of drinks from a dipper,
Eyes sparkling with joy,
As if the cool water
Was one more sweet toy.

He'd come from the cow barn,
Milk pail in each hand,
Then wade through his hay fields,
The lord of these lands.

He'd talk of a mansion,
Just over the hill,
And tell us he'd wait there,
Where time will stand still.

My cottage I've readied,
Rooms, cheery and bright,

Made fit for the coming
Of loved ones tonight.

We'll sing 'round the keyboard
And hammer out tunes,
Craft lyrics and music,
By light of the moon.

Tell tales for the grandkids,
Of deeds good and true,
Then smile as they marvel
And praise God for you.

So, thanks for the seeds, Dad!
And thanks for the love!
My garden you nourished
With help from above.

Lobster Love

Nonfiction

Vilma Blenman

I remember him coming to visit me in my third year at the University of Waterloo. I had moved out of the Mennonite residence at Conrad Grebel College by then and was living in what was nicknamed "Cockroach Towers," a set of white, student-infested high-rises near the university. I shared a one-bedroom apartment with two other girls from September to April.

The visit was both unexpected and unusual. My family didn't own a car, so ordinarily neither Dad nor anyone else came to visit me. My father must have taken the Greyhound bus from Toronto to the bus station in Kitchener, and then a taxi to the neighbouring city of Waterloo.

He must have, because I don't remember giving him bus directions to our apartment. And I don't recall knowing that he was coming. I just remember him showing up, a bulging black bag over his shoulders, and on his face, his impish schoolboy smile that even to this day assures me the sun will still shine, no matter how hard the rain is pelting.

"Jen, I brought you goodies," he said as he unpacked the bag. Just hearing him calling me Jen conjured images of my childhood home, a place of both comfort and calamity. No one in my extended family calls me by my legal name, in keeping with the Jamaican custom of often giving a child an alternative first name that is neither a nickname nor an abbreviation of the real name. The alternative name is completely unrelated in sound or sense to one's legal name, but is known and legitimized within the family and close neighbourhood.

The explanation I recall an aunt giving was, "If you know someone's real name, you have power over them. Understand? That's why you don't call out a person's true name in the dark." She'd delivered that lecture with hands akimbo on her hips and staring me straight in the eyes after I'd transgressed the rule and called out my cousin's full legal name one night, just for spite.

So to Dad I was always Jen, or Jennifer, pronounced with a full, cheer-filled "J" that reminded me of a firm handshake that says, "So nice to meet you!" And it *was* nice to see my dad!

From his black bag, Dad pulled out two fat yellow plantains, three fragrant red mangoes, a bottle of Peardrax, a sparkling fruit beverage, and two recently alive lobsters that stared straight at me as he held them up for me to admire. I remember their black, beady eyes. I pitied them.

But I pitied my dad more. For in that moment, I sensed his perennial need to get out of the paternal dog house and prove to his children that despite what may or may not have been said, despite all he had done or failed to do, he was not a failure at loving us. That was my assumption that day when my dad came to my university apartment with the gift of lobsters.

This extravagance is penance. Something must have happened back home in Toronto.

"Dad," I said after the shock of seeing the lobsters, "you didn't have to bring me lobsters all the way from Toronto. You know I love mangoes and would be glad for them. Lobsters are expensive."

"Jen, it's not every day I see you. And I didn't want to bring fish and smell up the bus."

We both laughed at that. In fact, I remember laughing a lot with my dad that day when he delivered the lobsters.

It was true. We didn't see each other much now that I was away at university. But it was also true that even when I was younger and growing up in Jamaica, I hadn't seen him every day. My dad was an addicted gambler. He often disappeared on pay day Fridays, returning on Monday mornings looking shamefaced and beaten down, like a dog that had lost the fight and returned home to lick its wounds.

I remember days and nights of hunger and anger in our home, my mom waiting and hoping for his return but knowing he'd gone off again—gone with the little money he earned as a sugar cane factory worker, gone with the children's bread. And in my head I hear, even now, the *whir whir* of my mom's Singer sewing machine late at night, and see her bent back in the grey shadows cast by the kerosene lamp as she sat completing a piece of clothing, hoping the owner would come and pay before Saturday's market day was done. At least there would be a decent Sunday dinner for her children.

And I remember the sound and the fury upon Dad's return. Mostly it was the sound of my mother's tirade, for my father rarely answered a word, except to beg for silence. "All right, all right. Stop nuh? I know. I know all you say. You say it already. What yuh want me to do?"

"Do what yuh *say* you going to do. Stop the gambling! For God's sake, stop! Look at yuh children and stop."

I didn't know what to do then, though I felt sure there must be *something* I could do to soothe my mom's ache and alleviate my dad's anguished regret. But I didn't know what it was, so usually I'd get a book and disappear into its pages, occasionally poking my head out to sniff the atmosphere for calmness. Once I happened to hear Dad say he'd sharpen his machete and kill himself, if that would prove to my mom he was sorry. Dad had a sharp machete, as I recall, but he never used it on himself—or on anyone else, for that matter. Only on the rich green grass that grew quickly around our house. As a child I was both anxious and grateful for this.

Even though he hadn't provided a stable home for us, he was still the gentlest, most loving father a girl could ever have. Strange, but true.

My family migrated to Canada in the mid-'70s when manufacturing jobs mushroomed in the Golden Horseshoe and Canada opened up immigration doors. Dad's three brothers, already settled in Canada, sponsored him. My mom and youngest sister came with Dad. A few months later, three more of us followed, and last my two older brothers, until we were all under one roof again.

Yet under that roof, there were still tensions. To be sure there was more food, but there were more arguments, too. Dad's addiction followed him to Canada, pursued him relentlessly from feverish tropical nights to snow-chilled mornings in Toronto. I remember looking around our new apartment one day, feeling the same old feelings and thinking, *Where's the big Canada change? We could literally wallpaper this place with the lottery tickets he buys!*

Once again, it was Mom who scrimped and saved and ensured the rent got paid on time, and Mom who had some money to give me when I went off to university, my hopes high for a better life for all.

But now, here was my dad, on a cool spring day in Waterloo, after the snow had melted and green had returned to campus. Here he was with mangoes, my favourite childhood fruit. And here too were lobsters, something I'd never dreamed of eating. Something he imagined I would love.

I don't know that I was grateful for the lobsters my dad brought me that day. They seem, even now, a strange gift for a financially strapped university student studying for end-of-term exams.

First of all, I didn't know how to cook lobsters.

I'd cooked for my family since I was nine years old—cooked dinner bending over cold charcoals, coaxing them to burn red hot, and later, as a teenager, delivered delectable meals from an unpredictable kerosene stove. But lobsters were not part of my repertoire of Jamaican dishes, and I'd not yet tried Canadian recipes. This was before the internet, so I couldn't just Google for a recipe.

Then there was the problem of sharing the two lobsters with my roommates. Would there be enough for the three of us? And how would I present them anyhow? Boil them and leave them in the pot on the stove? One of my roommates was quite squeamish. She preferred, for instance, fish sticks to real fish with real eyes. She'd screamed once when she saw a real fish on my plate. It was a crisply fried snapper adorned with sliced onions and red scotch bonnet peppers. My mom had sent the fish back with me after a visit home that Thanksgiving.

"That fish has eyes!" Karla had exclaimed, surveying my plate from a distance.

"Of course it does," I'd replied, thinking how strange these Canadians were.

"You eat the head? Don't you take the head off?" she'd asked, horrified.

I remember giving my roommate, who'd been raised in Sarnia, a lesson on real life and real fish from the perspective of an island girl. "Karla, cooking a fresh, whole fish like this red snapper here is a treat—an expensive treat. You can steam the fish, fry the fish, escovitch the fish, jerk the fish, or do whatever you wish with that fish. Just don't mince it up, put bread crumbs on it, and make fish balls out of it. And why cut off the head and throw it away? You can always make soup with it. But if you don't have green bananas or something else on hand ready to make fish soup, the only sensible thing to do is to cook the entire fish. And who purposely gouges out fish eyes, anyway?"

Eventually, we ended the fish-head discussion that day in classic philosophical mode, both of us agreeing that everyone has some strange food phobia.

To this day, I can't remember what I did with those lobsters. Even as I conjure the memory of that Saturday visit so long ago, I only recall Dad coming and me seeing the lobsters and seeing the pain he didn't show, and hearing the two of us laughing a lot. Just the two of us.

"Dad, you remember the time when I was in basic school in Jamaica, the kindergarten prep school down at Race Course?"

"Yah, that was so far to walk to, Jen, all the way from up Belle Isle Mountain, but you walk anyhow. You always been a walker."

"I remember one day when you were coming back from Grange Hill and you stopped and brought me a whole set of brand new slate pencils."

"Yah, I remember. I got them at Chin-Lee's store down from Grange Hill market. Dem did have a store and a patty shop near de bank. Dat store sell cloth an' pants an' pots, furniture, groceries an' everything under the sun."

I remembered the store well, and the patty shop. Many wintry days in Waterloo I'd wished for the taste of fresh, hot Jamaican beef patties, the flaky outer pastry melting in my mouth and the spicy beef filling sending shock waves to my senses. But in that moment, reminiscing with Dad, it was the image of the pencils that gripped my imagination.

"Well, I wanted to use all the slate pencils at once. They were so nice and new-smelling. I couldn't wait to write with them. I took one out and started writing, and then pop! That broke. So I took out another one, and pop! It broke too. I think I was breaking them just so I could take a new one from the box."

"Yah?"

"Yah, I think that was it. After a while the teacher said that if I broke one more she was going to take them all away and keep them and I would have to write with my fingernails. Well, I put them away so fast, Dad, and no more slate pencils broke that whole afternoon."

Dad had laughed loudly then, throwing back his head and slapping his legs, the way he often did. He had laughed remembering that day so long ago, remembering another of his finest hours. And I laughed too, remembering how I'd literally believed the teacher's threat that I'd have to write with my fingernails, and had pictured, in my five-year-old mind, my nails red and bleeding, and got such a fright.

On that Saturday afternoon, Dad and I kept trading comical, do-you-remember stories.

"Dad," I said, suddenly drawn back to the setting of our lives before Canada, "remember when you went to that justice of the peace for him to sign the passport papers, and it was election time, and you didn't want him to know who you were really going to vote for?"

"Yah, Jen. I was careful for a reason. You see, if a man's hand is in a tiger's mouth, he mus' tek time and draw it out. But your sister was vexed hearing him tell me in his big boss voice I must make sure I mark the X right and vote for the People's National Party, which she know was not our party. So when he offer food that was right there in the office, your sister answer back, 'No, we not hungry. Anyhow, we voting for—ah, who is it again, Dad?'

"So I just hurry up and say the name of the person the JP want to hear. That did it, Jen, and the papers got signed."

"That was scary funny, Dad. Do you think he would have refused to sign the passports if he'd known?"

"Of course he would. You know back home people take politics very seriously. Who you vote for could be life or death. So I jus' keep looking at you sister, batting my eyes and tapping my foot."

It's my youngest sister who usually tells this story at family gatherings, and we all laugh, thinking how a sassy seven year-old almost derailed our chance to come to Canada. I wasn't there with

  Hot Apple Cider with Cinnamon

her and Dad when she made this political faux pas, but I've always sensed it was a significant moment for both.

And here we were, Dad and I, having a significant moment in my apartment in Waterloo.

When one of my roommates got home, Dad said it was time for him to head back to the city. "Jen, I gotta catch that Greyhound before that dog runs away from me and takes off to Toronto."

I remember accompanying him to the bus station and waving to him as he sat looking at me, smiling from the window seat of the Greyhound bus.

I must have cooked the lobsters later that evening. Did I? Or maybe the next day, though I don't actually recall cooking a lobster dinner. I don't think I'd have thrown away those expensive lobsters, but I just don't know.

What I do know is that on Father's Day, and on ordinary days, when I count all the passionate ways my father loves me, the memory of that visit stands out. And then I count my blessings, given in divine, overflowing measure, because despite his past, Dad's love has been the most grounding, the most defining reality of my girlhood and adulthood, and also a bedrock for my theology. It is Dad's love for me that has helped me understand and accept the largesse that is God's love for me.

Today my dad is a transformed man, no longer addicted to gambling. Instead, he's a one-man meals-on-wheels elder-care provider for others, and for me a prayer counsellor and a confidante. Now we talk openly about those dark days of him wandering about, wasting money, and wounding his family. We talk about what drove him and what changed him.

"Jen," he told me one day when he'd visited me and we'd gone for a walk around my suburban Pickering neighbourhood, "I was always thinking of my children. I wanted more for them, more than I got from my father. My father wouldn't even give me a pittance from the money he and me work hard for, doing road work together with the other men, breaking rock stones to pave road. He get all the money. An' I just keep thinking that de next ticket, I'm going to win. De next game is going to pay off big time. An' den the next time and de next time."

"Did you ever go to rehab?" I'd asked him that day, thinking about the psychology of addiction, about the strangle hold a habit can have on a human heart and mind. "How did you stop?"

"Jen, my rehab was with God, down on my knees. Dat was it. Dat was the change."

As a family, we see and celebrate the changes in Dad's life. What has never changed for me though, is Dad's gift of unconditional love and his unwavering belief in my abilities. My knowledge of his affirmation has kept me secure even through so many insecure moments.

To the little 11-year-old girl wondering if she'd pass the big exam necessary for entrance to high school in Jamaica, Dad said, "Jen. Don't worry. I know you're smart. You gwine pass."

To the 31-year-old woman in Canada burying her second still-born baby, Dad said, "Jen, one day, one day, your baby will walk and talk. You don't worry. God have it all under control."

To the fledging writer holding her first published piece in her hand, Dad said, "Jen you always did love books. Read, Read. This chile was always reading. So I know you was gwine write one book, one of these days."

I explained to my dad that it was an anthology, and that the whole book wasn't mine. But it didn't matter. He already believes in my book. He's already seen it.

When I look back now, I realize that Dad's admiration of me, and his encouragement of all my academic and spiritual pursuits, gave me confidence as a girl, guidance as a wife and mother, and gumption as a teacher and writer.

Oh, and I should add that I know how to cook lobster now. In fact, I love lobster, with lots of garlic butter.

But sitting here on my patio, looking back on that Saturday in Waterloo, I begin to wonder what absurdly extravagant gifts I've given to each of my children. I'm not sure that I have. So I wonder, what could be my "lobster love" for them?

Going Home

Fiction

Darcy Elizabeth Neal

The last wisps of a pleasant dream faded away. Susan felt herself waking but lay still, eyes closed, savouring the lingering sensation of weightlessness and peace. After a moment she wondered what time it was. She listened for sounds of her parents in the next room and sniffed the air in case the scent of their coffee was wafting up from the kitchen.

Nothing. No sound of parents, no scent of coffee, only a dull humming from somewhere far away and a strange smell that she couldn't quite place. Her body felt heavy too, as if she'd slept too long, or not long enough. Perhaps it wasn't morning after all.

She opened her eyes and turned her head to see if any daylight was visible around the edges of her curtains, then raised herself up on her elbow in surprise. The window was in the wrong place, and instead of curtains there were only blinds. The kind with vertical slats.

She frowned. Sometimes if she fell asleep while her parents were visiting friends, they would carry her home and tuck her into her own bed without her waking; but she couldn't remember it ever happening the other way round. She lay back, waiting to see if someone would come and tell her where she was, but since no one came, and the light seeping between the slats of the blinds was becoming stronger, she decided to get up and explore on her own.

Susan was surprised to discover railings on the sides of the bed. She hadn't needed those in the longest time. This bed must belong to a very young child.

Carefully, she pushed back the covers and scrunched down past the end of the railing. She swung her legs over the edge of the bed and stood up. Mistake. Her legs felt unusually heavy, and her head was spinning. She held on to the end of the bed till the dizziness passed, then cautiously made her way to the door.

She opened it and peered out.

What she saw was a long hallway with many other doors. The corridor was dimly lit, but there was a warm glow of light at one end. She frowned. It looked a little bit like a hospital. Had something happened? An accident, maybe? That might explain her being here and not remembering. But she felt okay. A bit weak maybe, but nothing felt broken and there were no bandages. She reached up and tentatively explored the back of her head. No, it was fine, though her hair seemed shorter than it should be. Had someone cut it while she slept?

Perplexed, Susan glanced one more time at the strange room behind her, then looked carefully up and down the corridor. All of the other doors were closed. If she left hers open, surely she'd be able to find her way back.

She stepped gingerly into the hallway. The tile floor felt cool to her bare feet.

Not wanting to wake the other sleepers, she started slowly toward the light, keeping one hand on the wall for support, just in case. It wouldn't do to slip and fall.

Before she'd gone half way, a tall figure moved into the light and began walking toward her. She was dressed all in white and Susan wondered if she were a nurse.

"I'm looking for my mummy and daddy," Susan said. "Do you know where they are?"

The figure didn't appear to hear the question, because when she reached Susan, she took her by the arm and turned her around. "It's not time to get up yet," she said. "Come, I'll take you back to your room."

"But I want to go home."

"It's not time yet," the woman repeated.

When Susan next woke, someone was sitting in the chair beside the bed. He looked vaguely familiar and was smiling at her as if he expected her to know him. Perhaps he could tell her where her parents were. She smiled back.

"I want my mummy," she said. "Do you know where she is?"

The man's smile faded. He looked very sad. "Your mummy is in heaven."

"And my daddy?"

"Your daddy is with Jesus, too. Do you know who *I* am?"

Susan studied his face, trying to remember. He looked a little like her father. Perhaps he was one of her father's relatives. There were so many of them it was hard to keep them straight. She hesitated, almost remembered something, but then it was gone. She frowned and shook her head.

"Mom," he said, reaching over to take her hand in his. "I'm your son, Matthew. Don't you remember?"

She stared at him, astonished that someone so big could be the son of someone as small as she was. Then, in a sudden flash of recollection, she remembered the day of his birth. "Yes" she said eagerly, "I remember when you were born. You were so small and wrinkly and you were crying—"

He smiled and squeezed her hand.

"—and I held you in my arms and told you I loved you. And then your daddy—" She looked around wildly. "Where *is* your daddy? Shouldn't he be here with me?" She struggled to sit up.

"Dad's all right, Mom," Matthew said, leaning forward to put an arm around her shoulders. "He's with Jesus. You needn't worry about him."

She stopped struggling and let her weight fall on her son. "Oh— Oh, yes. That's right, so he is."

There was silence for a moment. Susan felt comforted by the strong arm around her shoulders, but she was having trouble remembering who it belonged to. She turned her head to look at him again.

"Did you come to take me home?" she asked.

"No, Mom. I came to visit. This is where you live now."

"But I want to go home."

"Soon, Mom. The doctor says you'll be going soon."

She slept some more and woke some more. How many days and nights passed, she couldn't tell. Sometimes there were people in her room. Sometimes she was alone. Sometimes it was hard to tell which people were real and which were only in her dreams. She tried asking some of them about going home, but nobody seemed to understand.

Then one night, while she was sleeping, the room suddenly filled with a bright light. Even though her eyes were closed she could see its brightness and feel its warmth. Her heart surged with joy.

She opened her eyes. A figure was standing in the light. He was dressed in white, and the brightness seemed to shine forth from him.

He smiled at her and she smiled back.

"Are you here to take me home?" she asked.

He held out his arms.

"Yes, my child, I am."

  Hot Apple Cider with Cinnamon

The Promise in My Hat Box

Nonfiction

Heidi McLaughlin

"Hey, lady! Where in the world are you going? Would you like a lift?"

What woman in her right mind would even consider the notion of getting into a noisy, rusty blue pickup truck on an uncharted road in the middle of the British Columbia mountains in the early hours of a Sunday morning?

As I wobbled back and forth on my fancy city flip-flops, which were coated in sweat and dust, I nodded. "Yes, can you please just drive me another eight kilometres down this gravel road?"

With one swooping gesture, an unshaven younger version of Clint Eastwood opened the door.

With a pounding heart, I strapped myself into the front seat of his rickety contraption. Torn between relief and uneasiness, I stared at the endless gravel road ahead of us and prayed, *God, I sure hope you sent him to get me there on time!*

The ride was welcome, the drama not so much.

I was the keynote speaker for a women's Spiritual Leadership Training Weekend being held at a forestry camp tucked miles into the majestic country of the interior of British Columbia.

It was a September weekend when the fragrance in the air tickled your nostrils and reminded you that the landscape would soon be painted with the gorgeous autumn colours of orange, red, yellow, and rust. The days were still warm, but the mornings invited you to throw a sweater around your shoulders to keep the unfamiliar chill away for just a little longer.

When I arrived that Friday afternoon and saw the sparkling blue sky and smelled the invigorating air, I knew this would be the perfect spot to train eager young women to trust God's love in spite of difficult circumstances. However, at the same time, something about the location troubled me. Just days prior to the event, I'd had a conversation with a woman who had attended meetings at that venue. "Did you know that there are mice running in the cabins?" she asked me.

I'm not a shrinking violet. I've slept on lumpy mattresses and lain awake all night shivering and listening to frogs. But after that conversation with her, I couldn't get the word "mice" out of my head. When I was eight years old, I'd experienced having mice run across my bed, and the sheer terror of this memory made me rethink my upcoming sleeping arrangements.

I came up with the perfect plan. The venue was close enough to Kelowna that I could leave the camp each night after the final activities and drive home to snuggle in my soft, comfy bed and get a good night's sleep. I'd then leave home early in the morning and arrive just in time for breakfast. No one even needed to know that I wasn't sleeping in one of those musty log cabins!

Friday night, I slipped out after the last session and walked to my car under the darkness of a sky that was as black as coal. Without street lights illuminating the landscape, I had to grope for a familiar pathway. Frantically clicking my remote car opener, and using the blinking light from my car to direct my path, my feet flew over the dirt trail. My heart pounding, I slipped into the car, rejoicing that my sly plan was going to work masterfully.

The drive back on Saturday morning was blissful. I sang songs of praise and expressed my gratitude for this glorious opportunity to speak at a venue nestled in the beauty of God's nature. I was rested and ready to speak all day on a passage in the Bible that teaches us to think about things that are excellent, true, and honourable. I knew this weekend would be a hallmark spot in my heart for years to come.

That night, I found my car with ease. And no one suspected.

Sunday morning was the last day of the conference, and by now the routine had become familiar, comfortable, and safe. I jumped into my car and confidently headed up the long gravel road. I had everything I needed for the last session with me: my laptop, digital camera, notes, Bible, and some props. I slid a CD into my player and sang songs at the top of my lungs while my eyes roamed over the perfect blue sky, the beautiful mountains, and the river running below.

The music was so loud that I didn't hear any unusual sounds, but as I neared the turnoff to the camp, I began to sense that something was wrong. My car seemed sluggish, and then it started swerving from left to right on the gravel road. I hit the brakes, gasped, and jumped out of the car to see if I could determine what was going on.

It didn't take a mechanic to find the problem. My left rear tire was as flat as a dried-up pancake. And no, I'd never learned how to change a tire. I tried using my cell phone to call for help, but I was out of range.

So there I was, helpless and miles from any kind of support.

I figured I was about nine kilometres from the camp, where I was scheduled to speak in one hour. In all the times I'd travelled this road over the weekend, I'd never seen another car, so I knew my options were limited. I'd have to start walking.

My mind swirled into action and I found a way to carry all my props. There was a hat box in the back seat of my car. It was a prop that was going to be an essential part of my last teaching session. So I placed all my other teaching materials, my laptop, camera and my Bible in my hat box and slung it over my right shoulder. I hung my purse over my left shoulder, and started walking.

Oops. My cute little summer flip-flops slipped in the gravel. This was going to be hard. I wasn't singing any more.

Before I'd gone more than a few steps, the purse and hat box had begun to feel heavy. Plus the straps were cutting into my shoulder.

Right about then it occurred to me that there were animals in the mountains. Animals much bigger and more dangerous than mice. I began to feel small and insignificant, and my heart started to pound as I fought back tears.

But in the absolute stillness on that mountain road, God had my full attention and I started to listen to His whispers. He reminded me that in my hat box were my Bible and my notes that I'd been speaking on all weekend. Women had heard me teach on the theme verse, Philippians 4:8, which says, "And now, dear brothers and sisters, one final thing. Fix your thoughts on what is true, and honorable, and right, and pure, and lovely, and admirable. Think about things that are excellent and worthy of praise." All weekend, I'd been teaching women that we cannot always change our circumstances, but we can trust God to help us change our thoughts. Maybe my flat tire was all part of God's plan to bring me to a place where I truly understood what I was teaching!

Trudging up that lonely gravel road, I had a lot of time to think about this verse. I realized that I had a choice. I could focus on excellence, truth, and peace, or I could feel defeated, get angry, and complain that life wasn't fair.

I stopped and looked at God's magnificent creation and felt the autumn air on my cheeks. I listened to the water gurgling in the creek and the birds chirping their harmonious melodies. I decided I would enjoy this glorious splash of time and allow God to get me to the camp in His timing.

As I slowed my steps and starting whistling, all of a sudden my hat box became lighter and my shoulders felt stronger.

At that moment, I saw a cloud of dust and heard the distant sound of a vehicle's tires crunching the gravel on a rough backwoods road. Through the brown haze, I saw the shape of a battered blue truck coming closer and closer. Then I heard those sweet words, "Hey lady!"

The Cat We Didn't Need

Nonfiction

Ruth Ann Adams

"Mom, come into the bathroom," my daughters called. From their voices, I could tell that something very suspicious was going on. Sure enough, in our bathtub was the ugliest cat I had ever seen.

"Why is that cat in the bathtub?" I spluttered.

"We found her trying to get in the back door of the apartment building," the girls explained. "We put her in the tub to bathe her and keep her away from Ascension."

I shook my head. "We can't keep this cat! Our apartment is crowded enough!"

My daughter, Andrea, pointed out logically, "We couldn't leave her outside! I'll ask around and see if she belongs to somebody in the building. If not, we'll put up signs."

Our resident cat, Ascension, a gorgeous, fluffy, tabby calico with white under her chin, swaggered into the bathroom and strode right up to the newcomer. "Grrrrr," she said, in a tone that was clearly threatening.

The ugly cat stood still, obviously afraid to provoke Ascension, perhaps feeling like prey about to be attacked.

I sighed. This cat was just another complication in my life. Our apartment was far too small for my husband and me, our three girls—Andrea, Hannah, and Susanna—and Ascension. We had no space for an unwanted guest.

Several years before, a heartbreaking financial loss had forced us to move from a spacious, small-town home with a huge backyard to a tiny, city apartment in Dartmouth, Nova Scotia. Some days, I stood at the barred windows in the staircase landing and wondered if we'd ever get out of the prison our lives had become.

Due to exceptional circumstances, I was the major family breadwinner, and the weight of responsibility was heavy.

As it turned out, nobody claimed the ugly tabby cat.

And the rest of my family fell in love with her.

I couldn't understand why. She had unkempt fur, her face and neck were longer than those of a normal cat, and she had long, spindly legs—the longest I'd ever seen on a cat. In addition to being unpleasant to look at, she made an odd bleating sound rather than a civilized meow.

Andrea, with her penchant for unusual names, called the cat Truffles, but my husband, John, in spite of the cat's scruffy appearance, preferred Princess. She became Princess Truffles.

John was the chief chef for the family, and while he cooked, this mangy cat sat close at his heels, presiding over the kitchen, ready to taste test any juicy morsels he could spare. She had a special love for cheese, yogourt, and ice cream.

Our two cats established their own areas in our small apartment. Ascension preferred the bedrooms; Princess Truffles stayed in or near the kitchen. And Ascension mostly ignored Princess, unless she invaded her territory.

The litter box was in the bathroom, near the bedrooms, and since Princess was afraid to encounter Ascension there, we had to put up with a second litter box in the dining room! Some days, this second litter box in a cramped space drove me crazy.

Besides keeping my husband company in the kitchen, Princess Truffles filled a more sombre role. On the day the girls had found her, our youngest daughter, 12-year-old Susanna, found out that one of her friends had died in a drowning accident.

We all struggled with the loss of this young life. As her mother, I tried to comfort Susanna, but I felt inadequate in trying to explain such a tragedy. Indeed, I wondered myself why this had happened, just as I wondered why we had ended up in such difficult personal circumstances. Nights were especially hard for Susanna. She became anxious and fearful in the dark. Princess seemed to know this, because she snuggled up with Susanna, shedding fur everywhere but giving comfort and affection.

This was one of the reasons I didn't insist on sending the cat away. I couldn't add to Susanna's distress.

Our personal circumstances were as unlovely and unexpected as our new cat. The year Princess joined us had been particularly difficult for me. I was struggling with hyperthyroidism, a condition that caused my heart to beat erratically and resulted in a number of trips to the Emergency. The health issues, plus the severe financial stress, took a toll. The hope I had left was flickering like a dying candle, still present, but threatening to go out.

However, our place of worship, New Covenant Ministries Church, offered us great support, encouragement, and a vision for a better tomorrow. I thanked God over and over for bringing us to this church, and teaching us how to exercise our faith to overcome the stress in our lives. We learned to look beyond our circumstances to God's promises.

Also, even though our apartment was tiny and cramped, we believed God had placed us there for a reason.

Gradually I began to see that it wasn't all about us and what we had lost. It was about where God wanted us for this season in our lives. A few pastors began a Christian coffee house in a room in the building, and we regularly attended. Susanna started a children's choir, and often the room was full of little ones singing songs of praise. John spent many hours walking the halls and praying. We saw much need and many people who were living broken and pain-filled lives.

On a July day, not long after Princess arrived, I received a phone call from a Zellers department store. I had almost forgotten that I'd put in an application. We'd been depending on the income from my substitute teaching, but that would be nonexistent over the summer months. Realizing we weren't going to survive financially unless I took on a second job, I'd filled out an application.

I was thrilled when I received an interview and job offer.

Although it was sometimes exhausting juggling two jobs, my time at Zellers changed my life in many ways beyond earning extra money. The staff became like a family, and the warmth and sense of friendship I felt there helped to heal my heart, and gave me hope that God would change our other circumstances as well.

Now that we had a little more income, John took Princess Truffles on a bus ride to the veterinarian. We found out that she was an older cat, probably 12 to 14 years old, and that she had hyperthyroidism. Ironically, she needed the same pills that I had taken to bring down my thyroid levels. I could certainly empathize with her condition!

We also learned that at one time someone had cared for her, since she had been spayed and received dental work. Where she came from will always be a mystery, but her presence in our family was by now very firmly established.

John looked after the medication detail. He hid her little pink pills in her wet food. However, she had a few tricks up her paw. Some mornings I would hear him say, "Princess, you have eaten all around your pill and left the pill sitting alone in the dish!" Sometimes, he would have to make numerous attempts before our sharp-witted cat would eat it!

While we believed we had been called to our building for a reason, the time came when we felt that season was over. Hannah had moved out to attend university, but Susanna was now 15, and she and Andrea really needed rooms of their own. I promised Susanna that by her 16th birthday, we would be in a new place, and she would have her own room.

I had no idea how I was going to fulfill this promise. Even with my working two jobs, money was tight. One day, while arranging a display of canned ham and corned beef near the cash registers at Zellers, I wondered, in frustration, *What are we going to do?*

As I stacked the cans, God spoke to me gently, "You have a choice. You can look at your circumstances and lack of resources, or you can look at Me, and what I can do."

Okay, God, I prayed, *I will trust you with this. I certainly have no answers of my own.*

One morning a few weeks later, a co-worker said to me, "You're looking for a place to move to, aren't you? My parents are renting the other half of their duplex."

"Would they accept cats?" I asked.

"I'll call them right now," she said.

They didn't mind cats.

I went home after my shift and told my husband about the duplex. We hurried over to look through the house. It was beautiful: three stories, three bedrooms, and a gorgeous backyard with a deck. It was everything I had dreamed of during the dark days in our apartment. We took Andrea and Susanna to see it, and they loved it, too.

"We'll let you know soon," I said to the landlady. This was exactly what we wanted, but I was afraid. Could we handle the additional expenses, the heat, and utilities? *God, please give me some reassurance,* I prayed.

"What should we do?" I asked John.

"I think we should take it," he said.

We needed to sign the lease, so I called the landlady and left a message on her answering service, asking what the exact amount of the deposit would be.

She called me the next day, October 8, which happened to be my birthday, and said, "We've decided to lower the rent."

God had given us the green light and the reassurance and peace I had prayed for!

On October 30, we moved into our new home. Twenty-six days later, Susanna celebrated her 16th birthday with her friends in the rec room of our new duplex. God had provided where I didn't see a way.

Since Princess Truffles was getting older, and was used to living in an apartment building, I didn't expect her to be able to manage the stairs. I had visions of us carrying her from floor to floor. However, she bounded from one floor to another, her long legs carrying her with apparent ease. Her only concern was Ascension.

One day, she started to climb up the stairs to the bedrooms and saw Ascension on the top. She stopped, wary of interacting with her territorial housemate.

Watching her, I realized how much I had grown to love this cat, how it was just as possible to love an older, unattractive animal as it was an appealing, younger one. She had won our hearts and truly become our Princess. It was as if she had lived up to the name John had given her.

Princess seemed happy and contented in our new home, but on the Ides of March, just a little over four months after our move, she slipped away.

She had taught us all that love can be found in unexpected ways. While I didn't want this old cat when she first arrived, God knew that we needed her in our lives, just as much as she needed us in hers.

As for the signs the girls put up, asking if anyone owned this cat—recently, Susanna admitted to me that she took them all down shortly after they were put up!

Trapped

Maureen Fitzpatrick

My room is in a dark basement
Where the walls close in on me and
I feel stifled, almost claustrophobic.

I thirst, but my cup is empty;
Tears fall but no one hears my silent cry.
I am trapped with nowhere to go.

I long to hear the birds twittering,
See the sun rise, view the sunset
Or the moon on a summer's night.

I dream I am in a beautiful house by the sea
Where splashing waves play music
And I dance on the smooth sand.

But a moment later I am awake, trembling,
Imagining a fire on the stairs—
The only way out.

Am I going to die here before God rescues me?
I pray—loose the chains of adversity,
Unlock the bars of despair;

Let me escape from the basement
Of my mind to the upper floor
So I can be free to live, to love, to laugh.

An earlier version of this poem was originally published in *A Cry for Love,*
copyright © 1997 Maureen Fitzpatrick (Watermark Press, Maryland, USA).

Learning to Love by Letting Go

Nonfiction

Lisa Elliott

Corrie ten Boom once said, "Don't hold onto anything too tightly. Otherwise, it hurts when God pries your fingers open." However, loosening your grip is easier said than done—especially when it's letting go of a child.

From the time I gave birth to them, I knew I was going to spend years releasing my four children—letting go of their hands so they could take their first steps, letting them go to school where someone else would teach them, letting them make their own choices in life. However, in spite of all my practice, I didn't understand what it was to completely let a child go until August 12, 2008, when my 18-year-old son, Ben, was diagnosed with an aggressive, high-risk form of acute lymphoblastic leukemia (ALL).[1]

That day began what turned out to be a year-long process of release until August 19, 2009, when I let him go one last time. Some might say that I lost him, but I know that in reality I *loosed* him. The entire year Ben battled his leukemia, right up until his final breath, we prayed for his healing and did all we could do to keep him alive, "hoping for the best while preparing for the worst."[2] That meant having to accept that we may not have the happy ending we were all praying for.

While I felt that holding onto Ben was how I needed to express my love for him, in the end, the opposite was true. I learned to love him by letting him go—one pried finger at a time.

I had discovered early in Ben's life that *time* was his love language. Thankfully, time is what I was able to give him, especially during this last year of his life. Immediately after his diagnosis, I let go of my day job in exchange for a full-time position as Ben's 24/7 caregiver. Since his leukemia compromised his immunity, I also opted to stay home from church for that entire year so that I could provide him with my company—a tricky feat for a pastor's wife.

I surprised myself by finding tangible ways to express my love for Ben. Some of them transcended my comfort zone and stretched me far beyond my limits. When he was being treated as an out-patient, I took him to his weekly cancer clinic visits, held his hand during painful procedures, administered medications, monitored side-effects, and even became trained to change the dressings for the tube carrying nutrients and medicine into a vein in his arm.

I did whatever I could to occupy my hands and to ensure a sanitary environment in our home. When he was an inpatient, I took up residence by his side and even stepped up to aid the nurses and hospital staff in whatever hands-on ways I could.

Throughout the year Ben was sick, I gathered and held onto each intimate, valuable, and necessary moment with him. I wanted to hold onto him for as long as I could. But with each moment we shared, I felt my grip loosening. That was especially true during one particular conversation. Ben asked me what my thoughts on heaven were. He relayed to me that he was beginning to see the colours of heaven in his sleep, and that there was nothing like them on earth.

As my heart welled up within me, I told Ben that, when the time came, I wanted him to go home to heaven quickly rather than trying to hold on for our sake. Then, with nothing less than God-given power, I told him that as hard as it was to let him go, some-how we'd learn to carry on without him, because we knew that we were leaving him in the trustworthy hands of Jesus.

I likened it to when he and his siblings were young. I explained that 95 percent of his dad's and my ability to go out and enjoy our-selves came with knowing we were leaving our children in the hands of a trustworthy babysitter.

Ben told me that he and his father had had a similar discus-sion in which his dad told him that we believed our children were on loan from God.

"So, Mom," he said with a grin, "when you think about it, you and Dad have really been the babysitters."

In that moment, God taught me the ultimate importance of loving Ben by letting him go. From that day forward, and into his final week with us, I began my final release. But it wasn't easy.

Ben wanted to spend his last days at home. I wasn't convinced this was the best idea. In fact, I rallied our medical team together to convince Ben otherwise. I had grown to appreciate the reality that we had help at our fingertips—literally—with a nurse only a call button away. (I was holding on for dear life!) But Ben had grown weary of simply existing. He wanted to *live* the rest of his days in the comfort of his own bed, savouring the sights and sounds of our home, and surrounded by those he loved. What could I do but consent to his wishes? We went home that day, but I must admit I wasn't happy about it.

So evident was my resistance that Ben's palliative home nurse picked up on it as soon as she walked in the door. She pulled me aside and privately asked me why I was struggling so much. I told her that I just wanted to be his mom and *not* his nurse in his final days. She assured me that I could still do that by simply loving him the way I had always done. She also assured me that the time we spent together as a family during Ben's last days would be something we would treasure and hold onto forever. And she was right.

As a family, we shared some precious moments as Ben prepared to leave his earthly home and go to his heavenly home. We spent hours on our backyard swing. There was always someone at his side—talking, laughing, or quietly watching over him.

It was during these final days together that God pried the last of my fingers open and I gradually and lovingly released Ben into His capable hands.

But we weren't the only ones doing the releasing. Ben needed to do some letting go of his own. Earlier, he'd made a list of things he wanted to do, people he wanted to see, and things he wanted to say before he died. He even planned his funeral and shared a powerful message with our church family only ten days before his death.[3]

Even so, there was still some unfinished business Ben wanted to take care of before he left us. Ben was aware that bringing him home for his last days had been stressful for me and that it had caused some tension between me and his dad. In our final conversation together, it became apparent that he needed assurance that we were all okay.

Ben turned toward me, and asked, through closed eyes, if I was still stressed.

Through tears, I said, "No, Ben. I'm *so* glad we brought you home." With those words, I gave him my final release and he gave me mine. No regrets.

Throughout Ben's illness, I learned invaluable lessons about loosening my grip, not only on my children, but on the things of this world. *Everything* is on loan to us from God. I learned what it is to "live in the moment,"[4] seizing, embracing, and savouring each and every second as God's gift. I also learned the importance of releasing each and every moment into God's hands to do with it as He pleases.

The Lord understands what it is to love by letting go. Our Heavenly Father released His only son into a dark and hurting world all because He loved each one of us so much. He loosened His grip in order to put Jesus into the hands of angry people. He is well-acquainted with loss and grief (Isaiah 53:3). As Ben would say, "He just gets it, folks."

When we release whatever it is we're holding onto, and entrust it to God's hands, He's able to fill our empty hands with more than we can imagine. In return for our letting go, He gives us a hope we can hold onto for life and eternity.

1. This is a type of cancer of the blood and bone marrow in which the bone marrow makes too many immature lymphocytes (a kind of white blood cell). It's typically found in children aged 2 to 5, and the older you are when you get it, the lower your chances of recovery. What made Ben's ALL high risk and rare was the further complication of a chromosome shift / translocation of cells.

2. *The Ben Ripple: Learning to Live through Loss with Purpose,* p. 21

3. A link to the message Ben gave to his church family ten days before he died. https://www.youtube.com/watch?v=rK4P3axkhag

4. *Dancing in the Rain,* p. 129

Alone, Again

Fiction

Carolyn R. Wilker

It had been a month since his wife died, but to 82-year-old Michael it seemed like yesterday. He'd been 18 years older than Laurie, who was in her early twenties when they'd married nearly 40 years ago. Naturally, they'd always assumed that he'd go first. More than once, she'd said, "When I'm here by myself someday, I'll miss you, but I'll be okay."

But now she was gone and he was the one left alone. And he wasn't okay.

They'd lived in this small southwestern Ontario city all their married life and liked it fine. His workplace had been only a few miles away, and it had worked well for her, too. Once the children came along, Laurie wanted to be at home with them, and she'd babysat when neighbours needed childcare for a few hours. It had been a busy household.

The small apartment they'd moved into after their sons were grown was quiet now except for the racket he himself made as his crutches connected with the wood floor of the hallway and then the linoleum as he picked up his cup of tea and took it to the living room. On the carpet, the crutches made only the slightest sound.

He set the mug on the table next to his chair, then sat down. While the tea cooled, he recalled anniversaries, birthdays, and dinners they'd shared with family and friends. He picked up the 35th anniversary photo that stood next to his steaming mug and looked first at the faces of his tall sons, then at Laurie's. She wore the determined look he knew well, but all who knew her were aware that she was deeply compassionate, always thinking of others first.

In the background, he could hear the radio. Some mornings he turned it on and left it going all day. Announcers made their statements and singers sang their songs, and he barely heard any of it.

  Hot Apple Cider with Cinnamon

At Laurie's funeral, he'd told a friend of hers that he'd just go back to being a bachelor. That's what he'd been before they met; he was already in his forties, and had managed quite well in spite of his physical limitations. He was shorter than most people—barely five feet tall, hairline already receding—and because of polio, he'd had only one leg since he was in his early twenties. He'd told the doctor that if his left leg wasn't going to be strong and healthy, maybe he was better off without it.

He'd tried a prosthetic leg, but it gave him sores, so he finally abandoned it and stuck with the crutches. Was it the right decision? He thought so.

Laurie, too, was short—only four foot four. She was a fair-haired beauty with a will the size of Goliath in her tiny frame. Her blue eyes and fine brown hair framed a usually serious face, but when she smiled, it radiated to her eyes and lit her whole being. Often wearing dress pants and a blouse or sweater, she was never given to excess where clothing was concerned. In fact she usually shopped in the girls' department of the clothing store, rather than the women's. For the most part, her watch and some earrings made up her jewellery, and later his ring.

They'd met at the long-term-care hospital situated on the outskirts of the city where he was the head accountant and she a librarian. Had she come to him with requests for additional funds for books for the library? Yes, that was it.

They had chatted as long as the opportunity provided, then planned to eat their lunch together the next day at the hospital cafeteria. The dates came after that, when they realized they might be in love. And later, the wedding with family and a small group of friends.

Age didn't matter with love.

Right from the beginning, she'd made it her business to watch out for him, asking if people had steps or railings on their porches when they were planning to visit. As they aged, she'd become even more protective of him.

They'd had a family—two boys. When the boys were babies, he'd lain his crutches on the floor and played with them, and when they were toddlers, they'd run around and around in their home and he'd chased them on his crutches, and caught up to them, and then they'd all collapsed in a heap of giggles.

He'd liked their building blocks best. He'd helped them build a tower, and then they'd knocked the tower down and rebuilt it.

The boys grew tall and strong; they passed him in height by Grade 5 or 6, but discipline was never a problem. They were good boys, and a stern lecture worked when it was needed, which was infrequently.

His wife—wonder woman that she was—had done the outside work at their home, and all the cooking. She had learned well from her mother. No one would go hungry while she was queen of the kitchen. Little ladders or step stools made her life more manageable and the kitchen cupboards easier to reach, and when the boys grew tall, they helped her get things up and down as needed.

He'd never been able to climb a ladder—just one of the things you can't do minus a leg.

His wife had loved having the house full of children, and she catered to them as best she could, but never at risk of spoiling them. The boys were men now with their own homes, and one was married and a father.

A few years after the youngest son was married, they'd sold the family home and moved to this apartment. It suited them fine. No more driveways and front steps to shovel in winter—not that he could do it anyway, and it was getting harder for her, too. No more outdoor work either, although she'd missed planting flowers in the front beds as she'd done for years.

And then she had gone into the hospital with a suspected case of pneumonia.

Thinking she'd be home in a few days, she'd arranged for friends in the building to bring meals for him in her absence. But that wasn't the way it had worked out. Her condition worsened, and doctors put her in an induced coma. In spite of all the medical intervention, she never regained consciousness.

Her time in the hospital had seemed so long, with him coming and going every day, but in reality, it had been only a few weeks.

Their sons had been at her side with him at the end, when nothing else could be done and the last surgery hadn't worked, and

  Hot Apple Cider with Cinnamon

her heart was giving out, too. In the end, the three of them had stood there silently, each reflecting on all she'd meant to him.

The funeral had come and gone, and everyone had gone back to their lives. Everyone except him.

The apartment was quiet, the way it had been when Laurie went on errands or to speak, as she sometimes did. He'd gone with her on some occasions, but most of those times he'd stayed home enjoying the peacefulness. But now the quiet lasted far too long.

Sometimes he actually forgot, and thought she'd gone on an errand, to church, out with her friends; and then he remembered she wasn't coming home.

He had lots of paperwork to do, the closing out of a person's accounts. The ending of a life—his beloved's. Not that paperwork was a difficult thing; he'd been doing bookkeeping since he was in his early thirties. But this wasn't paperwork he could enjoy.

It was too early, but he just wanted to go to bed and sleep.

He turned off the radio voices and sat listening to the clock ticking while he sat in his easy chair. He heard a few people pass in the hallway, talking on their way. He couldn't make out the words they spoke.

Quiet. She wasn't coming back. It was still hard to realize. Would the numbing grief hit him as he'd seen it do to others half his age when they lost their partners? Would he end up in depression or worse?

And then he saw something that he hadn't noticed before. Laurie's white sweater—the one she wore every day to keep her warm, lying neatly folded on the lower shelf of the end table at the side of the sofa where Laurie always sat. Someone must have found it lying on the couch and put it there. Not the sweater he'd given the funeral people to put on her for her last goodbye. It was silly, he knew, but he had wanted her to be warm. He'd even given them a pair of fuzzy socks for her feet, lest they be cold too. No, this was an old sweater she wore around the house when it was just the two of them.

He got up from his La-Z-Boy and made his way across to the sofa and sat in her spot. He put aside his crutches and picked up the sweater.

It was a sweater that a child could wear, she was so small. He held it against his face. The fibres still carried a familiar scent—that of the soap she used—gentle with only a hint of lemon, a scent he'd always liked.

He wasn't a man to cry often—his humour usually checked in—but now his eyes filled with tears. Just as they had on the day she died, and at her funeral.

Tears flowed more freely now, running down his face, and then he sobbed. Tears caught in the sweater he held to his face. It was soft, and he felt the warmth he'd missed so much.

After a time, he gathered up the sweater and looped it over one of his crutches and took it with him to the bed where he slept alone. He'd have it to remind him of her at night.

By day he had everything else—the furniture she'd chosen, her books and music collections, the Bible she'd read each day. He remembered her last words before the coma, assuring him that they'd see each other again soon. Surely he'd see her again, though it could be some time.

And then he remembered how she'd always said, "When I'm here by myself someday, I'll miss you, but I'll be okay."

But he was the one who was by himself.

Would *he* be okay? He took a deep breath, stroked her sweater, and prayed a quick prayer. Yes, yes, he would.

Weighted Down
(A Widow's Lament)

Brenda J. Wood

I'm weighted in the waiting.
The time drags heavy, hot.
I'm weighted in the waiting
'Cause time is all I've got.

My patience wears, my heart grieves,
I fear; I tremble deep.
But life goes on and I, too
My promises to keep.

To stand alone against trials
Seems oh, so very wrong
But God has tasks still left for me
And He will keep me strong.

And even though the waiting
Weights and wears me down,
I know we'll meet again in heav'n
And both wear victors' crowns.

Love from Beyond

Nonfiction

T. L. Wiens

The heavy-set man with the thinning hair held the young woman's hand in his as he guided her to a pew just a couple of rows up from where we sat. His face beamed with the pride of a father leading his daughter up the aisle on her wedding day. The expression on the young woman's face and the gait of her steps told me she had some form of disability.

Allan, my soon-to-be husband, leaned over and whispered in my ear, "That's Cornie Braun and his daughter Penny."

I saw a father who adored his daughter. During the service, he sat beside her, her hand still in his, patiently whispering to her. She let out the odd whoop of excitement during the singing, but although Cornie shushed her once or twice, he never became harsh with her.

This man with strong square shoulders and a smile that held a sliver of a mischievous smirk won my respect from the first time I saw him.

My respect for him only grew as I got to know him. Cornie may have slept through a few sermons, but his desire to live a life pleasing to God came through in every conversation we had. He held to his principles even when not the politically correct viewpoint.

Some years later, life pulled my family in a direction that involved a move to a neighbouring district. This took us to another church and away from building a stronger relationship with Cornie and his family.

I still saw people from our old church and heard tidbits of news. I was crushed when I heard that Cornie had cancer. Every report after the first one told a story of doom—the cancer was advanced and moving fast. I thought about this loving dad and

Hot Apple Cider with Cinnamon

husband. I remembered watching Penny on Cornie's arm as they made their way to their pew that first time I'd seen them. How would this family manage without Cornie? We all prayed.

Cornie Braun lost his battle with cancer on September 5, 2005. At his funeral, my heart went out to his family, and especially his daughter Penny. Having lost my own dad just a couple of years earlier, I knew the months of sorrow and grieving they faced.

"Fire!" The shouts from Katelyn, my middle daughter, pulled me from my slumber.

I'll never forget my 11-year-old's cry as she rushed up the stairs to our bedroom.

It was mid-afternoon, Easter Monday, 2006, and we were exhausted from a weekend of church services and family gatherings. Allan and I had lain down for a nap an hour earlier.

Katelyn's eyes bulged and her chest heaved as if she'd run a marathon. "The house is on fire!"

Allan and I jumped out of bed and, with Katelyn following, scrambled down the two flights of stairs to the only exit from our house—the door from the walkout basement.

As Allan hurried down the stairs ahead of me, flames shot out of the chimney vent in the wall. Allan's hair warped back into tight black curls as the flames sent the foul odour of singed hair into the air. Smoke had already coated the windows with a dark film that swallowed up the mid-afternoon sunlight that should have been cascading through the glass panes. Red licks of flame spread across the floor joists as we made our way to the basement where the door was located.

I put my attention on my four children. Katelyn was with us. She had assured us that Jenna, our youngest child, was waiting in the basement.

But where were Matthew, our son, and our oldest daughter, Kendra?

After a frantic, fruitless search of their bedrooms, which were in the basement, we headed outside. Matthew was in the back yard working on one of his cars.

"The house is on fire!" I screamed.

He looked up.

I didn't have to say anything more.

With Katelyn and Jenna out, and Allan and Matthew getting the hose working, I rushed back inside, frantically calling for Kendra.

The walls were hot. The fire was eating our house from the inside out. It was easy to see that the small trickle from the garden hose wasn't going to overcome this monster.

I suddenly remembered that Kendra had mentioned she was meeting a neighbour to go for a walk. I ran outside. At the same time, Allan and Matthew went from fighting the fire to pulling out whatever they could salvage.

I jumped in our car, and headed down the road. I found Kendra and her friend a couple of miles from the yard. I picked them up and we drove back toward the house, stopping at a neighbour's to call 911.

When we got back to the house, I expected Allan and Matthew to be standing outside with Katelyn and Jenna, but they were still going in and out of the house, pulling out belongings.

I knew that people died when they stayed in burning houses, so I hurried inside to find them. I found Matthew in his bedroom and pushed him toward the door.

Allan was upstairs. He handed me something and we headed down the stairs. But the water from the hose had made the steps slippery, and he tumbled down the last few steps. I was terrified he might be injured; I could never have managed to carry his 280-pound frame. I whispered a prayer of thanks when he managed to get back on his feet.

As we emerged from the house, trucks were arriving. Neighbours and friends, alerted by the thick column of smoke, had come to help.

We had to pull our small pile of belongings further from the house or they'd have melted in the heat. Thankfully, the barn was a good distance away so the animals were safe. By this time, the fire was too hot for firefighters to do much but prevent it from spreading.

  Hot Apple Cider with Cinnamon

Friends and neighbours offered words of condolence, but their stares made me feel uncomfortable.

We gave statements to the police.

The flames that now engulfed the entire structure created a red glow in the twilight when I took the children to my in-laws house, where we would spend the night. Time had ceased to exist. It felt like mid-afternoon, but in reality, it was almost time for bed.

Different kinds of fire have different smells. Some are even pleasant. But there was nothing pleasant in the acidy odour that clung to us. Only when I took the time to escape to the bathroom did the reality of it all set in. I stared at my image in the mirror. My eyes shone like beacons from my blackened face, revealing the fear that held me in its grip. I didn't care about the house—it's how close we had come to losing our lives that haunted me. But, thank God, we all survived.

I desperately wanted the smell off of me, but the sticky left-overs from the smoke and ash proved hard to remove, even with soap. Of course, the memory of that day would be around much longer.

Word had spread fast. Before we went to bed that night, neighbours had already dropped off clothes, food—everything we needed for a few days.

That night in bed, as I talked with Allan, we realized that God had something planned. It turned out He'd spoken to both of us in the two weeks before the fire.

Allan tried to hide his tears. "It was like He was asking me to be okay with how He decided to handle things. I gave Him the farm."

I'd had a similar experience. God had asked me if I was willing to let go of everything. I'd thought about that long and hard before answering. In the end, I'd said I trusted Him.

We couldn't turn back now that we really needed to trust Him, but where would we live? We needed to be at our farm, close to our animals.

The worry came and went. We told each other that God would take care of us.

The next day, we drove back to the scene. Our house was a smoking pile of rubble with some areas still glowing. I found a fine china teacup still intact.

During the day, people came over, each bringing something to help us out. It was overwhelming.

The biggest question, of course, was where we were going to live for the next while until we could rebuild our house. Someone offered us a house in town where we could stay, but Allan and I felt we couldn't be that far from the farm. Then we got a call from Cornie Braun's widow, who invited us over for tea.

With everything that had happened over the past 24 hours, our heads were spinning, and it seemed like we should be doing something to start the cleanup. But we decided that going to see this lady was more important than standing by the still-hot embers that now represented our home.

When we arrived, we sat down at a table and enjoyed lunch. Afterward, I took in the pictures—smiling faces of Cornie and his family. It still seemed unreal that he was gone.

The conversation drew my attention back to matters at hand.

"I have to tell you something." Cornie's widow teared up with her words. "Before Cornie passed away, we made many decisions. He didn't want to leave me with any loose ends. In the end, we'd settled everything except one detail. I wanted to sell the old trailer, but Cornie didn't want to."

Allan and I knew the trailer. We'd visited it on several occasions when Cornie's middle daughter lived there with her husband. It was built in the '70s and still had the wood panelling and carpet that went with that era. Even so, it was well maintained.

She kept going. "We bought it new, and it served as our first home. After we built the house, the trailer became a home for many people over the years, including our own children when they decided to move back to the farm. Now, it's empty. It seemed a waste letting it sit there, but Cornie was sure God had told him to keep it. He said someone would have need of it, and when the time came, I should give it to them. I believe that someone is you."

We were stunned. Months before the fire happened, God had known we'd need a home, and because of Cornie's obedience, He'd already provided for us.

In a daze, we thanked her, and arrangements were made to move the trailer to our farmyard.

By the time friends and neighbours helped us get the trailer into its new spot, we not only had furniture but every room had a co-ordinated colour scheme. The odds and ends donated by people from the community had come together as if an interior decorator had planned it.

Eight days after the fire, we moved into our new home.

I wish I'd had the chance to tell the man who made this possible how much I appreciate his gift, but I have a feeling he knows how his love reached out to us from beyond the grave.

Hot Apple Cider with Cinnamon

A Second Chance

Nonfiction

Frieda Martens

Steven, a 10-year-old boy, was one member of a group of ten 10- to 12-year-olds who couldn't read—a fact they were not proud of. It was my mandate to get them reading. Helping me in my challenge were a psychologist, a reading clinician, a social worker, and a teaching assistant.

All ten of these students had been diagnosed prior to entering the class. They had all been deemed capable of learning to read, but for various reasons, they had all failed to learn.

Their inability to read had set them back academically and caused them to have problematic social relationships, particularly at school. Naturally, this led to frustration, which often resulted in inappropriate behaviour.

These students had been teased mercilessly on the playground at recess and lunch hour. This deflated their self-esteem and led to feelings of low self-worth. Their grievances were often settled with their fists, the one weapon they knew how to execute effectively. But, of course, this brought only misery to themselves and others.

They were trapped in a cycle of failure, and I was determined to change that.

Before I could teach them anything, I had to make sure they knew two things. The first was that they could count on me to be "firm but fair." The second was that I cared for them as individuals. On occasion, it required a little juggling for me to keep those two things in the proper balance.

I tried to remind them of both my concern for them and my firm but fair attitude each day when they lined up to go home. My parting words were, "Love you. Tomorrow we start with a clean slate."

I found it helpful to have an incentive program with rewards for points earned. Of course, the rewards had to be things they

Hot Apple Cider with Cinnamon

wanted badly. My hope, of course, was that the good behaviour they demonstrated in order to get their prizes would become a habit.

This particular day, the prize was to get that afternoon off school to go roller skating.

Every day at the same time, each student had to give an account for whether or not he or she deserved to keep the point for the day.

The discussions were lively. Usually, the students told the truth. On occasion, other people, including the principal, the on-duty teacher, or students from other classes, were called upon to give evidence.

Up to the morning of the day we were to go roller skating, Steven had just barely managed to acquire the minimum number of points. Recess that morning would be the litmus test, because he couldn't afford to lose a single point. Before he went out for recess, I warned him of his conundrum.

I was disappointed, but not surprised, when I heard the din in the hallway a short time later.

"Steven was fighting…"

"He hit me…"

"Mr. Bollenbach had to stop him."

The accusations were flying.

A few students began chanting, "He can't go roller skating this afternoon."

Steven hung his head as he shuffled into the classroom. But to my amazement, he didn't defend his actions. He said that someone had teased him and he'd fought back.

The atmosphere in the class was grave.

My students, who usually showed some solidarity within the classroom, believed that he could have shown more self-control, especially since he wanted to go on the field trip.

After I talked to the teacher on duty and listened to my students, I concluded that Steven had lost his chance to go roller skating. The offence merited the punishment. Looking straight at his crestfallen face, I gave the official verdict: "You will stay at school and work."

That day, my regular teaching assistant, who always stringently enforced my rules, was absent.

An older lady, who had experienced a lot of trauma and hardships in her life, was substituting for him.

Earlier that morning, I'd been teaching the concept of God's grace, thinking it was a possible solution to some of my students' relationship problems. In an open discussion, the substitute teaching assistant had shared with the class some of her own struggles as a young person, and how she'd eventually overcome them with the help of kind and understanding people.

Unknown to everyone else, in keeping with our earlier discussion, I was now trying to come up with a way for Steven to go on the trip that would demonstrate grace. What made it more complex was the other students' assessment of the situation. I silently prayed for wisdom.

The talk that morning had caused sober reflection, but I was uneasy. I was afraid the students would see my forgiveness as leniency or weakness. But because of my own conviction and the time restraints, I forged ahead.

"Because of grace, Steven will be given a second chance."

Silence reigned as the entire class leaned forward to process my words. I watched Steven's reaction as well as the reactions of his classmates.

A grin lit up his freckled face as Steven raised his hand. He brushed his curly, thick, strawberry-coloured hair back and glanced at me confidently. "The teacher and I believe in grace."

I smiled and nodded at him.

Whether the meaning of the word was clear to him, I'm not sure, but his sagging shoulders straightened and his eyes sparkled.

Astonishingly, the whole class bought into it, and Steven went roller skating with the rest of the group.

As we stepped onto the city bus for the ride downtown, an elderly gentleman followed us in. He smiled at me and my young charges and wished us a good day.

"I wasn't supposed to go, you know," Steven blurted out. "I got to go anyway."

The kindly man nodded, as if he understood the situation.

There wasn't a happier boy at the roller rink that afternoon, despite Steven's inability to skate without falling down at every turn.

In view of the fact that these students were quick to exploit any exceptions to my rules as an excuse to get away with bad behaviour, it astonished me that the rest of the year went by without reference to this episode. That spelled out God's grace for me.

At the end of the term, I quizzed Steven on the meaning of grace. He responded by saying that it meant being able to go roller skating when you don't deserve to.

I believe that he did understand in his own way that it was love that wasn't deserved.

A transformation happened to Steven that year: he began to believe in himself; he learned to read; and he was transferred to a regular Grade 5 class in the school. I saw him becoming part of the games at recess and not just getting picked on.

I don't know for sure, but I think his success might have had something to do with his being given grace that day.

Although I lost track of Steven, I've never forgotten him and the lesson we all learned that day—to give grace to others.

Hot Apple Cider with Cinnamon

Love in Alignment

A. A. Adourian

I often feel blind
not seeing answers
not knowing what questions
to ask
wondering if and when and why
and everything all over again
going 'round and 'round in circles

And then
God sends a thought
telling me to
check my email, make a call, write a letter,
or—harder still—to
wait, be patient

The waiting seems endless,
but often, as I pause to
think things over
and try to trust…
my email pings, my phone rings,
a text pops up on my screen,
a knock sounds at my door—
Jackpot!

Those are the days I am tempted
to play multi-million dollar lotteries
but
He doesn't push me to seek
things, rather
He draws me gently
toward Himself
endlessly proving to me

Hot Apple Cider with Cinnamon

that I am
never forgotten;

Assuring me
I matter to Him

Even my thoughts count,
so He interjects,
reminding me to
check my email, make a call, read His Word,
connect with someone…

Though I often fail Him
He still speaks
into my thoughts,
grace—

Hot Apple Cider with Cinnamon

A White Piano Bench

Nonfiction

Rose Seiler Scott

I don't know who wrote it, but copies of a short typewritten essay, titled "Believe and Be Satisfied," have been making their way around the women's dorm. It's a reminder to young people to place their trust in God and pursue Him wholeheartedly for satisfaction and contentment, rather than expecting a future mate to fulfill all their longings. Folding the pages, I put the essay in my journal and consider its message.

Though I've tried not to wear my heart on my sleeve, I realize I've often been guilty of putting too much hope in the wrong thing. After two years of Bible college, I'm no closer to either finding that special someone or deciding what I want to do when I finish school. I love going to college, but my career direction lacks clarity and my wallet lacks funds.

I decide to focus my efforts on following and serving God as I figure out future education and career goals, whatever they may be. I'm only 19, after all. When tempted to mope, I tell myself there's lots of time.

I've been enjoying piano lessons with a part-time instructor at the college. At the end of term, my teacher invites me to continue lessons at her home studio so I can polish my pieces for a Conservatory exam.

I also have a job at my dad's auto-wrecking and repair business. I run errands, act as cashier at the sales counter, and help my mom with the bookkeeping.

Throughout the automotive shop, even in the office, a veneer of black dust coats the walls. This cloak of oil and grease is almost palpable. It permeates everything, and the odour clings to my jeans and hair.

The first day of piano lessons at my teacher's home, I drive straight from work and climb the stairs to her living room, where the Yamaha grand dominates the room. Its warm wood finish gleams in the sunshine. Even though I haven't practised enough, I know everything will sound better on this instrument.

The piano bench is padded with white vinyl. Pristine, white vinyl.

I prop my music on the shelf and sit down tentatively, wondering if I have any business sitting here in my work clothes. Mrs. Scott doesn't say anything, and it doesn't make sense for me to travel all the way back home to clean up—way too far in the opposite direction—so I continue to come straight from work once a week to prepare scales and arpeggios along with Mozart and Chopin for the exam in June.

The piano is located right by the stairs and the hallway. The family, including Mr. Scott, and their adult children, often pass by as I am having my lesson.

One day, their son, a recent university graduate, arrives home early from his new job. He pauses at the top of the stairs to greet his mom, and I shift around on the bench to face him. His mother introduces Andy to me.

From the sharp way he's dressed, it's obvious Andy works in a downtown office, not a grubby shop. But in spite of my old jeans and the *eau de automotive* I know is emanating from my direction, he flashes me a warm smile.

For weeks afterward, Andy often comes home in the middle of my lesson, but we don't speak much until one day when I'm running downstairs to leave and I hear someone coming down the stairs behind me.

I turn to see who it is.

It's Andy. And he's smiling at me. "Would you like to come to the graduation banquet at my church on Saturday?" he asks.

My heart beats a little faster. Really? He's asking *me* to his graduation banquet? The girl who looks and smells like a refugee from an automotive shop? "I'll check my calendar," I say, playing it cool but knowing I will make a way to do it, even if it means skipping my scheduled softball game.

That Saturday night, Andy arrives at my house to pick me up. He is wearing a blue suit and tie to match his eyes and holding out a corsage edged with pink, which will go perfectly with my cream-coloured dress.

I am adorned with lace and ruffles and quite sure I look and smell good this time.

In my excitement, however, I leave the poor guy standing in the doorway while I go back to finish getting ready!

When we go out to his car, a 1970 Chevelle, I'm not overly impressed. It has a beautiful turquoise paint job, but it's a *domestic* vehicle. Even though my own car is only a Volkswagen, one of the perks of my job is occasionally driving Porsches and Mercedes that my father has rebuilt.

I'm even less impressed when Andy invents some ridiculous function for some of the buttons on the dashboard to see if I'll believe him. I roll my eyes. I'm a mechanic's daughter, and I make sure he knows I'm way smarter than the average girl about that kind of thing.

In spite of my arrogance, my import car snobbery, and our questionable first meeting when I looked and smelled as if I'd been working in a garage, we enjoy the evening, and our relationship blossoms.

I continue my piano lessons, but now, when I come each week, little foil-wrapped tokens of candy or encouraging notes from my teacher's son wait for me on the white bench.

Mrs. Scott encourages me to take up teaching piano as a career—which turns out to be an excellent idea.

The rest, as they say is history.

Turns out that trusting God to take care of the details of my life was a good idea, too. I didn't expect to meet my future husband while pursuing my love of music, but I'm certain it was orchestrated by the great matchmaker Himself—with a little help from my father-in-law, who apparently coaxed his son down the stairs to ask me out that first time!

Twice, for Good Measure

Historical Fiction

Laura Aliese Miedema

Mary Jean Parsons eyed the apple slices in the measuring cup with a frown. *I really need two more apples to make my apple pie,* she thought, *but I don't have the time to go all the way to Graceson's Store for two measly apples, just for the likes of them. Probably they won't even notice it's a tad flat, just like they don't pay attention to anyone but themselves.*

She sniffed, dumped the browning slices into her mixing bowl, and tightened the starched apron around her large-boned frame. Her frizzy, black hair insisted on escaping from under her white cap, like the new growth pushing out from the groomed hedges she could see from the kitchen window.

The deep green hedges were living walls that guarded the ivory manor house, with its three stories and stained-glass front door. The hedges, along with the tall wrought-iron fence, kept the dirty people from the dirty streets of Halifax far away from this immaculate home.

Well, she thought, *if the Ladies' Christian Missions Society wants an apple pie for their annual meeting of 1916, by the blessed saints above and below, they'll get one. They'll get what's coming from a black lady who they don't treat very ladylike. "Orphans in Africa need to eat," my Mistress Teresa says to me. Humph! I may live in Canada, but I need to eat, too, and I would eat a lot better if she paid me more.* Mary Jean mixed the dough with a vigour that came from roughly 30 years of fighting to make sure she wasn't over-looked in Maritimes society, where black girls and women were often afterthoughts.

No. Miss Teresa is no saint. Her righteous friends may tell her she's better than the spineless wives who dawdle over needlework while their men bleed in the trenches, but I'm Miss Teresa's house-keeper. I know what's hidden in her closets.

Mary Jean slapped the pie dough on her mistress's marble counter. Mary Jean's brown arms were spotted with white flour, but the only white she was seeing was on the bulging white cheeks of the members of the Ladies' Christian Missions Society, as they chewed her pie.

If only those ladies really knew Miss Teresa! thought Mary Jean. *Why, I bet they would call down sulphur and brimstone if they knew how she used to play cards with her gardener, my Pop, at an ungodly hour on Saturday evenings, in order to fit in a wager just hours before Sunday. Of course, she was too good to gamble on Sunday, but what would the other ladies say if they knew she gambled at all?*

Mary Jean's eyes darted to the picture of her Pop set carefully on the window sill above the kitchen sink—dear Pop, who still grinned at Mary Jean from the picture frame, even after he'd left her, his only daughter, behind on this earth. Mary Jean's hands stopped and lingered in the dough. Pop seemed to be chuckling at her as she muttered Miss Teresa's name under her breath and felt her cheeks burn with anger.

Oh, Pop, she thought, *I can ignore or positively adore a good many folks, but this high-and-mighty pie isn't even the half of it. Miss Teresa went and hired back Alfie. Alfie! She said she hired him to renovate the kitchen cabinetry, for old time's sake. How could she do that when she knows what he did to you and me? She's acting more like a devil than a saint, bringing him back here!*

Mary Jean's thoughts didn't disturb Pop's picture-perfect smile. *Mary Jean,* his eyes seemed to say, *Alfie needs to work. He has to eat and pay his rent, you know.* And then Pop seemed to add, *Think how much you enjoyed the funny songs Alfie would sing when he worked here full time as the handyman. How he used to joke, his freckles nearly popping off his black cheeks because he smiled so big. Remember how he'd whistle through his teeth when he measured each board—only once—and then confidently cut.*

Mary Jean tore her gaze from Pop's soft eyes to look out the window at the bristles of grass. *I am remembering,* she thought. *Remembering how he kissed me quickly after that garden party, when he drank too much and embarrassed me. Remembering how he never replied to my letters after Miss Teresa fired him for getting*

  Hot Apple Cider with Cinnamon

drunk, even though I knew I had the right address. And I wrote three times. Remembering how, before that, he slipped you drinks, even after the doctor said you shouldn't have any more. How he held your hand when you were dying from cirrhosis of the liver, and sobbed for you to forgive him.

And now he's back and he says he's a new man, and he's conquered the drinking demon with God's help, and he wants to fix things. Like the cabinets. And Miss Teresa says she believes him, and he'll do a good job.

Mary Jean clenched the pie dough in her fingers without thinking. The soft pastry wasn't meant to be kneaded, and it grew tougher and tougher as she dug in her nails.

Miss Teresa has money and a mansion. All I have is my heart, and it's scuffed and dented just like those cabinets Alfie is tearing out over there by the oven.

Mary Jean glared across her sacred kitchen at the abomination of a carpenter.

Alfie was looking around for something, chewing on his thick carpenter's pencil, balancing it like a cigar between his teeth. He scratched his black hair, now sprinkled with more sawdust than grey, and picked up a bucket. "There it is," he muttered, and took a measuring tape out of the bucket. He whistled a few chirps to himself and then proceeded to hum a ditty.

Mary Jean turned her back to that tone-deaf man, and didn't notice him kneel down to measure the wood twice and cut it straight and true. She didn't see him smooth out the rough wood edges with gritty sandpaper. For all she knew, he just kept shuffling around the kitchen, lazier than a snail on a holiday. And he didn't stop his humming—which was blasphemy in the "holy," cold silence given off by Mary Jean.

Mary Jean felt deeply offended at the desecration of her sanctuary. The gospel song Alfie was humming was actually a favourite of Pop's. The last time she'd heard it was at his funeral. Mary Jean caught herself whispering the words, and forced her hips to stop swaying to its rhythm. With the speed of experience, she hid the naked apple pieces inside the pie shell and thumbed down dimples in the crust to seal them away from sight. With the pie balanced on one hand, Mary Jean stepped around Alfie's heap of timber to reach the oven.

As she waited for the oven to finish heating up, she looked at the clock. It was the household time for a hot drink.

Part of Mary Jean wanted Alfie to ask her for a strong coffee. *A decent man drinks tea,* she thought, *but* he *wouldn't ask for tea. A finely steeped tea would be lost on that kind of man's taste.*

When Alfie tapped her turned back, Mary Jean jumped.

"I'm sorry my supplies are in your way," he said as she whirled around, pie in hand. "I'll clean it up as soon as I can."

She brushed off the hint of sawdust he'd left on her shoulder. That man was sprinkled with sawdust head to toe!

Mary Jean sent an icy stare into his warm, brown eyes. "I know you, Alfie. You always leave a mess and make *me* clean it up. And I've done enough of that—okay?"

She strode to the counter, picked up her rolling pin, and pointed it first at him and then at the door. "Alfie, I want you out of my kitchen. Now!"

He blinked and cleared his throat. Then he smiled.

His slow voice poured out like molasses. "The way I see it, Mary Jean, you're like sandpaper. You rub rough on rough people. But it all smooths out in the end if you just put in the elbow grease. You'll see. And I promised your Pop I'd put in the extra effort to smooth things over with you."

"What do you mean?" Mary Jean pointed the rolling pin at his nose.

Alfie grasped the other end of the rolling pin. "Pop made me promise that I'd take care of you, because he couldn't any more. When you wrote me, Mary Jean, I was so ashamed of myself, I couldn't answer.

"And afterwards, the strong drink kept sucking me down through the bottle-neck, just as I was about to be free. But it eventually got tired, you see, and one day I got out.

"On that day, Mary Jean, I wrote you a fine letter. And I know you probably didn't open it when you saw my name on the envelope. But—please hear me out—I can't let your Pop down again." His eyes glazed with tears. "Your Pop forgave me—even *me*—on

  Hot Apple Cider with Cinnamon

his death-bed, Mary Jean. If *he* could forgive me, someone who helped kill him, can *you* find it in your heart to forgive me, too?"

Mary Jean felt like a frightened deer caught in a spotlight. Slowly, she lowered her rolling pin. Hot tears slipped down her cheeks.

Alfie came over and reached to brush away the tears with his handkerchief. He whispered, "Please, Mary Jean."

When he touched her, she cried out and stepped back, away from him. She felt the pie teeter on her palm, but, blinded by a blur of tears, she couldn't do anything. She heard the stupid pie splatter onto the floor. "Don't pick it up. I don't need you to be picking it up. Please, don't pick it up," she begged.

But Alfie scooped up the pale mess of pastry and apples with the empty bucket that he had used to hold his nails. Mary Jean wiped the trickles off her cheeks with the back of her hand. *I must look horrid,* she thought. Aloud she said, "Well, I guess I'm the one who is quite the mess now."

"I don't leave messes where I go any more," Alfie said. "I won't leave you as a mess, Mary Jean. I've changed."

"Changed? Look at how my pie just got crushed—all because of you!"

He stepped toward her, so close that Mary Jean could smell the fresh sawdust on his shirt. Her tired frown began to melt like butter under his warm gaze, and tears betrayed her again. He cupped her trembling chin in his calloused fingers. "Make a new pie, Mary Jean. Measure it out again. Twice, for good measure."

She moved her head. "I don't have any more apples—I don't—"

"Have the apple from my lunch."

"Oh, Alfie, I won't—"

But he was already paring it with steady hands, exposing the heart-shape he created from his apple, a little bit more with each sure cut. Mary Jean eyed his sawdust-covered head, bent over his quick hands. Her heart quavered. *Is he just being smooth?*

But Alfie placed his heart on the counter in front of her. Then he said, "If you still want me to leave your kitchen, I will. I will be on my way to Graceson's Store to buy more apples, and you may take them or you may leave them, Mary Jean, but know that I bought them for you with all I have left." He turned around to leave the kitchen, exactly as she had asked him to do. His lanky brown arms swung slowly at his sides as he plodded into the hallway.

Some deep part of Mary Jean shouted for him to stay, to touch her face again. But all she could do was whisper, "Oh, Alfie! I was wrong. I was so wrong about you."

His head perked up at her mumble, and he twirled around, searching her face.

"I was just saying—that is—I meant that— You should stay, for a little while."

Her gaze was drawn to his eyes—eyes that glinted just like Pop's with the same mischievous spark. "Alfie, forgive me—" her words clumped in her throat "—forgive me. I haven't offered you a drink. Would you like to have a cup of tea with me before your travels?"

Alfie's smile rounded his cheeks like apples. "Bless my head! I thought you'd never ask."

From the window, Pop's picture watched the two of them making timid small talk, sprinkled with awkward pauses and nervous laughter.

Mary Jean could almost feel Pop's gaze, as if he were somehow alive again, grinning back at her through the spaces in Alfie's big-teethed smile. Mary Jean poured a second cup of tea for Alfie, and he slurped it down before leaving for Graceson's.

When he got back to work, Alfie sang like a speckled songbird, making the time fly by. Meanwhile, Mary Jean measured the pie ingredients a second time. Into the mouth of the oven she gingerly placed her new plump pie, like the "humble pie" she had to eat in her own mouth. Soon the sweet smell whispered through the kitchen that the steaming pie was ready for Miss Teresa to take to the annual meeting.

After the refreshment period of the Ladies' Christian Missions Society, the general consensus of the saints was that Miss Mary Jean's apple pie was the best pie in the county. Miss Teresa moved that they should ask Mary Jean for her recipe so they could

  Hot Apple Cider with Cinnamon

make more apple pies to auction off for the Halifax food bank. The motion was passed as quickly as the pie had disappeared.

Later, Miss Teresa sashayed into the kitchen, waving the empty pie dish in her gloved hand, to ask Mary Jean for her recipe. She found Mary Jean humming Pop's favourite gospel song and stirring a new mix to its beat. Alfie was packing up his saws and sandpaper, humming the same song.

Miss Teresa raised an eyebrow. "Alfie, my good man, are you going so soon? You haven't finished the work I brought you here for, have you?"

"What do you mean, Miss Teresa?" he said, gesturing to the completed redwood cabinets.

"Silly man, I'm talking about Mary Jean. You're not done fixing things here until there's a wedding band on Mary Jean's finger. I guess you'll just have to stay around as the permanent handyman again." She winked. "I won't take no for an answer, and neither should you."

Both Mary Jean and Alfie stared in disbelief, but Miss Teresa was apparently serious. She shook Alfie's hand, and then took Mary Jean aside into the corridor to talk about the pie recipe.

Mary Jean barely heard the words tumbling out of Miss Teresa's red lips. She could only feel a smile tickle the corners of her mouth. She was half-surprised that she could actually be happy. *Oh, Pop,* she thought, *I may have been a little rough on Alfie. And on Miss Teresa for bringing him back for me. Yes, Miss Teresa really is a saint!*

Of Sparrows and Children

Nonfiction

Marianne Jones

Have you ever seen a bird fly into a window with enough force to stun or injure itself?

For some years, we lived near a lake where we were surrounded by birds. Whisky-jacks, blue jays, grackles, grosbeaks, and hummingbirds took turns at our feeders. Loons, with their timorous laughter, and merganser and goldeneye ducks drifted gracefully into our bay.

When one of the birds flew into a window, my tender-hearted husband would fret, hoping it would recover and fly off.

I would think of the hymn we used to sing when I was in Sunday school.

> *God sees the little sparrow fall,*
> *It meets His tender view;*
> *If God so loves the little birds,*
> *I know He loves me, too.*[1]

But instead of comforting me, those words had angered me every time we sang them. If God was really watching over me, then why didn't He protect me from the stranger who had lured me into his house and abused me when I was eight years old? Where was He when the man threatened to kill me if I ever told anyone? Did God not care? Was I not valuable enough to protect?

Church attendance was a regular part of my family's practice, and I gave outward assent to its teaching. But deep inside, my innocence and trust in God were shattered from the day of my secret trauma. God might be watching over the birds, but it didn't appear that He was looking after me.

As I grew older, I came to believe that the world was on the side of the strong and powerful. As far as I could see by the evidence, so was God.

Hot Apple Cider with Cinnamon

I knew from Sunday school that Jesus had said, "Let the little children come to me."² But I wasn't sure what He meant by that.

I also knew that the Bible states that God is on the side of the underdog. Psalm 10 portrays God as one who listens to the cries of the afflicted and defends the fatherless and oppressed. Jesus identified his ministry from the book of Isaiah: to preach good news to the poor, freedom to prisoners, and release to the oppressed.

But how are we to reconcile what we experience in our own lives, and what we read in our newspapers and see on our television screens with what we are told of God's love and compassion? If we judge by the evidence of our eyes alone, we would have to conclude, as many have, that a loving God is not in charge of the universe, that might makes right, and that smart people look after Number One.

For me, the revelation of God's concern began in a counsellor's office. It was the means God chose to break the restraints that had kept me locked in a prison of shame and fear for three decades. Finding the courage to tell my story broke the power of the death threat that had caged me for so long.

The journey to healing was neither swift nor easy, but I sensed that God was with me in it. He led me to safe friends I could share my story with, who prayed for me and with me, and who allowed me to cry my grief out. He showed me that I had built walls to keep Him out. He helped me take down those walls, brick by brick.

At one point in my healing journey, I took our rowboat out into a private marsh on the lake near our home. It was a spring morning, shimmering with heat.

The only sound I heard was the tranquilizing music of the birds from the trees on the shore. As I listened to them, the words of that childhood hymn came back to me.

> God sees the little sparrow fall,
> It meets His tender view;
> If God so loves the little birds,
> I know He loves me, too.

An image came to my mind of an injured bird being lifted from the grass with infinite gentleness by a large pair of hands. The bird was still, sensing that these were the safe hands of a healer. And I knew that I was that wounded bird, and that I was in the hands of a God who did care, and who promised healing.

1. "God Sees the Little Sparrow Fall," Words by Maria Straub, Music by Soloman W. Straub, 1874.

2. Matthew 19:14

3. Psalm 10:17–18

4. Luke 4:18; Isaiah 61:1

From Poison to Passion

Fiction

Grace K. Chik

Sitting in his office, 53-year-old Richard Terca gulped down some of his coffee, then set the large paper cup down hard onto his desk. He shook his head as if he were trying to stay awake.

I must have gone through twenty meetings in the past two weeks and I've barely had time to do a quarter of what I'd set out to complete this month. We'll all have to work like crazy for the next two weeks.

Glancing at the small stack of mail in his in-basket, he picked up a small, light-blue envelope with no return address, and frowned at it. He almost tossed it out, but at the last moment, slit it open and pulled out a card with three yellow flowers in a red pot. On it, in writing, were the words

> *Dear Richard,*
> *I forgive you.*

It was signed with an ink blot in the form of three leaves joined by their stems. Likely done with a rubber stamp.

Richard's face grew red. "What is this? A joke?"

He ripped both card and envelope into pieces and tossed them into his recycling bin.

At that moment, his new assistant, Tancredo Tugend, opened the door and popped his head inside.

"Morning, Mr. Terca. How are you doing?"

Richard looked up. "There was a letter in my inbox with no return address. Where did it come from?"

"It was in the mail, sir."

Richard grunted.

"Do you need me to do anything, sir?"

Richard started to shake his head, then changed his mind. "Get me some fresh coffee and a doughnut."

"Yes, sir."

As Tancredo turned to go, Richard frowned. "Is that a new suit? It looks much better than what you usually wear."

The younger man chuckled. "I bought it yesterday. I'll be right back, sir."

As soon as Tancredo was gone, Richard breathed a sigh of relief. He looked at his recycling bin.

"I hope I won't be seeing any more of your kind."

When Richard came into his office the next morning, the first thing he did was scan his mail. There was a small red envelope with no sender's address.

Rolling his eyes upward, he tore open the envelope and pulled out a white card with a circle of three embossed doves; the tips of their wings touched each other's. Richard opened the card.

> *Dear Richard,*
> *I forgive you.*
> *May your happiness be based*
> *on more than just your success.*

Beneath the words was the same three-leafed plant as on yesterday's letter.

Richard crumpled the card and envelope, threw it onto the floor, and stomped on it.

"What are you trying to do?" he demanded. "Curse me?"

Tancredo burst into Richard's office.

"Tancredo, what are you running away from? A tornado?"

His assistant stepped back. "I'm very sorry to rush in, Mr. Terca. Mr. Jerry came to my desk early this morning. He wanted me to tell you that your evaluation has been moved up to today at ten in his office."

"What?" Richard frowned. "You must be mistaken."

"No, sir, he asked me to tell you as soon as you came in." Tancredo studied Richard. "Are you okay? You look as if you've had a shock."

"I'm fine. Just had a terrible commute this morning."

A few minutes before ten, Richard hurried along a hallway, passing several doors until he came to the corner one, which bore the name "Alaric Jerry. Senior Manager." He knocked.

"Come in!" called a man's voice.

Richard opened the door and walked into an enormous office. Along one wall stood several filing cabinets and a bookcase filled with books. The outer walls had large picture windows, through which morning sunlight brightened the room.

From behind his desk, a stout, balding man in a blue suit looked up and smiled. "Hello, Richard. Thanks for coming today. Sorry for the unexpected change. Have a seat."

Richard sat down on the vacant chair in front of the desk and settled back. "Thanks, Mr. Jerry."

Setting his paperwork aside, Alaric opened a drawer and fished out a red file folder. He adjusted the position of his small desk lamp, then opened the folder and studied it for a moment. Then he looked up. "Tell me about your results, Richard."

Richard settled back. He always enjoyed this part. "Our department amassed the highest amount of profit in the entire company during the last quarter. We exceeded the quarterly goal by quite a bit. We had a lot of positive feedback from conferences where I represented our company as an exhibitor and also where I gave seminars and appeared as a panellist. In addition, my webinars have made our company very well known. We have a lot of new clients who have told us that they were inspired by me to invest with our company."

"Yes, you're making a positive contribution to the company. Tell me about your people."

"I think everything is good. I do sometimes have to push them to meet our quarterly goals."

Alaric appeared to hesitate. He cleared his throat. "Are you aware that for the past few years, your department has had the highest number of employees who have left the company?"

Richard shrugged. "I know some people have left. Their spouses were transferred to another city; they accepted a new position elsewhere; they had a personal reason, such as having to look after a loved one."

"That may be what they told you. However, I asked Human Resources for a report from the exit interviews. Can you guess what they told me?"

Richard frowned.

"Apparently, not wanting to work for you was the main reason most of them gave for leaving."

"What?" Richard's eyes widened in disbelief. "They're lying."

Alaric shook his head. "The report referenced times when you forced them to change their evening plans at the last minute, insisting that they work overtime. You apparently threatened them with job termination and poor work reviews if they didn't comply or if they complained. And you didn't approve overtime pay. Not only that, they said that you often degraded them for the way they looked and worked."

Richard was barely holding in his anger. "They're making excuses for being lazy! They don't care about the company!"

Alaric stood up and paced around the room for several minutes. Finally he faced Richard and said, "Last month I went to Jerry Connory's funeral. He was one of your employees. And he committed suicide. But you weren't at the funeral. And when I talked to several members of your team who were there, they told me that you'd been on him a lot for not doing things right. They told me you seemed to enjoy insulting him, as if you'd chosen him as your personal scapegoat."

"I—I couldn't go to the funeral because I had an important meeting with a client."

"And the insults?"

"If I hadn't pushed him once in a while, he'd never have finished anything. He always had excuses for his delays!"

"How often is 'once in awhile'? Every month?"

Richard hesitated. "No. Something like once or twice a year."

"Well, what about this? Yesterday, I received a call from Valeria Porteric's sister. She said that Valeria has been sunk in depression since leaving the company. She says that you were always telling Valeria that she'd never be good enough for any guy unless she lost weight. Richard, the lady wasn't close to being obese, yet according to her sister, you made her believe she was! Now she's anorexic, and her doctor has her in the hospital being fed through an IV!"

Richard's mouth fell open. "And you think all that is because I said she could stand to lose a few pounds? The woman's crazy. I should sue them both for libel!"

Alaric stood up. "You'll do nothing except improve your relationships with your workers. You're one of our best people in sales and customer relations, and we don't want to lose you. But you need to learn how to treat your employees with more respect."

Richard opened his mouth to complain, but Alaric shook his head. "I'm sending you for sensitivity training. After that, I'll be watching you. If I find out that you aren't behaving in an acceptable manner, you're gone."

Richard sat there in stunned disbelief. No one had ever dared to speak to him this away before. Not even his parents.

Alaric sat down. "I think your job evaluation is over. Thank you for coming. I hope you'll consider what I've said. We value you as an employee, and we want you to value those who work for you in the same way."

Taking his time, Richard rose from his chair and put his pen and pad into his jacket pocket. Nodding at Alaric, Richard walked out of the office without speaking. He was afraid that if he gave even a hint of what he was thinking, he'd be fired on the spot.

He just barely managed to shut the door without slamming it.

As he made his way back into his office, the burning fury inside him grew stronger. He ignored the puzzled reaction of a few colleagues whom he passed by without a word.

When he entered his office, he closed his door without making a sound, sat in his chair, and allowed free reign to his angry thoughts.

When Tancredo knocked on the door 20 minutes later to remind Richard he had a lunch appointment with an important customer, Richard let him know in no uncertain terms that Tancredo was not to bother him when his door was shut.

When he came into his office on the following morning, Richard spotted a lone envelope lying on his desk.

His meeting with Alaric had made him forget all about the anonymous letters! Was this another one of them? No, this envelope had a return address.

He quickly put down his briefcase and his coffee and hung his coat on the hook near the door. Sitting down, he picked up the letter and opened it. He smiled as he read the engraved card.

"You are invited to attend the Gerrard Timberback 25th Annual Charity Dinner on Saturday November 15th, 2014 at 6:30 p.m. You are welcome to bring a guest."

He'd wanted to be invited to this event for years! But, who could he bring? He'd been so focused on his job that he still hadn't found someone he wanted to marry. He knew a few women, of course. Independent ones who didn't want a relationship with strings any more than he did. Ah! He knew just who to take as his guest!

Putting down the card, he picked up his phone and dialled. He waited with a grin.

A woman's voice said, "Hello."

"Hi, Rochelle."

"Is that you, Richard?"

"The one and only."

"What do you want?"

"I've been invited to Gerrard Timberback 25th Annual Charity Dinner, and I'd like you to be my date."

"No way!"

Richard frowned. "Why not? Didn't you enjoy the last fundraising event I took you to?"

"Not at all! As soon we entered the place, you hurried off to be with your friends and left me to fend for myself."

"But we sat together for dinner."

"And that's the only thing we did together! You ignored me the rest of the evening, and when I tried to talk to you, you told me to 'hush up'!"

"I thought you'd be impressed by my association with the important people in the city!"

"You asked me to be your date, not an observer!"

"All right, Ms. Nutcase! If you don't want to go out with me, that's fine!"

"Fine! Goodbye!"

"Goodbye!"

Richard slammed the phone down. Taking a few deep breaths, he picked up the phone again and dialled another number. "Please, let this be a better conversation," he said aloud.

Another woman's voice said, "Hello?"

Richard tried his best to smile. "Hi, Sharon."

There was a moment of silence.

"Sharon, are you still there?"

"What do you want, Richard?"

He hesitated. "I was wondering whether you're free on November fifteenth."

"Really? Don't you remember the last time you asked me out?"

He pretended to think. "I'm not sure what you mean."

"When you came to my house to pick me up, you laughed at my dress. You said that I looked more like a streetwalker than a date. I told you to get lost."

Richard sighed. "All right, what do you want from me?"

"I'm waiting for an apology for the whole thing."

"Okay, I'm sorry for calling you."

"That's not quite the one I'd hoped for, but it's about what I'd expect."

Richard heard a click. The phone went silent.

What's with women these days?

He heard a soft knock on his door. He was ready to yell at Tancredo when the door opened and a brunette woman looked into the room. She held a small yellow envelope. "Mr. Terca, do you have a moment?"

"Daisy, what's up?"

"I was going through my mail and found this letter. It's addressed to you, Mr. Terca. One of the mail sorters must have put it into my in-basket by accident."

He tried to hide his disbelief as he glanced at the envelope. It had no return address.

He forced himself to take it and say, "Thanks, Daisy."

When she was gone, Richard tore open the envelope and pulled out a card with a drawing of two hands holding one another.

Now what?

He opened the card.

> *Dear Richard,*
> *I forgive you.*
> *I hope your personality is*
> *enjoyable to those around you.*

As before, an ink blot in the form of three leaves, joined by their stems, was at the bottom of the small note.

Richard dropped the note, and slammed his right fist into the top of his desk, accidentally knocking over his paper cup of coffee. "Ouch!"

The next morning, Richard found a green envelope on his desk. Without meaning to, he yelled out loud in anger.

A hesitant Tancredo popped his head inside the room. "What's wrong, Mr. Terca?"

Richard lifted his head. "I'm being stalked."

"Stalked? By who?"

Richard held up the envelope. "By whoever's sending these harassing cards."

Hesitantly, the young man entered the room. Taking the envelope, he studied it. "You don't know who sent it?"

"I have no idea. Go ahead and open it."

Tancredo obeyed, then looked at Richard. "Who did you make fun of 40 years ago?"

"What?" Richard seized the card.

> *Dear Richard,*
> *I forgive you for teasing me*
> *40 years ago.*

As before, an ink blot in the form of three leaves, joined by their stems, was used as the signature.

Richard gazed at Tancredo. "Forty years ago? I'd have just started junior high. Whatever I did or said to anyone back then shouldn't matter now."

Tancredo shook his head. "Mr. Terca, I learned in my psychology classes that childhood incidents can have a profound effect on a person's outlook in life."

"But—" At a loss for words, Richard asked, "How can I figure out who this person is? There's no name or anything to give me a clue."

"How many people did you tease back then?"

Richard started to deny teasing anyone, but remembered his talk with Alaric the day before and thought better of it.

Tancredo pointed at the card. "I think that little picture is meant to be a hint. It may be based on either the person's actual name or the name you gave him or her."

Richard studied the inked image on the card. "Nothing comes to mind."

"Do you still have your junior high school yearbook?"

That evening, Richard dug through his bedroom closet and dragged a large blue storage container toward his bed. After opening it, he took out books and small boxes. Finally, he found a soft-covered book, Knights of Coxwell. Yearbook 1974–1975. Sitting on the edge of his bed, he leafed through the book until he came to the students' black-and-white photos. He flipped forward a couple of pages, then stopped and stared at one of the photos on the first row on the left page. It showed a girl who was making no effort to smile. From her neck to her left cheek was an unusual birthmark that looked like three leaves, joined by their stems. Below the photo, her name had been covered with ink, and beneath it, written in blue ink, was "Poison Ivy."

Richard felt his heart sink.

He fished out the last card, opened it, and stared at the inked picture.

"That's poison ivy," he muttered.

He glared at the photo. "Poison Ivy, you sent those cards to me."

From his pants pocket he fished out his cellphone. He punched a phone number and waited for a response.

"Hello?" said a man's voice.

"Hi, Kirk."

The man sounded pleased. "Hey, Richard. How have you been?"

"Fine, Kirk. Listen, I need to tell you something. For the past few days, I've been receiving cards that say 'I forgive you' and—"

"You too, huh?"

Richard sat up straight in surprise. "You've been getting cards from Poison Ivy, too?"

"We're not the only ones. I heard that a lot of our friends got them, too."

Richard sighed. "Do you remember her real name?"

"I do. And I know where she is now."

A few days later, at the Viveca Charles Plastic Surgery and Skin Cancer Treatment Centre, a nurse in blue medical scrubs led Richard into a large room where several patients were lying in beds. A number of medical staff attended to their needs.

The attendant pointed to a blonde woman in a lab coat whose back was facing them. "She's over there, sir."

"Thank you, miss," Richard said.

Hesitantly, he approached the blonde woman, stopping a foot behind her.

"Dr. Passion Elliot," he said.

When the woman turned to him, his eyes widened in amazement at the sight of her birthmark. It was still there, but very faint. Only an echo of what it once had been.

"Richard, it's good to see you. How did you find me?"

"Kirk Farland was one of your patients."

She nodded. "He had a very serious melanoma, but he received a clean bill of health a month ago."

"How did you locate me?" Richard asked.

"Why don't we talk in private?" Smiling, she took his hand and led him into an empty room. She closed the door. "I asked Kirk if he knew where you were. He gave me one of your business cards."

"Passion, why did you send those cards?"

She put her head to one side. "I don't suppose you'll understand, but I needed to be fully free."

He was puzzled. "Free? From what?"

"From the pain of what had happened to me."

"You mean your birth mark?"

"Well, I had to accept that, too. And I did. Even when it became possible to remove it through plastic surgery, I wanted to leave a little of it there. So I never forgot."

"You look—beautiful."

"Thank you."

"If it wasn't the birth mark, what did you need to be free from?"

"From what you and your friends did to hurt me."

Richard hung his head.

"When I met you in junior high, at first I liked you a lot. But from the day you and your friends began to laugh at me and called me 'Poison Ivy' because of my birthmark, I battled depression. That name made me feel as if I were untouchable, unapproachable, and unlovable.

"Whenever we passed by in hallways, you jeered at me and pretended to itch. Even though the teachers and the principal told you to stop, you continued to taunt me privately."

Richard tried not to shake at the memory. "I know," he whispered.

She sighed. "I was fortunate because my parents decided they didn't like the house we were renting and they found another one, and so I changed schools. It was better there, but I mostly kept to myself because my self-esteem was still fragile.

"My real name is Passion, and it fits me well. I'm very passionate about the well-being of others. That's why I became a plastic surgeon and counsellor. I want to see people healed, both inside and out. And over the years, I've had a good life, and I know I've helped many people.

"But every once in a while, my mind would go back to those days when you boys teased me. Whenever that happened, it would take me a while to regain my focus. There were even nights when I couldn't sleep.

"I tried to push those memories out of my mind, but I couldn't, because each time they came back, they seemed stronger than before. Worse than a nightmare, even. But that no longer happens."

"When did you start feeling better?"

"After I told God how much being called Poison Ivy had hurt me, and felt the pain all over again, and forgave God for allowing it to happen. And then forgive you—each one of you—for every single unkind thing you said or did. After I did that, I was free from the pain of the memories."

"Why did you send the cards?"

"Because I wanted you to know I had forgiven you, and I wanted God to bless you."

Richard thought for a moment. "What can I do to make it up to you?"

"Nothing. When I forgave you and everyone else to whom I sent the cards, I let go of the hurt I'd experienced over the years." She smiled. "I'm free. But I wanted to make sure you were free, too."

He walked to the window and took a deep breath. He felt as if a steam roller had just driven over him. His mind was going in crazy circles.

At last, he said, "I have a confession to make. When I first saw you, back in junior high, I thought you were beautiful. I wanted to ask you out. But my friends told me that I would be an embarrassment to them if we were to become a couple. When they started teasing you because of your birthmark and calling you 'Poison Ivy,' I joined in because I didn't want to lose my friends. But even though we acted tough and mean, I always felt guilty. I even went over to your house to apologize to you in secrecy, but I found out you'd moved the day before."

"Really?" she said.

His back still to her, he nodded.

"I didn't want my friends to think I was a wimp. So we kept on making a lot of our schoolmates' lives miserable. But I'm so sorry for doing that. And—and the truth is, I've just this moment realized that I've continued that behaviour toward my employees and the women I've dated. I'm the real Poison Ivy."

There was a long silence.

Richard turned to face Passion. "You wouldn't have more of those cards you used, would you? I might need to send some out. Except I need to ask for forgiveness instead of offering it."

She giggled. "I'd be happy to give you as many cards as you need."

A thought came into his mind. "Passion, Kirk said you aren't married. Would you by any chance be free on November fifteenth?"

"My husband died a number of years ago." Pulling a Blackberry from her pocket, she checked it before saying, "Yes, I'm free that night."

"Would you like to go out with me?"

She thought for a moment, then nodded. "Yes, I believe I would."

Richard smiled. "Thank you. You won't regret giving me another chance. I promise."

> "The tongue that brings healing is a tree of life, but a
> deceitful tongue crushes the spirit."
> —Proverbs 15:4

Reconciliation

Janet Sketchley

Do you have a minute?
    It's important.
I feel I need to ask
    your forgiveness.

Your eyebrows mime surprise.
    "What's to forgive?"
But your smile thins,
    your eyes skirt mine.

I don't meet your fondest
    expectations,
Don't always live my life
    the way you'd choose.

Your mute disapproval
    is crushing me.
There's no way to please you
    the way I am.

But God is making me
    more like His Son.
I know He's in you, too.
    Could we make peace?

Would you please forgive me
    for being me?
As I'm forgiving you
    for being you.

The Handshake

Nonfiction

Beverlee Wamboldt

One spring morning in 1930 on a farm in rural Nova Scotia, 16-year-old Ned finished hitching his father's two big draft horses, Jim and Bill, to the wagon. He hopped up on the seat and gave the horses a light tap on their backs with the reins to urge them forward. They trotted along the tree-lined lane to the main road, where Ned pulled the reins gently to the right. Jim and Bill took their cue, turned right, and headed in the direction of Caledonia and the feed store, ten miles ahead.

Ned relaxed the reins and let the horses choose their own pace. Since they knew this path meant a light load and fresh oats at the feed store, they picked up speed, and clouds of dust poured out around the wagon wheels as they moved quickly along the gravel road. This promised to be an easy day for both the horses and Ned. Most days required heavy work and few treats.

As was the custom in the rural areas at that time, if the families needed extra money, young boys went into the workforce early to help out. Ned had been just 11 years old when he had taken Jim and Bill into the woods camp deep in the forest of North Queens to work. They'd left home in the fall of the year and returned to the farm in the spring.

Each morning that winter, he'd fed the horses, harnessed them, and hitched them to one of the sleds in the lumber yard before he headed out to the woodlot, where the choppers cut down and limbed the trees. Ned and another young fellow loaded the sled and hauled the logs to the sawmill three miles away. On a good day, they made four or five trips. At day's end, it was Ned's chore to groom, feed, and settle the horses in their stalls. Only then could he eat his supper and put his head down on his hard cot for the night. It was a long, demanding day's work for a man, let alone a young boy.

During that winter, when he'd had time to dream of better things, Ned set a goal for himself. He would save any money he earned to buy something he'd always wanted.

One cold morning on his way to the stable, his eye caught an extra bright glint in the snow. Upon further investigation he discovered an empty "tobaccie" can. It was flat and rectangular, small enough to fit in his shirt pocket. Just what he needed to hold his savings! He could visualize his paper money folded neatly and tucked inside the little can. Dad would need the bulk of the money earned to pay farm expenses, but surely at the end of the winter, Ned would have some money to put in the can.

But by that winter's end, with the heavy work behind him and Dad's farm expenses paid, Ned had only a few coins in his tobaccie can. Plus he had grown taller and more muscular. Since he was now three inches taller than his older brother Joe, and 20 pounds heavier, there was no way he could continue to wear Joe's hand-me-downs. He needed new clothes and work boots. How his feet had grown over the winter!

Dad promised him a young piglet when the next litter arrived. Ned planned to fatten the little fellow quickly, sell him, and use the proceeds to buy the clothes he needed. Even with that money, buying new clothes would clean out his savings.

He was disappointed, but he vowed to persevere.

One year went by and then another and another. Ned managed to find part-time work on neighbouring farms and save a little money, but there were more coins than paper money in the tobaccie can. And it was paper money he needed to build up his savings.

Now, five years later, the tobaccie can was full. As the horses came nearer to town, Ned patted the old can in his shirt pocket. It held his precious treasure—$40 in paper bills. On his last trip to the feed store, he'd gone to the bank and changed his remaining coins into paper money.

He flipped open the top of the can and scrunched the money between his fingers. It crackled and sent a thrill of joy up his spine.

Hot Apple Cider with Cinnamon

Not being a young fellow to sing, and never having mastered the art of whistling, Ned didn't display his joy outwardly. However, his heart sang and he thought it might even whistle from time to time.

His light-hearted mood even seemed to affect old Jim and Bill as they neared town and the feed store.

Ned's first duty when he arrived in town was to visit the dry goods store. Before he'd left home, Mother had carefully tied four wicker baskets packed with jars of maple syrup to the wagon floor. Each spring, she sold her maple syrup to the shopkeeper and used the money to buy fabric, often for a new dress.

Ned had helped Mother and his sisters tap the trees along the lane and collect the sap. They then boiled it down into beautiful amber maple syrup. However, the cold nights and warm days that produced the most syrup had been scarce this spring, and the sap hadn't run as freely as in other years. It bothered Ned that his mother might not have enough money to carry out her plan. On the rare occasions when he'd been in the store with her, he'd noticed that when she ran her hand over the bolts of cloth, a dreamy expression would cross her gentle face. He knew she'd already picked out the paper pattern for her dress and she had planned to get the fabric next time she was in town.

After depositing the maple syrup at the dry goods store and receiving payment, Ned went to the feed store. He placed his order, and the storekeeper laid out the bags of feed by the outer door. Ned signed the credit slip and hurried outside where he hustled Jim and Bill around to the back. While they munched on fresh oats, he loaded the wagon.

The feed store was always Ned's last stop before he started back home, but not today. He had to take care of one more errand—a very important errand.

He walked across the lane to Mr. McGuire's garage.

When he entered the building, Mr. McGuire greeted him with a smile. "Hello there, Ned. How're you doing today? Fine day, it is."

Ned passed his own greeting along to Mr. McGuire and then got down to business. "Mr. McGuire," he said, "I'd like you to order me a bicycle from your Eaton's catalogue. I got the money for it right here." He patted his shirt pocket proudly.

"Well, that's great, Ned. I can order it for you. It'll take about a month to arrive. Has to come all the way from Moncton on the train. Probably cost you between thirty-five and forty dollars, including delivery costs. No need to pay me now, though. It's best to wait until it's here. Come in next month when you come to town."

His business finished, Ned strutted back to where old Jim and Bill were waiting, turned the team around, and headed back to the farm.

While he waited for that month to pass, Ned dreamed of his new bicycle and quietly counted the days until he could complete his purchase.

But one evening toward the end of the month, as Ned finished his barn chores, Dad called him aside.

He looked grim, worried.

"Dollars are scarce, Ned," he said. "I can't pay all my bills this month. Can you help me out? I hate to ask you. I know you've been saving your money for something special. But I'm really in a jam. Mother has already offered to help, and you know what that means. She won't be able to buy her new dress fabric."

Ned's heart sank into his boots. He knew his dad wouldn't ask for money unless he was desperate. His dad had fed him and put a roof over his head for more than 16 years. And his mother worked hard—he didn't want her to be disappointed. Her needs were always close to Ned's heart. He knew he had no choice but to help out. That's what families did—helped one another.

Ned looked down and scuffed a toe in the hay scattered haphazardly across the threshing floor. "I've got forty dollars. You can have it. Do you think there'll be enough left over after your bills are paid to help Mother buy her cotton?"

Two days later, Ned urged Jim and Bill along the tree-lined driveway, on their way to the feed store. He still had his tobaccie can in his breast pocket and the money was in it, but his plans had changed.

Ned did his duty at the feed store, and the storekeeper scribbled "Paid in Full" across the invoice. There was three dollars left over. Ned was determined that it would go toward Mother's cotton.

He knew he should have felt good after paying off what his dad owed at the feed store, but he didn't. His heart was heavy as he shuffled across the path to Mr. McGuire's garage. The door was open and, as he walked inside, the first thing he saw was a shiny, black bicycle standing against the far wall. My, but it looked grand!

Mr. McGuire greeted him with a hearty laugh. "There she is, Ned. Just waiting for you to hop on and take her for a spin."

Ned bowed his head. "I can't take her home with me, Mr. McGuire. I don't have the money to pay for her. Dad fell short of funds and needed my money. I'm really sorry, sir."

Tears stung his eyelids and there was a big lump in the base of his throat. He couldn't cry in front of Mr. McGuire. It wouldn't be a manly thing to do.

Keeping his head down, Ned slowly turned toward the door. He'd leave quickly before Mr. McGuire got angry with him for falling short on his end of the deal. But before Ned reached the door, a big hand settled gently on his shoulder, turned him around, and brought him face to face with Mr. McGuire.

"Take the bicycle home with you, Ned. I'll give you credit. Your dad's a well-respected farmer around these parts and I believe you're an honest young man. You can pay me whatever you have when you come to town to buy feed each month."

"But, Mr. McGuire, I don't earn much. It took me almost five years to save enough to buy the bicycle in the first place. It doesn't seem right to make you wait for your money."

"Take the bicycle, young man." Mr. McGuire extended his hand. Slowly, Ned reached out and gripped it in as firm a handshake as he could muster. His knees were weak, but his heart was strong.

"It's a deal, Ned," Mr. McGuire said. "Your handshake is your word."

During the summer months, Ned made regular but meagre payments to Mr. McGuire. He worried he might never pay off his debt. Come fall, the apple crop was good and he made slightly better progress. Then a miracle happened—he was offered a full-time job on a nearby farm. Before winter's end, he had paid Mr. McGuire in full. More importantly, he had kept his word.

And that's how young Ned got his first bicycle.

Several years later, in the spring of 1934, Ned met a pretty young girl named Flora, who was visiting her sister on the farm adjacent to Ned's. It didn't take long before the young man's heart turned to romance.

The summer flew by and it was soon time for Flora to return to her family, approximately 35 miles away—what was considered a long-distance romance back in the '30s. Since Ned wanted to continue his courtship, and his father's horses weren't available for such long treks, he had two choices—feet or bicycle. He chose his bicycle.

Ned and Flora (my parents) were married four years later in the United Baptist Parsonage in Caledonia, Nova Scotia, and were together for 64 years.

Hot Apple Cider with Cinnamon

Mary's Dream

Fiction

N. J. Lindquist

It was raining. You might have said "like cats and dogs" if you were inclined to use clichés. Mary Rogers was not so inclined. Furthermore, it occurred to her that there were 364 other days in the year for it to rain, and the choice of this day was sadly unforgivable.

Crouched on her knees on the small window seat at one end of the upstairs hallway, Mary willed the rain to stop. She shut her eyes and demanded that the rain stop. But when she reopened her eyes, the dismal scene remained the same.

Rain streamed out of the skies, dripping from the tall elms in the front yard. Puddles grew until they burst forth to join with other puddles to form one vast, shallow river of flowing water. The muddy water glistened with rainbows of oil from the many cars that daily passed by the house where Mary had lived since birth.

"Mary, you need to get up and moving!" Her older sister, Ellen, who was to be matron of honour, bustled down from the attic, her arms filled with assorted linens. "You've got to get dressed. The photographer will be here in less than an hour!"

"I know," Mary said vaguely. "I was just watching the rain. Isn't it a bad omen or something?"

"Of course not! I've no time for that nonsense. Superstitions are for ignorant people who don't know better!"

"I guess," Mary said, not moving from her perch.

"Get a move on! You don't want to keep everyone waiting at the church, do you?"

"No." Mary turned and set her feet on the floor. "Where's Mom?"

"Still at the hairdresser's. She'll be back soon, though. I'm just going to put these in the kitchen. Mom wants them for the tables the gifts will be put on. Now, hurry! I've got to get Dad out of whatever book he's reading so he'll be dressed."

Mary slowly stood and stretched. Her dad told her she was like a contented cat—slow-moving and lazy, yet graceful. He said she never seemed to get excited, the way Ellen and their mother did. But shouldn't she be excited now? After all, today was her wedding day. Hadn't she looked forward to it for months? After all the planning she'd done (with a lot of help from her mom and sister, of course), shouldn't she be excited instead of just annoyed with the rain?

She wondered how Rob was doing. He was pretty laid back himself. He would take this wedding in stride just as he did everything else. He wouldn't even be upset if she was late.

She went up on her toes and hummed the wedding march. But her stomach remained calm and unexcited.

Maybe it was the rain's fault. She'd read that weather could do things to you—sunshine making you happy and rain making you depressed. Well, if any weather could make one depressed, this downpour of rain ought to do it! Tears filled her eyes. It wasn't fair for this to happen on her wedding day!

She turned back and stared out of the window, knowing she was being foolish and that she'd have to rush to get ready, but still not moving.

Ellen came halfway up the stairs to yell at her. "Mary, for goodness sake, hurry up! Stop daydreaming!"

Idly, Mary wondered how many times in her life she'd heard those words. A million? Probably more.

After a last, beseeching look out the window, she headed for her bedroom. But once there, she flopped onto her back on the bed. The gown was hanging on the hook behind her door. It was a beautiful dress. Ellen had teased her about how fancy it was.

It wasn't her, of course. She was just Mary, plain and ordinary. This dress—all satin and embroidered flowers and yards and yards of lace—belonged to someone else. A fairy-tale princess, not plain Mary Rogers.

She put up her hand and touched the back of her head. Yes, the two silver combs that held her mousy brown hair in a svelte braid were still there. She had no idea how the hairdresser had worked his magic. Or what the woman who did her makeup had

  Hot Apple Cider with Cinnamon

done to her face. She hadn't recognized the girl who stared out of the mirror at her when they were finished. The girl had seemed sophisticated and rather attractive. Actually, quite attractive. Not like plain Mary Rogers at all.

Mary Rogers wore pants or skirts with blouses and sweaters and sensible shoes, and she kept her hair long and free so it would help her hide from the world—help her keep her thoughts separated from the ordinariness of her day-to-day life. Up in the morning and then off to work in the factory, where she could lose herself among the rows and rows of workers. Then home to eat supper and spend the evening curled up with a good book. Sneaking off to her room to scribble down her crazy ideas before going to bed.

Dates were rare. "You refuse to try," her mom and Ellen said.

But it wasn't that. She simply didn't know how. Oh, she'd read some of the flashy magazines that told you how to get a man by dieting, buying sexy clothes, going where men were, learning about sports, and all the myriad other tips that successful women offered to their poorer sisters. Most of the things she couldn't have done. The others she wouldn't do.

And then Rob had entered her life. Ellen's husband Tom worked with Rob at the garage, and one night Tom brought Rob home for a drink. Rob was single, which made him an instant success in Ellen's eyes. She encouraged him to come again. And later on he met the rest of the family. Her mother and dad liked him, so why shouldn't Mary like him, too?

He liked Mary. He teased her about being shy and made her laugh with his silly jokes.

Then one day he told her it was time she thought about getting married and having a home of her own. And she said, "Yes." Automatically. Knowing everyone would be pleased. Not knowing, really, what else she could do. If she didn't marry Rob, wouldn't she just drift into nothingness?

It had seemed so odd that anyone actually wanted to marry her. Almost too good to believe.

Mary rolled off the bed, walked over to the door, and took the dress off its hanger. Hastily, she undid the fastenings, slipped off her shapeless sweat suit, and stepped into the dress. When it was fastened, and not before, she looked into the mirror on her wall. Annoyed, she realized she could see only from her waist up.

There was a full-length mirror in her parents' room. Willing her mother not to be there, she ran lightly down the hall and through the end door. As she entered the room, she was met by a girl dressed in white—a beautiful girl in a beautiful dress. Cinderella. Ready for the ball!

She floated up close, staring, not at the dress, but at the face of the girl wearing it. Who was this beautiful person who had apparently stolen her mind?

For several long minutes she stared. Then she heard voices coming up the stairs—her mom and Ellen.

Like a wraith, she slipped back to her own room and locked the door. She needed to be alone now, to study this person who was her but wasn't her.

What had happened? What force had overtaken her, changing her from caterpillar to butterfly?

Was it Rob? The fact that someone actually wanted to marry her? Or was it something else? Something within?

She shook her head, weary of her thoughts, and went over to the window.

Rain continued to cascade from the skies.

But the rain no longer depressed her.

She stepped back and did a pirouette. She remembered movies with ladies in ball gowns doing the minuet, and she began to dance, gracefully, joyously, now holding the fingertips of her phantom partner, now flirting coquettishly with her fan.

Someone tried to open the door and found it locked. "Mary!" her mother's voice called. "Are you dressed? You must hurry!"

The dancing stopped and Mary hurried to her mirror. She saw the beautiful stranger there, eyes glowing, cheeks pink, lips parted in a delightful smile. She felt a small bubble of joy in her heart.

"Mary, stop daydreaming and open this door!"

As she heard her mother's words, Mary saw another girl. Plain Mary working at her job, trying not to bother anyone else because… because she wasn't important enough for others to have to worry about. Plain Mary, letting her mother and Ellen have their way because it wasn't worth the argument. Plain Mary, agreeing to marry Rob because… because it was easier than not marrying Rob.

"Mary!" Her mother's voice was high-pitched with urgency. "I know you're in there! Open this door! You're going to ruin everything!"

"Don't be so selfish!" Ellen shouted.

"Selfish?" Mary whispered. "Is it selfish to want to know this strange girl who is apparently part of me? To want to let this girl live?"

Suddenly, she was fully alive to the choice she must make. If she opened the door and went to the church and married Rob, that was the end. She would always be plain Mary.

But she wanted to get to know this new, beautiful Mary. This Mary who laughed at the rain and exulted, like the newborn butterfly she was, in life itself.

For the twentieth time, she remembered the sermon from four weeks ago. How we can't really love others as they deserve to be loved unless we're first able to love ourselves. The sermon had bothered her ever since, like a pebble in the bottom of a shoe. She'd never loved herself. So how could she ever hope to love Rob?

But this new Mary she saw in the mirror—she might be able to love this Mary. If she had the chance.

One part of her mind was aware of the strident voices at the door alternately threatening and pleading. The other part made her take off the dress and rummage in her closet for a decent pair of slacks and a blouse. When dressed, she glanced around the room. Was there anything here that belonged to the new Mary? A loving glance at a small ornament her dad had given her for her birthday. It was a ballerina, dainty and filled with joy. Yes, Mary wanted that. And the Japanese box made of cherry wood that her dad had given her years ago—the one with the delicate bonsai tree engraved in its wood. Several of her favourite books.

She found a suitcase and quickly put the items inside, wrapped in some of her underclothes. She chose a skirt, some jeans, a dress, a few tops and a blouse, a sweater, a pair of slippers, shoes, a few odds and ends. Finally, she stood on a chair to reach onto the back of the shelf in her closet and brought out a box that had once held winter boots, but now held many small notebooks filled with her scribblings. She scattered the notebooks throughout the suitcase, and then hid the suitcase in the back of her closet. She took a deep breath and opened the door.

"What on earth do you think you're doing, young lady?" Her mother's furious voice exploded in her ears.

Ellen shouted in horror. "You aren't even dressed!"

"Where's Dad?" Mary asked quietly.

Taken by surprise, her mother answered. "In the basement. No doubt reading a book. I suppose that's what you've been doing, too. Well, you march right back in there and get dressed!"

Mary slipped out of her room. "I need to talk to Dad about something first."

Ignoring her words, they urged her again to get dressed, but Mary eluded them and ran quickly down the two flights of stairs to her father's small basement office.

"Dad!" she said breathlessly, shutting the door behind her. "The money you were going to give us for a wedding present! Will you give it to me?"

Her father looked up from his book and stared at her. "The what?"

"The money. You were giving us money to buy furniture. Will you give it to me instead?"

"But—what are you doing? I don't understand!"

"I'm running away, Dad. Will you help?"

"Will I...? Then you aren't going to marry Rob?"

"No. I can't. I have to—to find out who I really am first. Maybe someday. Who knows? But not now. Oh, please, will you help me? They'll be coming soon to get me, to make me go through with it. I don't know if I can be strong. Please hurry."

He was pulling his chequebook from his desk drawer before she finished. His hand shook while he wrote. As he handed the paper to her, he said, "Cash it immediately and get a new account in a different bank."

"Dad?" she hesitated.

"Go quickly, Mary. And may all your dreams come true."

She thrust the cheque into her pocket and edged past her mother and sister, who had indeed come to find her. "Yes, I'm going to my room," she said.

"Well, hurry up!" Ellen said. "You don't want to keep Rob waiting or he might change his mind!"

Mary tore up the stairs to her bedroom.

Her mother's voice trailed up the stairs like Tinkerbell might have followed Peter. "That girl has been nothing but a millstone around my neck since she was born. Always daydreaming. Not a practical bone in her body."

Mary took a last, loving glance at the fairy-tale wedding dress. She'd have liked to take it with her, but there was no room. Maybe someday she'd have another one like it. One she'd chosen herself.

Remembering the cheque in her pocket, she pulled it out and absently glanced at it, then stared. Instead of the one thousand dollars her dad had promised as a wedding gift, this cheque said five thousand! Joy filled her as she recognized her father's love and confidence in her. After placing the cheque in her wallet, she took the suitcase out of the closet. Picking up her purse, she took a deep breath before opening her door a crack.

It sounded as though her mother and sister were in the kitchen. They were complaining about her.

Knowing they would be coming after her any second, she crept down the stairs and eased out the front door.

On the porch, she paused for a moment, dismayed. Rain thundered onto the roof and she had neither hat nor coat. But that couldn't stop her.

Her sneakers were drenched within five feet of the porch. As the rain soaked her hair, the silver combs loosened. She stopped to put them safely in her pocket. Her flowing hair clung to her head in wet ringlets.

A tremor of joy went through her body. The old Mary would have gone home by now—no, would never have begun this journey. But the new Mary exulted in simply being alive.

She skipped down the street, taking deep gulps of the fresh, clean air.

No more need to daydream. The butterfly was in flight.

A Baby Named Hope

Nonfiction

Carmen Wittmeier

The Consult Room next to Diagnostic Imaging on the second floor of the hospital in Calgary, Alberta, had a black recliner, three wooden chairs, and a small table with a box of tissues sitting on it. The cardboard box's cheerful goldfish pattern did nothing to offset the starkness of the small room, or to quell the nerves of those confined within it.

To one-year-old Sadie Koslowski, that box of tissue was irresistible. She'd been in the ultrasound clinic for four whole hours. She'd seen the image of her yet-to-be-born sibling wriggling on the screen. She'd tugged on machine cords, eaten the crackers a nurse used to distract her, and amused herself with stickers and the few toys she'd found in the waiting room. Now she wanted to go home. She looked over at her daddy, who was sitting quietly, and her mommy, who was wiping at the water that kept dripping from her eyes, and sighed. No one seemed to be going anywhere. So Sadie tore into that box of tissues.

Amy Koslowski stared at the box, wishing that the tissue it contained was truly absorbent. The 27-year-old Calgary mother had shed enough tears to give those cardboard fish a place to swim.

The visit had started out as a routine ultrasound for an ordinary pregnancy, Amy's second. As Amy held her husband, Shawn's, hand, and a wriggling Sadie sat in Shawn's lap, the technician had cheerfully speculated that their baby was a girl, although at 19 weeks it was a little too early to tell for certain.

The baby's spine, brain, liver, and kidneys appeared to be flawless. When the technician began examining the heart, however, she lapsed into silence. She spent nearly an hour scanning the baby's chest; but no matter what position she guided Amy into, her puzzled scowl remained. Then, after hastily placing a wad of paper towels into Amy's hand so that she could wipe the cold jelly from

  Hot Apple Cider with Cinnamon

her bare belly, she'd asked the family to wait in the Consult Room and left abruptly, fumbling with an excuse.

Only one month earlier Amy and her extended family had rented a bungalow on the tropical island of Kauai. One afternoon, while Sadie napped nearby, Amy had embraced the quiet. Relaxing on her bed, she'd opened her heart to God.

As her mind drifted, she'd thought about how happy she was, and how she had everything she could possibly want. Although her family was spread across Australia, the United States, and Canada, her parents and siblings were tightly bound.

She also had a wonderful husband and a growing family. Amy had come to know Shawn when they were engaged in ministry together in Maui, and with time and persistence, he'd not only become her closest friend but her life companion. They'd settled in Calgary and purchased a home that had become a central meeting place for the friends they easily attracted. When their daughter Sadie arrived, as if by chance, her charming ways made parenting a breeze. Life was simple—almost too easy.

I've chosen God through all of this, Amy had realized that day. *But it's been easy. I've never actually* needed *Him to get through any difficulty.*

An inexplicable fear had gripped her then. But her uneasiness made no sense. She was surrounded by beaches and trees and sunlight and the warmth of those she loved most.

Is something going to happen? Is He preparing me?

Now, contained in the Consult Room, Amy and Shawn watched a man enter the room. He was middle-aged, with some wisps of white hair beginning to show, and a pair of glasses that gave him a scholarly air.

He introduced himself as a neonatalist, smiled at the scattered tissues, and made a joke as Sadie stared up at him from the floor. Then, sitting down heavily, he pulled out a clipboard. On a piece of paper, he sketched something that looked like an apple. With broad, rough strokes, he crossed out the left portion of what Amy suddenly recognized was a heart.

"Your baby is basically missing the left half of its heart," he said. "This is a condition known as hypoplastic left heart syndrome, or HLHS. If your baby should survive the pregnancy, it would require immediate open-heart surgery. If it survived that, it would require two more surgeries by age five."

He stood up. "I'm sorry to have ruined your lives with this news." He edged toward the door. "The choice of what to do next is yours, of course. But if you care about your marriage, and your daughter here, you'll do the humane thing and end the pregnancy. There's no hope here."

No hope here.

As Amy and Shawn sat in stunned silence, unable to move, a second doctor, this time a cardiologist, entered the Consult Room and pulled up a wooden chair. Leaning forward, she smiled at Shawn and then looked Amy directly in the eyes before reaching out to touch her quivering shoulder. She explained that HLHS was a rare and serious congenital heart condition, and that the left side of their baby's heart was too underdeveloped to provide adequate blood flow to the body. Such babies, she said, faced a daunting set of challenges: three gruelling surgeries followed by the ongoing risk of heart failure and even the need for a transplant. Many HLHS babies had lower-than-average IQs. Contact sports were out of the question.

Then the doctor said the words that Amy and Shawn desperately wanted to hear. "Some make it. For whatever reason, they thrive. They fight through those early years. They survive adolescence. They take ballet, and go to college. One of my patients is now 23 years old. You never know what's going to happen," she said. "Don't give up hope just yet."

On November 18, 2011, two days after the ultrasound, Amy sat in front of her laptop. She was exhausted—bone-tired and emotionally depleted, but she knew that her family needed prayer and support.

Hot Apple Cider with Cinnamon

She had decided that a blog would be the easiest way to update everyone, and to answer the questions of the dozens of people she knew would want to support them through this ordeal.

"Our baby has been diagnosed with HLHS," she wrote. "We believe that God is in control and will use our situation to glorify His name. As we take this journey, we invite you to join us on our knees and pray for a mended heart." Believing that God would perform a miracle on her unborn child, she titled the blog, "Mending Hearts and Bending Knees."[1]

Amy placed her hands on the small bump of her belly and wept. She knew there would be more than one heart in need of God's mending.

Three days later, a follow-up ultrasound confirmed that Amy was, indeed, carrying a little girl.

Amy and Shawn knew that their baby would need anything they could give her to help face the challenges that awaited, so on that chilly winter day, "Hope" received her name.

The latest ultrasound revealed that although Hope had a tiny left ventricle, it pumped no blood whatsoever. While she'd have major surgery only three to seven days after birth, and another surgery four months later, the defect was so significant that Hope would likely need a new heart as a teenager. She'd never become a soccer player like her dad; nor could she ever risk carrying a baby of her own. So many of her parents' dreams for her were already crushed, and Hope had yet to take her first breath.

Still, as if working at a jigsaw puzzle that just didn't seem to fit together, Shawn and Amy began to move the pieces around—to create a new picture. Maybe Hope would prefer Keds to cleats. Maybe she'd be content to nestle next to her mom on the couch, bonding over a shared television drama. Shawn pictured his radiant daughter on her wedding day, clutching the arm of a groom so taken with her that it didn't matter one iota that his bride couldn't bear his children. Amy thought they'd adopt. Hope's little ones would feel such love that they'd never guess their Mommy had only half a heart.

As her parents' dreams for her continued to grow and change, so did Hope. And on a Sunday morning in mid-December, Amy felt her daughter kicking for the first time.

Knowing they might never come home with this baby in their arms, Amy prepared a tiny room in their house for her. She scrubbed every inch of the hardwood floor. She wiped down the white crib, the matching dresser, the bookcases. She carefully arranged the pink and white quilt, lovingly stitched by Shawn's mother, on the chocolate brown recliner. Then she slumped into the recliner, placed her hands on her swollen belly, and prayed for the sweet baby girl within her.

Hope nestled safe within her mother's womb. But Amy knew that when Hope entered the world, she'd know pain for the first time.

Longing to meet their baby, but dreading the obstacles ahead, the family prepared to relocate to Edmonton. They would stay at the Ronald McDonald House—thrilling news—but it wouldn't be home. Hope knew nothing of her parents' anguish, or their joy when she moved into position, making a natural birth possible. Soon after, Amy, Shawn, and Sadie, accompanied by Amy's mother, left Calgary for Edmonton to await her arrival.

Sadie was already in bed the evening Amy felt some cramping. Only two days before, she'd been duped by a full bladder into believing her water had broken, so it was with some embarrassment that she informed her mother that it might really be labour this time. To be safe, the two left for the hospital, leaving Shawn to wait for the aunt and uncle entrusted to care for Sadie.

Since she wasn't in significant pain, Amy soon begged her mother to take her back to the Ronald McDonald house. As they stood up to leave, however, Amy's name was called. Reluctantly, she allowed herself to be guided to an examination room.

Minutes later, the first contraction hit—a seven-minute doozy. She was in labour. The next morning, as the neonatal and cardiology teams hovered nearby, and with Shawn at her side, Amy began to push. On April 4, 2012, at 10:08 a.m., Hope Taylor Koslowski drew her first breath.

Amy was given only seconds to gaze at her miracle baby before Hope was whisked into another room, her father and grandmother following closely. Left behind, Amy received stitches and an uninspired meal of tuna and pretzels.

The tug she felt for her broken baby was relentless. But it was a full hour before she could finally cradle Hope in her arms for a few minutes.

Amy was shocked to discover that her fragile newborn weighed more than six pounds. Hope was lovely, with a widow's peak and the long fingers of a musician. Her baby toes curled under, just like her sister's. Just like her dad's.

Amy cried as they wheeled her baby away in an incubator that looked, to her, like a coffin on wheels. While Hope left in an ambulance for the Stollery Children's Hospital, Amy was wheeled down to Postpartum. However, within 45 minutes, and against the advice of staff, Amy checked herself out and her mother drove her to the Children's Hospital to rejoin Shawn, who had trailed behind the ambulance.

Amy spent the first day of Hope's life at her side.

The next few weeks were a roller coaster of emotions. Within the first days of Hope's life, Shawn and Amy were not only forced to contend with a car breakdown and a spring snowstorm but a raging infection that delayed their newborn's surgery. Shortly after Hope's tiny chest was finally opened for the gruelling eight-hour operation, Amy fell ill with two brutal infections.

The family could do nothing but try to survive the challenges each day brought.

During the Koslowski's initial stay in Edmonton, Shawn was able to return to his job at Interpipeline, working remotely and spending any spare time he had at the hospital. Nearly a month would pass before the family could return home to Calgary, where their long hours would now be spent at the Alberta Children's Hospital.

All the while, Sadie was shuffled between Amy's mother and other relatives and friends.

Amy, sleeping fitfully at night and trapped by cords and monitors within the four walls of Hope's hospital room by day, started to feel a profound isolation. Nothing had prepared her for the impact of Hope's suffering.

On one occasion, it took six people 14 attempts to put in an IV as her baby cried soundlessly. Another time, she was unable to console Hope as she screeched and thrashed about, trying to evade the medical staff who laboured over her tiny body.

Amy knew that the road to her daughter's second surgery would be long. And yet she wrote in her blog, "When I sit and look into her eyes, I can't help but believe that God never makes mistakes."

At first, Amy couldn't bear to have anyone but herself, her husband, and her mother care for Hope. Then, after Hope came home when she was nearly two months old, the reality of her overwhelming needs set in, and Amy and Shawn decided to allow a night nurse to administer medication, nourishment, and love while they slept nearby.

When Hope's condition deteriorated six weeks later, and she was moved back to the Alberta Children's Hospital, the nurse they had hired offered to continue caring for Hope free of charge. She organized an army of volunteers, for an army was needed.

They were called the "Hope Cuddlers." Like a colony of bees surrounding a Queen, they served baby Hope with a regimented order and a fierce loyalty.

Amy could reconnect with Shawn and Sadie over supper, knowing that a volunteer would be cuddling her baby. Another volunteer would begin the night shift, watching over Hope as she drifted off, cradling the tiny infant when sleep evaded her. Amy, returning in the morning, would often meet a stranger who'd held her baby through a long night.

Hope, as one "Cuddler" described her, was a baby of no words but considerable wisdom—and the occasional smile from behind her soother.

Another volunteer was baffled by Hope's ability to silently speak volumes. She said Hope had stared into her eyes whenever a

  Hot Apple Cider with Cinnamon

doctor or nurse came close, as if searching for reassurance. Then, trusting this stranger with her entire being, she'd relaxed, completely at ease in loving arms.

One "Hope Cuddler," who'd recently lost her own baby, crept into Hope's hospital room with fear and stepped out with renewed courage. No one left unchanged.

For just over a year, Hope bravely endured the incomprehensible. She was placed under anesthetic 17 times. She survived two major open heart surgeries as well as two heart surgeries performed through her leg. She pulled through a double hernia repair and two schlerotheraphy procedures to repair damaged blood vessels. But in spite of all the doctors' efforts, her heart was failing, and she was placed on the transplant list.

Sister Sadie, perfectly at ease in the hospital, where she received stickers and Popsicles from doting staff, was Hope's most loyal companion. The two girls would snuggle up together in Hope's bed with Sadie chattering relentlessly, or lie in rapt silence in front of their favourite cartoons.

Daddy Shawn had a knack for making his daughters smile, and he had the honour of making Hope laugh for the first time. They were like reflective lights, one beaming at the sight of the other.

Whenever Amy entered the room, Hope would scream in rapture. She wouldn't be silenced until she had taken her rightful place in her Mommy's arms.

Like any baby, Hope could be set in her ways. She was enamoured with a grey Jelly Cat rabbit that became a permanent fixture in her incubator or bed. And Hope could not—would not—do without one of the muslin blankets from her vast collection. She needed a blanket, however filthy, to stroke against her face at all times, to sleep with tucked in between her legs and nestled soft against her cheek.

On May 21st, 2013, Amy arrived at the hospital to spend another day at her daughter's side. But when she entered the room,

Hope failed to respond. Instead of calling out with joy and squirming in her bed as usual, Hope looked into Amy's eyes with an expression that said, "I am *so* done. I just don't care any more."

That afternoon, doctors made the decision to airlift Hope to Edmonton.

Amy had driven from Calgary, and was on the outskirts of the city when her favourite cardiologist called, imploring her to hurry.

The doctor was waiting at the door to the Intensive Care Unit when she arrived, and he immediately put his arm around her. She panicked and nearly went into hysterics when he said, "Amy, it's too late to save her. Take the time you have with her."

Amy stepped into the room where baby Hope lay unconscious on the bed. Her heart had been jumpstarted and was beating only because of the adrenalin injections that were keeping her alive.

Amy took her baby's limp body into her arms and, over the next hour, clung to it as her little girl's heart rate slowly dropped.

In those last moments, as she stared into her daughter's exhausted face, Amy had a profound sense that Hope had been given a choice that cool spring day. Her little girl had come face to face with Jesus and had been shown the impact of her time on earth—the people she had moved. And she had been given the choice to stay or to go Home.

Amy knew, from the look she'd seen in her baby's piercing blue eyes early that morning, what Hope's decision had been.

Sometimes, in order for one heart to become whole, countless others must be broken. Amy, gripping that tiny failing body in the last few minutes of her daughter's life, whispered, "You are free from the hell that is your body." But relief for Hope meant an indescribable pain for the one who had carried her in her womb.

For Daddy Shawn, the pain of saying goodbye after Hope had already left was unfathomable: his final act of love for his daughter was gently carrying her body to the hospital morgue. At Hope's funeral, he told her, "Life with you was not easy on us, or our family, but you were worth every stress, every lost freedom, and every tear."

  Hot Apple Cider with Cinnamon

Sadie, missing her little sister, asked her mother one day if Jesus had baby wipes. When told that Jesus had everything He needed to take care of Hope in Heaven, Sadie said, "But He doesn't have us."

Even on the good days, Amy found that she needed God for the simplest of tasks. Putting dinner on the table could be an insurmountable challenge.

She never carried bitterness or anger at God. Nor did she ever sense that He was deliberately slamming her with hardship, even when one daunting challenge followed another. But she did sense that He sometimes chooses not to step in—not to mend that which is broken. That He sees a much bigger picture, embracing those who leave this earth while sheltering those who are left behind.

I've chosen God through all of this, Amy realized one day. *I couldn't last a day without Him. And I'm okay with that.*

Over the year, many of the Hope Cuddlers had told Amy or Shawn how much being with Hope had affected them. But her influence didn't end there.

Countless family members and friends prayed for Hope throughout her journey. Every time Amy posted a blog entry, nearly 200 people shared her words with others. When Hope fought the hardest, as many as 100,000 people shared in her struggle. Strangers approached Amy in public to share words of encouragement or to describe the impact Hope was having in their own lives; people she had never met gladly took shifts to watch over her baby.

One evening, shortly after Hope had been put on the transplant list, Amy sat surrounded by her small group from church. "I know that Hope is having a huge impact," she said. "But it's hard to grasp. I won't really know her legacy until I get to heaven. Most of the people she has impacted are complete strangers."

Wanting to let Shawn and Amy know the impact much sooner, one small-group member asked readers of Amy's blog to describe how Hope had transformed their lives. Letters immediately started pouring in. A lengthy book of compiled letters and photos was created. Still the entries kept pouring in.

Hope's reach was indeed staggering:

A 17-year-old "Hope Cuddler" applied to nursing school because this baby had given her a sense of direction.

A three-year-old, upon praying for Hope nearly every night for six months, declared her love for God and accepted Christ after learning that Hope had died.

A stranger suffering from postpartum depression was pulled from her suicidal thoughts, and credits God for using Hope to save both her and her infant son.

As one woman aptly said, the baby who lived a mere 412 days "touched more people than most people can hope to do in 100 years."

In life, hope comes in many forms. On March 10, 2014, a baby girl named Stella Hope entered the world, her heart beating strong. Stella, the spitting image of her big sister Sadie from day one, cried lustily every night. Amy, unhindered by a mess of plastic feeding tubes and pumps and sterilization equipment, gently pulled her baby into the warmth of her bed to nurse.

And yet, there remains a space that cannot be filled. The memory of a beaming baby with only half a heart can never be erased. Amy, though grateful for her family, can't shake the feeling that she now has one foot placed firmly on earth, and another directed toward heaven, where one of her daughters resides.

1. Amy's blog is still up: www.mendingheartsandbendingknees.blogspot.ca

  Hot Apple Cider with Cinnamon

Until Death Do Us Part

Nonfiction

Ray Wiseman

"Don't you love me any more? You don't show affection; you never hug me." The note inscribed in Anna's flawless handwriting contained no salutation or signature. She had left it with the pen on her bedside table as though planning to return and write more. But the chances of that happening were one in a billion. She would no more remember writing the note than she would remember my hug that morning, or the "I love you" I had whispered in her ear.

When she wrote that note, I had loved Anna unconditionally for more than 60 years. But she had forgotten. And I had much more to learn about love.

We met in 1954 in a youth group at Oxford Church in Woodstock, Ontario. A year later, on the 8th of October, we promised before witnesses and a minister to love each other unconditionally as long as we lived. "For better, for worse, for richer, for poorer, in sickness and in health…"

Anna and I enjoyed a life of excitement, and often high adventure, with Anna contributing as an equal partner. Soon after our marriage, we started a television service business. While I did the service calls and major bench work, she looked after the books, did secretarial work, met customers face to face, and often helped at the workbench by soldering components into television chassis. She did all this without letting the birth of two sons seem any more troublesome than a bump on a busy road.

But things changed, mostly for the better, although our lives became even busier.

We sold the business and headed west to Briercrest College in a too-small trailer and an ailing truck. During our trip we had tire trouble, brake trouble, hitch trouble, transmission trouble, a broken truck frame, and a slipping clutch. We had planned for a three-day journey, but it expanded into ten, all in pouring rain.

When we arrived, the trailer sank up to its axles in mud in the newly-created trailer park.

For the next three years, while I studied for a pastoral diploma, Anna kept house, cooked meals, looked after the boys, added a third son, and earned numerous college credits. My love for her grew, along with my admiration.

After my graduation, we headed back home to Ontario where I accepted a pastoral charge. Over the next two years, Anna made a great pastor's wife, kept the family together on a fraction of the promised salary, and added a fourth son.

Then, realizing that pastoring a church wasn't for me, I dragged her through another career change, returning to electronics.

Within a few years, we managed to pay our debts and accept a call to Africa as missionaries. There she did the tasks of a missionary wife and mother: language study, teaching, writing and voicing a radio program, and keeping an office typewriter warm.

After five years, we returned to Canada, and I made another occupation change, which soon morphed into a writing career. Anna took over the business aspects of my career, developed fame as a proofreader, and in her spare time volunteered at hospitals. She kept that up for 30 years.

Is there any way I could not keep falling in love again and again with this amazing person? I found it very easy, with a wife like that, to have what I thought of as unconditional love.

But gradually Anna began to change. She was still the same person, but one day she decided to quit her volunteer position because she could no longer find her way around the hospital. Soon, she began losing herself in her own kitchen.

I took over the bookkeeping, paid the bills, and ran the household.

Eventually, a gerontologist diagnosed Anna with probable Alzheimer's. Anna remained at home as the illness progressed. Often she wakened with strange requests: "Can I go home? Where is my Mother? Isn't she here? Are you my dad?" Some mornings she would say, "Who are you? I want Ray, my husband."

Her questions, growing from her confusion, sometimes resulted in deferred laughter. One day while soaking in the bath, I noticed the door handle turning. Anna's face appeared in the crack of the door, and she said, "Who are you?"

More often, our experiences provoked something other than laughter. One day as I was dressing, Anna walked out of the apartment. From the doorway, I saw her hurry down the hall and enter the stairway leading to the outside door. By the time I had pulled on my clothes, she had disappeared down the street.

"She went that way," said a friend, walking his dog. "Look, my daughter is bringing her back."

Fearing she would leave the apartment another time without my knowledge, I used a small padlock to shorten the safety chain on the door. With the chain hooked and the lock in place, no one could leave without the key to the padlock.

Not many days later, a woman's voice coming from the living room awakened me at 2 a.m. The voice wasn't Anna's.

In one smooth motion, I rolled from the bed, grabbed a robe and rushed to the living room. Anna was there, but so was a neighbour lady, also robed, who said, "She knocked on my apartment door and asked if I could take her to her mother and father. It took me some time to convince her to come here, because she insisted she didn't live in this building. She wanted to go home."

I stood dumbfounded for a moment before going to the apartment door. Lying nearby I found a pair of pliers and a broken padlock.

Anna might have lost her memory, but she had retained the manual skills learned from her father decades before.

Soon after this, life changed again. On November 4, 2014, when my health began to break, I had no choice but to move Anna to a long-term care facility.

In her first days there, whirlwinds of words and emotion swirled around us.

"Why have you brought me here? Why can't I stay with Mother and Dad?

"Your health problems need attention. Doctors and nurses here will help you."

"I don't like this place. Where is my family? I want to be with you."

"Your sons live far away. And I can't stay here now—possibly in the future."

"Do I have to stay alone? How long will I stay here? I want to live with Mother and Dad."

"You're not alone. And you will stay only for a little while."

"Don't you love me any more?"

"I do love you very much! I'll visit every day."

"If you loved me, you would take me back to Mother and Dad."

"Your parents are no longer with us."

"What do you mean, my parents are no longer with us? Do you mean they're dead?

I sucked in my breath, then opted to tell the full truth. "Yes, they are both dead."

Anna dissolved into tears. "I didn't know. No one told me."

I realized I had fluctuated between truths and half-truths and should have avoided speaking about her parents. She lost them years ago; now I had caused her to lose them again.

I walked away from Anna's new home in the clutches of guilt, fear, and loss.

I had faced loss before: my father to a mental hospital, my brother to an early death, my mother to heart failure, and friends to a heavenly summons. I had faced fear in dangerous physical situations: I had been shot, suffered a head-on car crash, walked away from an airplane crash, and survived open-heart surgery. But never before had I felt such tension, sorrow, guilt, and fear of the future. It seemed I had walked away from 60 years of what I thought had been unconditional love. By leaving her in this place, could I continue to give her the love she needed? Would others accuse me of abandonment?

I visit her often. She repeats the same questions, and I leave her each day with the same sense of loss and guilt. I can't convince her that I, too, am alone and lonely. Most days, as I leave, she plucks at my sense of guilt by saying through tears, "Have fun."

Back in my apartment, if I simply glance into Anna's empty bedroom, loneliness tramples over all other emotions.

Recently I picked up the phone and called a neighbour lady to ask about the time of a church function. She told me, but I already knew. I called because I desperately needed to talk to someone, and I managed to keep the conversation going for 20 minutes.

Then the guilt returned. I owe my love and fealty to Anna, but I had just eased my lonesomeness by sharing time with, and seeking comfort from, another woman.

I climb into bed in the stillness of an evening. It is cold. I'm cold. Anna is not here—she will never join me in bed again. My half-asleep mind drifts to someone else. In my half-conscious condition I pull her to me but awaken empty-armed and sink into depression as more guilt floods over me.

Self-reproach strikes me every time I feel I'm not telling Anna the truth. The professionals who work with Alzheimer's patients try to convince me to use a therapeutic lie when sharing things with her. Most days, as I prepare to leave, I say, "I'll come back later," when I really mean, "I'll come back tomorrow." I comfort myself by calling that a half-truth, an acceptable therapeutic lie. But I still feel guilty. Anna and I were always honest with each other.

However, I lie outright when someone asks me how I feel. I want to answer by adopting words from the Apostle Paul: "I am hard pressed on every side… perplexed…persecuted…struck down…" But I don't say anything like that. I lie, using those popular words we all depend on, "I'm fine."

I've committed myself to visiting Anna every day, but other things often threaten that plan. I dream of making a trip west to visit a son, a young woman who is like a daughter, and old friends. I plan it in three ways: by car, bus, or air. I dream and plan, but then my aspirations come crashing down like an unbalanced tower of blocks. I can't go. I couldn't leave her for even the time it would take to fly. On the other hand, if I did choose to leave for a few days, she might not even realize it.

I ask myself, *Do I still love her? Does unconditional love exist between us? Or anywhere?* Anna is somebody different now. Maybe I'm in love with an accumulation of memories that I keep alive as we share old diaries and snapshots. But even as I review old memories, I realize that whatever my love is costing me now pales in comparison to the many wonderful years of our married lives. Anna had so many admirable qualities and lovable traits; even though she is no longer the partner she once was, she is still my Anna.

Regardless of what the future holds, I now believe that God has put me in my present circumstances to learn the meaning of unconditional love. One day, with His help, I may even learn to practise it.

  Hot Apple Cider with Cinnamon

The Launch

Heather McGillivray-Seers

I wonder if the arrow

ever wonders at the

goal

of the unrelenting Archer

as He pulls back on the

bow.

Back...

No!

Back...

No!

Back...

No! This is not the way to—

Back...

Go!

Loving Enemies

Fiction

S. M. Shigemitsu

Basil Ibrahim Ahmed sat in Rose Kira's living room. Across from him sat Rose's two children: ten-year-old Noah (her son from a previous marriage) and eight-year-old Kay Drake (Rose's niece, whom she'd adopted three years ago when her sister and brother-in-law died in a car accident).

All three sat on couches separated by a low coffee table that held a cup of green tea for each of them.

This was not a simple dinner invitation. Basil was here to ask Rose's children for their blessing for him to marry Rose.

While Rose was in the kitchen preparing the meal, Noah and Kay were entertaining their guest. To Basil, it felt more as if they were interrogating him.

"So, you were saying you want to marry Mom," Noah stated, a hint of suspicion in his tone.

"Yes," Basil replied.

"Do you like sushi?" Kay suddenly asked. Though she was eight, she was the smartest, prettiest, and toughest kid in Grade 3.

"I guess I do."

"You'd better, because Grampa is a sushi chef."

Basil took a sip of his tea. Silently, he prayed that he would stop shaking like a leaf. *They're only kids, for crying out loud!*

Another question came from Noah. "What do you do?"

"I teach math and history to high school students."

"Do you teach the part that Japan bombed Pearl Harbor and because of that everybody thought it was a good idea to drop the atomic bomb on Japan?" Kay's question rattled like a machine gun.

"Um…" Basil gulped. Hard to believe this girl was only eight!

The little girl wasn't done. "Because of that, the Canadian government put all the Japanese people in Canada in a prison camp and made them stay there until the war ended. It's like the government wanted to give the Japanese here a time out even though they weren't the ones who bombed Pearl Harbor."

Basil nervously cast a look at Noah.

"She likes history," the boy explained, as if this kind of conversation was normal.

Kay kept going. "Did you also know that the Taliban who bombed the Twin Towers got the idea from the Kamikaze pilots at Pearl Harbor?"

"Kay!" Rose had come into the room during the question. Seeing her niece's downcast face, she immediately changed her tone. "Everyone—dinner is ready."

Basil eyes met hers and he smiled. A blush spread across her cheeks.

Noah stood. "Come on, Mr. Ahmed. Let's go wash our hands."

Basil smiled at Noah. *Only ten, and he knows how to be a gracious host. What a wonderful job Rose is doing as a mother!*

When Noah and Basil had left the room, Rose knelt to be at the same level as the little girl and asked gently, "Kay, why did you say those things? Why did you say that the Taliban got the idea from the Kamikaze pilots?"

"Jamie Russell told me."

Rose sighed. Jamie Russell was the student who had gotten into a scuffle with Kay during recess yesterday. Both Kay and Jamie had ended up in the principal's office. "Is that why you kicked Jamie where it hurts?"

"He started it! He said because Grampa Toshi is Japanese, he was one of the bad guys during the war." Kay's eyes began to water.

"Well, *you* know that's not true. For one thing, Grampa Toshi was born *after* the war. Besides," Rose added, "those who make such comments don't know what they are saying. Kay, do you think you can forgive Jamie?"

"Jamie didn't stop saying those things until I kicked him. He never said 'Sorry.'"

Rose rubbed her forehead. This was one of those moments when she wondered if she was raising her niece right. She silently prayed for wisdom. She decided they'd talk about Jamie and forgiveness later. Right now, it was about Basil.

"Sweetie," Rose said kindly, "when Jamie said that the Japanese were bad guys during the war, how did it make you feel?"

"Sad."

"How do you think Mr. Ahmed felt when you mentioned the Twin Towers?"

Kay looked at her feet. "Sad."

"What do you think you should do?"

"Say 'Sorry.'"

"Can you do that?"

"Yes, Aunt Rose."

At that moment, Basil and Noah came back into the room.

Kay approached their guest tentatively. "Mr. Ahmed, I'm sorry for what I said about the Taliban and the Twin Towers. I shouldn't have said that."

Basil looked at Rose, then back at Kay. Crouching down to the little girl's level, he spoke in a soft voice, "It's all right, Kay. I know you didn't mean to be unkind."

Over their meal of rice and curried stew, Basil answered questions about his education, his job, and his hobbies. When those subjects seemed to be covered, there was a lull.

"Mr. Ahmed," Noah asked, "do you know of any good stories about unknown heroes in history? I'm doing a report about them."

"I know a story about my uncle," Basil began. "When he was a young man in Saudi Arabia, he met a young Christian girl whose life was in danger. She had run away from a country where Christians were being killed. She escaped with her family, but in the end she was the only one who made it to safety.

"But even though she had escaped to Saudi Arabia, she still wasn't safe on her own. So, although he was a Muslim, my uncle married her. Because he loved her, he protected her, and they later immigrated to Canada."

"Did your uncle become a Christian?" Noah asked.

"He did; although much later in his life."

"Mr. Ahmed, are *you* a Christian?" Kay asked. "Aunt Rose needs someone to marry her, but the guy has to be a Christian."

"Yes, I am a Christian. And," Basil added, "if it is all right with you and Noah, I would very much like to marry your aunt."

Kay thought for a moment. She glanced at Noah. "Do you think he'd make a good dad?"

"I guess we'll have to see," Noah answered. Turning to Basil he asked, "Will you go out on dates with her? My mother is a lonely person who probably would like someone to talk to and take care of her."

"Yes, I'll take her out," Basil said as he struggled to keep a straight face. "And I'll talk to her and do my best to protect her." He smiled at Rose. "Although, I think she's done a very good job of looking after both herself and you two."

Kay piped up. "Aunt Rose is a good cook and she is always very nice. We really like her, and we like you too."

Basil hesitated, unsure what to say.

"Well, aren't you going to ask her?" Kay inquired impatiently.

Basil looked over at Rose, who was smiling shyly at him.

"What do you think, Rose? Would you like to marry me?" Without waiting for her answer, he smiled at Kay and Noah. "I would also be very happy to help you raise Noah and Kay as my own children."

Rose looked down and nodded.

"Is that a yes?" he teased.

Rose raised her face, tears of joy glistening in her eyes. "Yes. Yes, I would very much like to marry you."

Kay jumped up. "Wait, Mr. Ahmed! You need a ring! Where's your ring?"

"I didn't bring one. I thought we could choose one together."

Kay ran out of the room.

Rose called after her. "Kay, where are you going?"

The little girl returned with a small ring made of tiny red beads. "You can borrow my ring until you get her a real one."

They all burst out laughing.

Basil carefully took the ring from Kay and placed it on Rose's pinky.

Such a Cute Face

Nonfiction

Elizabeth Kranz

Do you believe in love at first sight? Even more, do you believe someone could fall in love with a face in a black-and-white photo?

The moment I saw the picture of this little boy with short, black curls, a dark complexion, brightly shining brown eyes, a sweet smile, and an impish dimple, I knew he was the one I had been looking for. I should say the one my husband and I had been looking for.

I truly believed it was God's will for us to adopt a child.

Yes, we already had two children. And yes, we knew parenting can be a challenge. Before our children were born, we were, of course, certain that we would make excellent parents. After these babies arrived, the enormity of this great responsibility for other lives astounded and humbled us as much as the delicate, resilient, beautiful gifts of God's creativity awed us. Now our seven-year-old son and three-year-old daughter brought us great joy and fulfillment, and we loved being their parents.

When I was a young teen, a friend who was a foster child told me something profound. He said, "No one cares enough to look after me unless they are being paid."

Perhaps this statement was the reason I felt God wanted us to give another child a secure home. I don't know. But my husband and I believed it was God's will for us to have a couple of biological children and then to adopt.

We passionately wanted to bring home another child who desperately needed us. However, we had no idea how to go about finding him or her. So we prayed and asked God to lead us to the right child.

Then we contacted the local Children's Services.

"No, I'm sorry," the woman said. "It's against policy to have a child adopted into a family that already has biological children."

That door closed, we were uncertain what to do next.

Then came the day I saw the picture of that cute boyish face staring up at me from a Toronto newspaper. I knew at once that this was our child.

In the accompanying article, the journalist explained that there was a great need for adoptive homes for children such as this adorable little three-year-old. While couples wanting to adopt a baby had to endure a long waiting list, there were many older children living with not only the burden of a troublesome beginning but also the insecure limbo of foster homes. These children long to "belong"—to be part of a loving, caring, and committed family with "for better or worse, till death do us part" parents.

I *so* desired to adopt this child!

Since the local social worker had turned us down, we contacted the social agency mentioned in the newspaper article and were given a time for a meeting.

Travelling the almost two hours to Toronto from our country home near Waterloo, Ontario, added more suspense to the adventure.

But more than one meeting was involved. The team of social workers scheduled meeting after meeting: we talked to them as a couple, individually, in the city, and in our home. At the meetings, they nearly drowned us with questions, self-examinations, and evaluations.

Were we scared? Yes. What if we were denied? The little boy with the endearing face needed a home, and I needed to be his mother. Did we pray? Of course. We prayed for him—that God would do what was best for him; and we prayed for our worthiness to be his parents.

Members of our family were skeptical. "We've heard of adopted children becoming uncontrollable and violent." "You won't be able to manage the possible problems of health, mental, or racial difficulties." "Adopting strange children will be detrimental to your biological children."

There was too much to think about! Too much to consider! Too much to analyze! But through all the confusion, through all the babble, God's call beckoned to us.

Then came more warnings—this time from the social workers. "This child may have difficulties socially, developmentally, and physically."

We continued to trust God's call throughout the litany of fearful possibilities.

We proceeded, having yet more meetings with different social workers, who had more questions and different cautions.

One day the echoes of all the warnings and cautions began to muffle the "still small voice" for me. Fear clouded my faith and fogged my determination. I couldn't think clearly. The two corrosive words "What if?" gnawed at my certainty and created space for doubt to grow.

Craving clarity, I sat on our front porch in the quiet and the clean fresh country air. Turning to prayer, I sought reassurance. "God, please, show me a sign. What should we do? It's all so confusing and scary!"

Glancing to my right, I noticed a ladybug. Because, many years before, God had answered a specific prayer for help with a ladybug, they are very special to me—a sign of God's miraculous presence.

Then I saw another ladybug, and another. As I looked at the floor of the porch and the railing, I realized I was surrounded by a loveliness of ladybugs. Immediately, I felt my courage renewed. God had heard my plea and responded before I'd even asked for help!

Later that day, I picked up the newspaper and was amazed again. The entire front page was filled with a story about a couple with four biological children who had adopted ten children, all with various handicaps. The mother was quoted as saying, "We've never, ever regretted it."

"Thank you, Lord," I said aloud. "What more reassurance do I need of Your call?"

The worrisome waiting finally ended when the agency gave us approval for our initial visit. At long last, we met our cute little boy.

But when we visited him, the foster mother threw more warnings at us! "He's very hyper and possibly destructive. You'll have to watch him every minute."

  Hot Apple Cider with Cinnamon

What three year-old boy isn't hyper? I thought. *Watch him? Of course, you must watch, be with, and mother any young child. Not a problem!*

We drove the long way to Toronto to visit with him several times so that he could get to know us and so his new siblings could get to know him.

I'm very grateful for the dedicated adoption worker who drove him to visit us at our home a few times, too. I consider her my midwife because she helped to "deliver" our son.

The day finally came when he moved into our home, our family, and *all* of our hearts.

After the insecurity he'd felt as a foster kid, it took six months for him to realize that he really belonged—to stop asking, "Me too?" whenever I said "We're going someplace" or "We're going to do something." At last, he understood that he truly was part of "we."

He eagerly accepted his new brother and sister. Our seven-year-old son didn't have much time for three-year-olds, but he accepted his younger brother with as much tolerance as he did his busy sister.

Now that I had two three-year-olds, I pretended they were twins. They enjoyed each other's company and became best buddies.

Our new son loved music and laughter and hugs. He had difficulty walking at first, but new shoes that actually fit solved this problem and he soon could easily keep up to his sister. He also had difficulty speaking when he arrived, but soon he could keep up to his sister's constant chatter.

After all the warnings we'd received that he was hyper, I felt a bit of fear about how he would behave during church services. This hadn't been part of the routine of his foster family. But the music mesmerized him, and he sat still to enjoy it.

Every day when I told him, "I love you," his response was always, "I love you more."

Now I weep with the joy and fulfillment these memories bring to me. I'm also filled with humble pride and contentment to see the confident, happy, healthy young man he has become. He received honours all through high school. His teachers and employers praised him for his hard work, morality, and conscientiousness. He won awards in track and field, Judo, wrestling, and mountain biking. And he has many long-lasting, loyal friends.

As an army reservist, right now he's far from home, but he'll be back soon to go to university. When he *is* home, the phone rings often for him, with calls from many young ladies. After all, who can resist such a cute face?

Kosovo Canteen Concert

Nonfiction

Adele Simmons

Two soldiers at the guardhouse peered at us through the open windows of my red Honda Civic. I smiled from the driver's seat. "We're here to do an event for the Kosovo refugees. In the canteen." My pretty, red-haired niece Laurie leaned forward and smiled from the passenger seat.

It was clear they didn't know we were coming. We weren't on their list. Might be a threat to the Canadian Forces Base.

Bending over, they could see our musical instruments, sound equipment, suitcases, and open boxes of gear and props. The car was stuffed to the ceiling, like a red pimento.

Beads of perspiration rolled down my left temple. I tried to look innocent and non-combative. Yes, I like a man in uniform, but these ones had guns.

One of the guards called someone on the phone while the other scrutinized us and our driver's licences.

These were troubling times, with war and genocide in the Balkans. Canada had peace-keeping forces over there with the United Nations, but here at home Canadians lived in peace.

We were proud that Canada had welcomed some Kosovo refugees into protection here, safe and distant from the war. We wanted to do our part to make them feel welcome.

Laurie and I drooped with the humidity. Did our glistening brows suggest we were nervous?

But we must have looked harmless enough, because the soldiers allowed us to enter the compound and pointed us in the direction of the canteen.

A few lefts and rights, and we saw the big blue H for the hospital. The canteen was in the basement.

The time was 11:45 a.m. on July 26, 1999. We had two and a half hours to prepare. We parked and strolled over to do recon. We would unload later.

The canteen, a square room with some loose tables and chairs and a kitchen to the side, echoed hollow and empty. Was this the right place?

Stage? Check.

Piano? Check.

Power outlets? Check.

Chairs and tables? Check.

But where was the rest of our team?

We intercepted a passing soldier, and he led us outside and around the block to the mess hall.

From there, after uttering a big "Uh-oh!" a Red Cross worker walked us to the Commissar in another building so we could get ID tags.

Relieved, we found the other six women and one husband from our ministry group there, already ID'd and anxious to set up for our party.

Laurie and I hung ID badges around our necks, and then a soldier escorted us back to the same canteen in the hospital basement where we had first stopped. In all, a hot, steamy eight-block walk in the southern Ontario heat and humidity.

We peppered the soldier with questions.

"Yes, ma'am," he said. "We nicknamed it the Kosovo Canteen. It's their place while they're here in Canada."

It was now 12:40 p.m. We'd lost an hour finding each other and getting processed. And we'd lost our window for lunch.

No time to worry about that. We needed to set up.

Laurie and I lugged in the gear for my concert, and the other seven members of our team set up the food and gift tables. Bright yellow and white tablecloths appeared, then cupcakes, cookies, muffins, veggies and dip, cheese, nuts and chips, coffee and tea, juice and soft drinks, paper plates and cups—all set out attractively on the long tables.

We needed food and drink enough for 100 women and children.

The heat and humidity stuck our curls to our foreheads, and perspiration sparkled on pink cheeks as we scrambled to prepare for our party and afternoon concert for the Kosovo refugees.

War makes news in Canada. We all knew the stories. United Nations forces had rescued these Albanian civilians from the devastation of a war in which thousands of their people had died, murdered by Serbian and Yugoslavian forces in an ethnic "cleansing."

Here at the Canadian Forces Base in Kingston, although safe, the Kosovars were living as virtual prisoners. Unable to speak French or English, not allowed to leave the base unescorted or take jobs to fill the time, they were held under guard in a fenced-in military compound. During many of those long hours, listeners would hear desperate moans and weeping for their homeland and loved ones—so many people missing; so many dead.

And we were here to have a party and give a concert!

What were we thinking? Who did we think we were? How trite, how frivolous to try to make a party for them.

But the national executive of Women Aglow[1] had felt led, by inspiration and prayer, to do it. So, our chapter in Oshawa had purposed to take point and carry out the mission. The honour and weight of the entertaining had been offered to me. It was a compliment to be asked, a blessing to serve, a conundrum to plan.

My niece Laurie had joined me to be my roadie. She knew Kingston well from having spent several years at Queen's University. Laurie, on her way to becoming a teacher, had been eager to experience this challenge of international communication along with me. I valued her eyes and ears on the situation, and her positive attitude and energy.

We'd stayed in a Kingston motel the night before, in order to have the morning for last-minute tasks that couldn't be done in advance, including inflating 100 colourful, three-foot-long pencil balloons and stuffing them in large garbage bags. As I looked at the bags, I wondered how the guards at the gate would have reacted if one of the balloons had popped.

Not allowed to share the gospel in words with the refugees, our Women Aglow team had prayed and planned, planned and prayed. Our goal was to show love in every way permitted.

My puzzle? How would I communicate with war-traumatized refugees from Kosovo who didn't speak English? What songs could

I sing to touch our rescued Muslim friends? Surely not "Jesus Loves Me."

What would lift their spirits? What might offend? And, if we handled it poorly or touched a nerve, might any of our team be in physical danger? Soberly, we considered the perception that "Christians" were the enemy in Serbia.

Now, Laurie and I commandeered the stage, which was at the far end of the canteen. It was only 20 feet wide but, at 3 feet high, it would feel like a real concert to my audience.

I set up three microphones, amps, and stands, and tuned my guitar and ukulele. Out of the boxes came every prop and instrument I thought might help our audience participate. They didn't speak English and I didn't speak Albanian, so slapstick, curious props, comedy, and smiles would have to make our party. Surely among 100 people, some knew how to play the guitar, ukulele, accordion, harmonica, kazoo, flute, recorder, or musical saw. And anyone can play a tambourine, maracas, and drumsticks, or blow a train whistle or thump a hillbilly gutbucket.[2] I was ready for any scenario.

We laid out the instruments on a table where I could reach them quickly as I sang. We set up another table with cowboy hats, neckerchiefs, trick lassoes, a Mountie hat, small Canadian flags and a dozen other potential mood-lifters.

My grandpa puppet Reuben, with the fluffy white beard, hid out in a fat red box. His only routine is laughing. That works in any language.

I cued my accompaniment tracks and set the sound levels.

Two ladies on our team set out 100 song sheets on the chairs. The Kosovars could follow along and keep the song sheets for souvenirs. I had puzzled for days over the song choices. More than an ordinary singalong, the songs had to represent Canada's roots and flavours, yet avoid triggers for upset.

When I beckoned her, the translator assigned to us joined me onstage. She would explain for me as I entertained.

Her eyes fell on a bag of our sculpting balloons, already inflated, ready for me to hand out and teach people how to make balloon animals. Her hands flew up and her eyes blazed. "NO! NO!" She snapped and pointed. "NO BALLOON!"

I gaped at her fury and gasped.

She touched my hand. "I am sorry. No balloon. When pop, it is gunfire. Like shooting. They cry. They hide." She made a gun with her thumb and index finger and jerked it in the air.

In a flash, we stashed those balloons behind the piano, out of sight. Whew. I thanked her for her wisdom and thanked God for the intervention.

The Women Aglow ministry team prayed for me before our guests arrived: for good voice, for wisdom under fire, for nerve. We prayed for the witness of the team.

The translator answered our many questions. How many Kosovars? What ages? Children? What did they do with their time here? School? Cautions? Even with all our questions answered, we knew there would be something we'd missed.

As one of our Aglow gals, Barb, scurried with another armful of goodies to the tables, I saw the translator scowl and make a bee-line for her. She intercepted Barb and blocked her path with her body. With a harsh finger, the translator poked Barb's chest. She was stabbing at the gold cross on her necklace.

"NO CROSS! Serb wear cross! NO CROSS!"

My astonished teammate set down her load and tucked her necklace inside her blouse. Eyebrows raised, she said nothing, but she sucked in her breath. Her jaw hung open in disbelief.

My blood chilled to ice from my belly to my toes as I witnessed the skirmish. Emotion choked in my throat. What we do in God's name… we kill with hatred, greed, and power, and say it is God. This same cross a symbol of death to them, but a symbol of life to us. "Oh, God," I prayed, "protect them from us, from our thoughtless error and ignorance."

The cramp of fear curdled in my gut. It was way past time for me to dress.

Nerves intensified as I took cover backstage and drew on my red dress, red sandal pumps and red lipstick. No matter that I had forgotten my curling iron; it was useless now. The humidity had turned my hair into a frizzy chia pet.

The aroma of fresh brewed coffee wafted backstage from the food tables. I wanted one. Yes, I coveted my neighbour's coffee. But no, not for me. No time now. Tick tock, tick tock.

At 2:30, the women, teen girls, and children began to trickle in. The bright pink in their cheeks was the only colour on the women. They were fully covered in the black skirts, black tops, black jackets, black hose, black shoes, and black head scarves that formed their cultural uniform. I wondered how they were coping with the heat in such heavy garb.

But the teenage girls, in clothes donated by the Kingston community, were dressed like Canadian teens: red sweaters and yellow tank tops, hot-pink T-shirts and sky-blue cotton slacks. Some older girls wore their own head coverings, patterned in reds and greens. Two dozen smaller children were dressed in colourful donated clothing.

The Kosovo men could not join the women—a cultural thing. Women could not entertain men. Since teenagers were considered adults, all the teen boys had stayed with the men, leaving only young boys to come to our party.

We treated 100 women and children to afternoon tea and dainties, sweets and savouries. But none for me; I can't sing on a full stomach.

As they chatted and ate, our ladies distributed gift bags and toys. The refugees stretched out timid hands. Then, screeches of surprise and laughter echoed off the brick walls of the Kosovo Canteen. In a stroke of brilliance, our team had raised money to buy knitting and sewing crafts and tote bags as gifts. Balls and balls of wool, yarns, and threads in glorious colours, knitting needles, crotchet hooks, sewing needles, scissors, buttons, and thimbles. And every child received a toy.

The Canteen rang with joy as the guests of honour accepted their gifts and explored their bounty.

Then it was showtime! At three o'clock, I began my concert, on the crest of the delight from thoughtful gifts. The group was at ease with us now.

I stood with open arms and a smile, always my chief weapon of success.

The translator came on stage with me, interpreting my greeting and instructions. But she gave up translating the first number, "Ticklish Reuben," as my old man puppet brought everyone to belly laughs. "The Lion Sleeps Tonight" and "Somewhere Over the Rainbow" were familiar to them, and I heard 100 tuneful voices as they followed the lyrics on the song sheet.

I knew by advance research that Celine Dion was popular in Kosovo, so I included the lyrics for "My Heart Will Go On" in the song sheets.

When I announced the song, some teenaged girls on the side squealed and smiled at me. I beckoned them to come on stage with me, and three giggling girls were brave enough to join me. I arranged them around a mic and played guitar for them while they pressed their faces into the lyric sheets and sang with me, carefully, tentatively to start. But they gained volume and soon drowned me out. Their strong Albanian accent added flavour.

Sensational! The mothers and grandmothers were ecstatic! They threw up their hands, clapped on their own faces in delight. Applause and cheers demanded an encore.

"Again?" I said, nodding to the girls. The interpreter called them back on stage.

The three girls cuddled the mic and sang full voice, swaying their cute budding figures just like pop stars. Soon we would be famous!

With perspiration trickling down my forehead and into my eyes, I pulled out the skiffle[3] instruments. Not timid any more, a few Kosovars helped the ministry team spread them around the room. From hand to hand went the kazoos, drumsticks, maracas, tambourines, shakers, train whistle, gutbucket, ukulele, accordion, recorder, harmonicas, musical saw, and spoons. The young women knew which older ladies were too shy to play something, and coaxed them to participate.

One woman could play the accordion, so I prompted her with my eyebrows and accompanied her on guitar. She played tunes from her homeland and the group sang along and harmonized.

Others crashed and bashed out rhythms on percussion instruments. When I held up a harmonica, a lady's hand shot up, her face lit up, and cheers went up as she played. Grandmothers chuckled at the gutbucket, perhaps remembering their own stories.

Feet tapped, hands clapped, little girls and boys danced. Singing and laughter filled the canteen. A big happy noise.

People tell me I have a knack of drawing unexpected response from a group when I lead. I'm not sure if it's natural, or developed in the trenches when I taught music to youth and children, and worked ten years as a special educator and music therapist for mentally delayed adults. Certainly, I learned to drop my own inhibitions to illustrate non-verbally how a motor skill or dance or song could be done. Connecting with the Kosovars now relied on non-verbal communication. As in hundreds of other concerts, I charged in, armed only with a heart for the people and trust in a smart, kind God who paid attention and could turn me on a dime.

What is Canada without its cowboy heritage? I singled out three bold gals and dressed them in cowboy hats, scarves, Mountie hat, and the trick lassoes. Every party needs a trick lasso. Anyone can do it! I wailed into "Ghost Riders in the Sky." We howled like coyotes, mooed like cows, and clop-clopped like horses for sound effects. They caught on quickly: "Yippee-i-ayyy, yippee-i-ohhh!"

They looked and sounded hilarious, and seemed to enjoy when I pointed and laughed at them as we horsed around. I showed a pair of lassoers how to circle together while holding left hands and twirling the lassoes in their right hands on the outside. The ropes travelled around the curious group to words in Albanian that sounded to me like, "Let me try! May I try?"

Because I'd had to drop the balloon segment from my set list, I stretched out the skiffle and cowboy segments and did more singing. Some old songs were familiar. The Aglow ladies gave me a couple of breaks while they gave out door prizes, one of which was my CD, *No Ordinary Miracle*.

By the end of the hour, we were friends. Without language, we were friends. In my spirit, I felt God moving among us. His answer to our prayer. I had forgotten any nerves by the time my teenage trio sang Celine Dion with me. And when the moms and grandmas erupted in rapture over showcasing their girls, I realized they were on our side and would forgive any political error or stings we might naively inflict. God makes the way.

After an hour, I wrapped up my concert with "Bless This House"—a prayer for them all—and "Skinnamarink," which I correctly guessed they would know. Finally, the translator stood beside me for "O Canada." That's how we finished our party, with the whole room at attention and the refugees waving their small Canadian flags.

As they left the canteen, our Kosovo friends shook hands and hugged us. With wide smiles, bright eyes, and bobbing heads they left with their treasures: the needlecraft supplies, tote bags, song sheets, toys and flags. Some young boys clamoured around Laurie and me to help us pack up. We accepted their help, glad for their energy. Sticky, hot and flushed, I felt like a limp dishrag. The boys gathered up skiffle instruments and cowboy props and helped us carry boxes to the car. The flags were theirs to keep. But we kept the balloons hidden until the children were gone.

As the Kosovars crowded around us on their way out, our translator shared their comments—amazing, excellent, a blessing, loved it! The best they've had, wonderful, children joyful, teen girls sensational. Happy, funny, fun. Gifts excellent and meaningful. Skiffle instruments and cowboy songs happy and noisy.

"Thank you," they said. I saluted the Women Aglow who set us on this crusade of hope.

When almost all the Kosovars had gone from the canteen, a smiling, wrinkled, plump, grey-haired woman planted herself before me. She took my hot, flushed face in her two hands and squeezed my cheeks. She leaned into my face and said something in Albanian. The translator's expression was soft.

"What did she say?" I looked at the translator.

She said, "Te dua."

"Te dua?" I said, and looked at the old woman.

"Te dua," the old woman repeated, still holding my face.

"What does that mean?"

The translator said, "In Albanian, *te dua* means 'I love you.'"

And the old woman said, "Yas, I lawv you."
My heart melted. I took her hands in mine, then hugged her. I whispered in her ear, "Te dua."

There is an old saying, "It is better to light a candle than to curse the darkness."[4]
That day, we lit a candle.

1. An interdenominational organization of Christian women and men, now called Aglow International.
2. Poke a hole in the bottom of a big, old tin wash tub. Turn it upside-down and run a thick cord or gut string from an old bass fiddle up through the hole. Tie the string to one end of a mop stick, and hook the other end of the mop stick in the bottom rim of the inverted tub. Pull the string taut with the mop stick and pluck it to make a bass note. Ga-thump, ga-thump, ga-thump—the musicality of plucking a stretched rubber band.
3. A music genre with jazz, blues, folk, and roots influences, usually using homemade or improvised instruments.
4. Adlai Stevenson, Nov. 1962, in tribute to Eleanor Roosevelt. Also an old Chinese proverb.

Passing by the Father's House

Violet Nesdoly

On the sidewalk beside St. Joe's
while heading to his spot for the night
he stops pushing the lumpy cart
loaded with his earthly possessions
to blow warm breath on stiff fingers.

People stream past him to the church
eager-stride as if meeting someone inside
or stroll hand in hand, laughing.
Some smile at him as they pass
others turn away.

Light glows from within
the old stone building
as jewel windows
shine ancient stories
into the twilight.

Arched wooden doors
open, close
as old and young hurry in
families, singles
all together now.

What if he were one of them again
showered and dressed nice
knowing people
would be happy to see him
that someone had saved him a spot?
The big doors would open
pull him into the honey light
of the wood-panelled foyer.

There a painting of Jesus with outstretched arms
would welcome him in.

Down the aisle of the hushed sanctuary
people would glance up from prayers
as he passed by, smile a greeting…
Now bitter cold seeps in
He pocket-fingers his one-coffee coins

and nudges his cart
to get it moving again
but is halted by "Stop!"
A young boy is running toward him
while behind a smiling woman looks on.

"This is for you!"
The kid presses a bill into cold fingers,
eager eyes meet his.
"Get yourself a burger and fries
and remember, God loves you."

  Hot Apple Cider with Cinnamon

My Mother, My Hero

Nonfiction

Les Lindquist

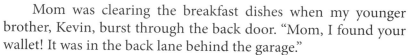

Mom was clearing the breakfast dishes when my younger brother, Kevin, burst through the back door. "Mom, I found your wallet! It was in the back lane behind the garage."

Mildred Lindquist, Kevin's and my mother, felt a sinking feeling cascade over her. She took the wallet from Kevin and opened it, then shut her eyes. Her cards, cheque book, and driver's licence were still there, but her money was gone.

The previous day, she'd taken money out of the bank to pay some bills, so there had been a lot more money than usual in the wallet.

"Mom?"

"It's okay, Kevin. I'm glad you found it. Get going to school or you'll be late. It'll be all right."

My parents, Kevin, and I had moved into Swift Current from the farm several years before, when we'd sold some of our land. We'd had a number of crop failures, so cash was always short.

After Kevin left, Mom tried to figure out what might have happened.

She'd left her purse on a chair in the hallway when she came home the day before, and it was still there.

Ah, yes. The day before. She remembered that two young children had knocked on the door selling raffle tickets for a charity. She'd been downstairs, and Kevin had let them in and sent them down to see her.

Mom was usually sympathetic and liked encouraging people who campaigned for charities, but she wasn't sure about giving money to young kids. Besides, this was a charity she didn't particularly like. So she'd sent them away without anything. There was a good chance they'd gone up the stairs and out the back door on their own. Right past the chair with her purse on it.

Normally, she'd have accompanied the kids back upstairs, but that day she'd been deep in thought about a talk she would be giving and hadn't paid enough attention. Besides, this was small town Saskatchewan in the 1960s where people didn't lock their doors.

Armed with this idea, she headed to the police station. The officer she spoke with was sympathetic but resigned. "I realize the kids probably did it. They're what some call 'known to the police.' But the evidence is all circumstantial, and there's really nothing we can do."

Mom wasn't satisfied. "Well, could you at least go with me to the corner store near our place? I'm sure that's where they would have gone if they had money. I need to know if they're the ones, or if someone else did it."

The police officer reluctantly agreed.

The trip was fruitful. "Yes, two kids came in with an unusual amount of money. They bought candy and cans of soup."

Soup?

Mom asked the policeman to visit the kids' home with her. "Maybe we can still recover some of the money."

The officer knocked on the door of a ramshackle house in a poor part of town. Mom was surprised people were living there, since it was little more than a shack. When David[1], a 15–year-old, responded, the officer asked to see the mother or father.

"Our father has been gone for years. Mom went down to the beer parlour on Saturday. She must have gone out to her boyfriend's farm with him. I'm in charge while she's gone."

The officer wasn't surprised. He knew the woman was a "practicing alcoholic," often off on a binge with men who would buy alcohol for her in exchange for "favours." He also knew there were seven kids, and David was the eldest still at home.

Maybe it was seeing the jeans drying on the oven door, or maybe it was the fact that the kids had bought soup, but at that moment Mom's mothering instinct overcame her desire for justice. She realized that if she pursued this crime, these children would likely be taken away and sent to different homes because nobody would take all seven of them. Maybe David was under age, but the kids seemed to be trying to function as a family.

So, feeling that they probably needed the money more than she did, she decided not to press charges.

In the following days, the kids stayed on her mind. Finally, she made a trip to Social Services. "Couldn't this family get some money so the kids wouldn't have to steal for food?"

"They are getting funding. But Jane, their mother, can't be relied on to use it wisely because of her addiction to alcohol."

Mom thought out loud. "What they need is a supervisor to manage the money for them so it won't be wasted."

Perhaps she should have known to be careful what you ask for. The call came a few days later.

"We've been thinking about what you said, and we'd like to ask you if you would be willing to act as a supervisor for the family."

"What about Jane? How does she feel about it?"

"She'll cooperate. She does love the kids—she just can't handle the responsibility. We've explained that the alternative is that the kids be taken away. The children's welfare cheques will be put in your control to spend for them."

"Let me pray about it and I'll get back to you."

Mom talked it over with the family.

Kevin, who was in junior high, was their only child at home now that I was away at college. He fully supported her taking on the family.

Dad, who was still working long hours on the farm, wanted to make sure she was fully convinced. "It certainly sounds as if it's needed, but are you sure that's how you want to spend your time? You've already got a lot to do. You wanted to focus on your home-products business this year."

"I've been thinking about that, but those kids need a chance."

"You know I'll support you whatever you decide."

"I think… maybe… Yes, I'll accept the challenge."

One of the first things Mom did was sit down with David and the older girls to talk about the money allocated to their clothes.

"I'm not going to just spend the money for you," she said. "You need to learn how to handle the money and make decisions for yourselves."

"How much do we have?"

Mom told them.

"Wow! That's a lot."

"Yes, but it needs to cover your clothes and other items you'll need for school."

They worked on a budget.

Twelve-year-old April piped up. "I want to use my clothes money to buy those nice boots all the girls have."

"But if you do that," Mom asked patiently, "how will you save up money for the new coat you'll need this winter?"

Planning ahead was an entirely new concept for them. The example they'd grown up with was to splurge whenever you had some money. It took time and a lot of patience to help them understand how to budget their money.

Some days later, Mom visited the home.

"Kids! Why are there half eaten apples all over the place?"

"Don't worry—there are lots of apples. You bought us that big case, remember?"

"We bought the big case because it was less expensive, and you need to have healthy snacks around. But if you only want half an apple, cut it first and put the rest in the fridge for later. For now, I guess I'll have to bring them over a few at a time."

Another day Mom noticed April sporting the new boots she had wanted but couldn't afford. When pushed, April admitted that they'd been visiting someone at the hospital and she'd seen the boots standing alone, so she'd taken them. She said she felt bad for taking them, but that she really wanted nice things so that she could fit in at school.

The trip back to return the boots and apologize to the owner produced many tears, but also a sense of pride in doing the right thing.

  Hot Apple Cider with Cinnamon

By now Mom had decided that they needed a much better house. The place they were renting was a dump that could only be bad for their self-esteem and their health. She approached a landlord who had a good place to rent.

"Well, I don't know. I'm not sure I want to rent to that family. Those people can't be trusted."

"I'm working as their supervisor so the rent cheques will come from me."

"Okay, but they'd better behave. I'll hold you responsible."

She took the kids shopping for clothes they needed. "Why are they staring at us?" the kids complained.

"You see, they don't know you. When you touch everything, the clerks are suspicious that you might be picking up items to shoplift. Perhaps it would be better to just look and not touch."

Going around town with Mom, they met a different group of people from those in their previous circles. They were surprised to learn that there were people who didn't drink to excess. They were impressed with a way of living that was so much different from what they'd experienced.

Before too long, however, Mom learned that David, the 15-year-old boy, had been expelled from school for poor attendance. She talked to the principal.

"Okay, we'll reinstate him. But this is the last chance!"

"I'm working as a supervisor with the family. If he misses again without permission, please contact me rather than call the boy's home. I'll get to the bottom of it."

To help David fit in with his classmates, she took him shopping to buy proper clothes and new shoes to replace the ones with the flapping soles.

A few months later, she visited the home during a school day. "David, what are you doing here?"

"I was expelled again because I missed school."

"David, why? We tried so hard. And it was going well."

"My stupid mother went to a party on the weekend and never came back. I couldn't leave my three-year-old sister here alone. The school called to talk to my mother, but…."

Mom pleaded with the principal, especially since they hadn't followed her request to call her first.

"I'm sorry. It's our policy to talk to the family first. We warned you that it was a last chance."

Then came the day Mom learned that David had been arrested.

"What happened?" she asked him.

"I was so bored. Me and my friend decided to go hunting. I learned to shoot at the farm when I went with Mom to her boyfriend's place. But we didn't have a gun and didn't have any money, so we thought we would borrow one from the pawn shop. But he had a stupid alarm, and the police came."

Mom stood with him in court. "Your honour, in spite of this mistake, David has demonstrated responsibility in looking after his younger siblings. They need him. And his intent to use the gun was not for criminal purposes. Please give him another chance."

The judge was firm. "David, stealing a gun is a serious offence. I find you guilty. But because of what has been said, I will give you a suspended sentence. Don't take it lightly. If you get in trouble again, the sentence will be carried out."

David was relieved and grateful.

Some time later, however, David went to visit an older sister in Moose Jaw. Again, he was bored. He stole a radio to have something to listen to. When caught this time, his luck ran out. He was sentenced to three months in custody.

At this point, Mom decided that continuing to try to keep the family together might prove counterproductive. The younger boys looked up to their big brother and would likely follow in his footsteps if they stayed with him. For nearly three years, Mom had done her best to help the kids, but she realized the situation was now too complex for one volunteer to deal with.

  Hot Apple Cider with Cinnamon

It was a sad decision. There were a lot of "what if" thoughts. What if the school had followed the plan and contacted her before they expelled David? Might he have avoided the trouble he'd drifted into as a bored teenager with nothing to do? What if the mother could have stayed sober? Her attempts to stop drinking by attending Alcoholics Anonymous meetings seemed to work for a while, but then one of her boyfriends would ply her with free booze, and she'd be off on another binge.

Mom visited her contact at Social Services. "The younger boys, especially, need more guidance than I can supply from outside the home."

"I understand. I'll arrange for an orphanage and let you know."

David was still in jail, and the youngest girl could stay with her mother, who was now living with the girl's father on his farm. That meant give kids still needed a home.

The call came. "We've found a place. It's in Punnichy."

"But that's 400 kilometres away."

"I know. But there aren't many places that can take five kids."

"I guess."

"Also, we have a huge favour to ask of you. Would you be willing to drive the kids there? We think that would help them get used to the idea."

Of course, Mom agreed.

When the time came, the five kids piled into the car with Mom and away they went.

When they stopped for the night on the way, she decided to crowd them all into one room. She was afraid the kids might decide to run away because they were upset about leaving their mother.

She gave the kids a tape recorder to play with and settled into the cot she had placed near the door. They spent the whole evening recording each other's voices and laughing and having a good time.

The next morning, they piled back into the car for the rest of the trip. Given the circumstances, the kids were remarkably well behaved. Life had made them resilient, and they seemed to accept anything.

At Punnichy, the staff welcomed the kids and introduced them to their new surroundings.

In some ways, the lonely drive home was a blessing—400 kilometres to process the tears and the relief and the hope and the prayers for their future.

Fourteen-year-old April ran away after the first night. When the police eventually found her, they were concerned that she'd run away again, so she was taken to a lock-up facility in Moose Jaw.

Mom made the two-hour trip to visit her.

As Mom was being escorted into the facility, walking past all the bars, the feelings that wafted over her were heart-wrenching. This was her "little girl" in there.

However, Social Services soon found a group home for April. She loved the structure and thrived in that environment.

Some months later, Mom was pulled out of a meeting in Regina by a phone call from Dad. "I didn't want you to just hear the news on the radio. Jane was killed by the man she was living with."

Jane was the mother of the family. The man she was living with was the father of her youngest child.

"That doesn't sound like him," Mom said. "He's a good man when he's sober."

"They'd both been drinking, and she decided she was going to leave to see another boyfriend. They fought, and when she started packing her things into a small suitcase, he shot her."

"Was David there? Last I heard, he'd been released from jail and was staying at the farm."

"They never said."

The man was eventually convicted of the murder. Presumably because he was intoxicated at the time, he was sentenced to three months. Three months! Mom wondered what the kids made of that. Their brother had served three months for stealing a radio, and this man was given three months for killing their mother.

Mom prayed that the people who were in the kids' lives then would be able to help them deal with it.

  Hot Apple Cider with Cinnamon

Years later, one of the younger boys contacted Mom. He was trying to reconnect with his roots and didn't remember much of those days other than that she had helped them.

Mom told him stories of some of the happy times they had together in those years. And she was able to show him (and give him) photographs of him with members of his family.

To this day, Mom continues to pray for these kids, whom she now envisions as grandparents.

Though this story doesn't exactly have a happily-ever-after ending, Mom had seen a need and done her best to make a difference in the lives of these kids. She had broadened their experience, kept them together as a family for a number of years, and given them a glimpse of what might be.

The need for help of this type stayed in the back of her head. When she was serving as president of the Local Council of Women, Social Services asked if the council might sponsor a program of "homemakers" who could essentially provide the kind of things Mom had done, but with a support system for the caregivers.

Because of her experience, Mom supported it, and the council agreed to go ahead.

She couldn't find anyone who would take the training in Regina in order to teach it in Swift Current, so she decided to take it herself. Over the next three years, she set up the program and recruited and trained 25 people to serve as homemakers in the community.

From a small robbery came meaningful help for many people in the community.

I don't think Mom thinks of herself as a hero. She was just trying to live out her faith. But she's my hero.

> "And if anyone wants to… take your shirt,
> hand over your coat as well."
> —Matthew 5:40

1. Names of the members of the family have been changed

Carlos

Nonfiction

Rob Harshman

It was one of those days in early June in the Toronto, Ontario, area where the hot, humid air hangs heavily.

In our school, which had no air conditioning, everything seemed damp, and you stuck to any chair you sat in. It was a Friday, just one week before final exams were scheduled to begin. And it was the last class of the day.

I'd been teaching geography for ten years and had learned a lot about students—which ones should do well and which ones seemed headed for failure.

My Grade 11 students drifted listlessly into Room 28 for their geography lesson. With only a week to go before final exams, I was trying to finish up the course as quickly as I could so we'd have time in class to review the important elements for the final exam. Needless to say, my students weren't exactly enthusiastic learners that afternoon. Their minds were focused on the heat and on getting out of school for the summer and leaving their studies behind for a couple of months.

When everyone was seated, I noticed that one of the students who really needed to prepare for the exam wasn't in his seat. Carlos. He wasn't a bad student, but over the past couple of months he'd put almost no effort into his school work. I'd also noticed that he'd begun to hang around with a group of guys who I was pretty sure were smoking pot and who frequently skipped school. I'd felt for some time that I needed to talk to him, but the opportunity had never come up.

I was about ten minutes into the lesson when Carlos wandered into the room. Seemingly unaware that he was late, he took his seat and dropped his backpack loudly on the floor beside him.

I cleared my throat, but he didn't look at me, so I decided not to interrupt the class to confront him about his tardiness.

Through that whole class, he sat at his desk saying nothing and doing nothing, despite the fact that exams were just around the corner. It was obvious that geography was the furthest thing from his mind.

When class was over and he was making his way to the door, I approached him and asked if I could talk to him for a couple of minutes.

He shrugged his shoulders, but stayed beside me while the rest of his classmates made their way to the hall and their lockers.

When the students were gone, I turned to him.

Carlos stood looking down at his shoes with his hands in his pockets. He said nothing. His jet black hair was long and unruly and looked like it hadn't seen a comb in a few days. His T-shirt had several large stains, and his jeans were dirty and ripped. His track shoes were covered in dust, and the laces tumbled untied onto the floor.

"Carlos, I'm very concerned about your mark in geography. You started off the year so well and your marks were good. You were working hard and you participated in class. But—" I hesitated a moment to collect my thoughts. "The last three months, your effort and your marks have gone down the tubes. There's a good chance you won't pass."

Carlos stood still, unable or unwilling to look at me.

"I know you're capable of so much more. You could have one of the top marks in the class. You've got the ability, but I'm afraid you're wasting it. But beyond that, Carlos, I'm concerned about you. Most of the time, when I say 'Hi' to you in the halls, you don't even look my way. And—can I be really honest with you?"

Carlos didn't respond.

"Carlos?"

He nodded weakly, still not looking up.

"Some of the friends you're hanging around with aren't good for you. They're into drugs and I've noticed the smell of pot on your breath some days. You know this isn't good. You could ruin your whole future."

I paused for a moment to see how he'd react, but he just stood there, eyes focused on the floor. He didn't move.

"Carlos, I suspect that you're not very happy. You spend your lunch hours hanging around the back of the school smoking and whatever." I paused again. "Am I wrong?"

Carlos shook his head very slightly.

"I'd suggest you take a hard look at your life and decide what you want. Do you really want to keep going this way? Do you want to keep hanging out with your current friends? What happens if you keep smoking pot, skipping school, and failing your classes?" I stopped talking.

As I looked at him, I tried to determine whether he was even listening to what I was saying. I wasn't sure.

"Look, I'm very concerned about you, and I want you to know that you can come and talk to me any time you want." I waited a few moments more, and when Carlos didn't respond, I extended my right hand to him.

He hesitated and then took my hand and weakly shook it. For a brief moment, his eyes met mine. Then he let go and turned to leave the classroom.

"I hope you have a good weekend, and I hope you do some serious thinking about your life."

I watched as Carlos walked straight out the door without looking back. I had no idea whether he'd heard anything I'd said, but I was glad I'd said it.

I prayed for him that night, and for the next few nights, knowing I couldn't do anything more to change him. Only God could do that.

After the final exams were over, I didn't see Carlos again. He did manage to pass my geography class, by one mark.

When the new school year began in September, I didn't see him at all. Since I was very busy with my new classes, after a couple of weeks, I assumed he'd moved or dropped out of school.

A number of times over the next year, I reflected on my last conversation with Carlos. I knew I'd taken a chance talking to him the way I did, and I wondered if I'd said too much. A number of contradictory thoughts ran through my mind.

I was too hard on him. I should have softened the message. Maybe he'd taken what I said the wrong way and decided to change

schools to avoid me. But could I have lived with myself if I hadn't told him my concerns?

Since I didn't have the answers, I eventually managed to push the whole situation out of my mind. I believed I had done what I needed to do. The rest was up to God.

Almost a year to the day after the conversation I had with Carlos, I was on hall duty in the high school during the lunch hour.

I was walking the halls and came to the main entrance of the school. As usual, clusters of students were gathered there, talking, joking around, and slurping soft drinks.

Out of the corner of my eye, I saw a young man come through the front doors and head straight for me. I didn't recognize him. His hair was cut short and neatly trimmed. He was wearing a white shirt and a tie with black pants. His shoes were polished, and they clicked as he walked over the terrazzo floor.

As he drew nearer, I studied his face to see if I could recognize him, and then it came to me. It was Carlos!

He walked straight up to me and shook my hand while he looked me in the eyes.

"Carlos, what are you doing here?"

"I came to see you." His voice was firm and confident.

"Me?" I'm sure my surprise showed in the tone of my voice.

"I wanted to thank you."

"Thank me? For what?"

"For talking to me that day last year. You told me what I needed to hear even though I didn't want to hear it."

I struggled for words. "I'm glad you listened. I was concerned your life was coming apart." I took a breath. "Where are you living now?"

"Last summer we moved to London, Ontario, and in the fall I started at a new school. I decided that I was going to start a new life, so I stopped hanging around with guys who skipped classes and smoked pot. I got my hair cut and changed how I dressed. I worked hard at school and I got accepted at university for next September."

His forehead was furrowed as he talked, but he had a confidence I'd never seen in him before.

"That's great. By the way, I almost didn't recognize you when you walked through the front door." I smiled. "You look great."

The corners of his mouth turned up into a slight smile. "I'm glad I found you. I was afraid you might have moved to another school."

"No, I stayed right here. So what are you doing the rest of the day?"

"I'm going straight back to London. You see, I came here just to see you. My dad is waiting in the car, so I've got to go."

"Wait. You and your dad made the two-hour trip from London just so you could thank me?"

"Yes."

Carlos shook my hand once again. His handshake was firm and he looked me straight in the eyes. Then he turned quickly and left.

"Thanks for coming." My voice cracked as I spoke, and I knew he probably didn't hear me. When I turned to walk back down the main hall again my vision was blurry. There were rain clouds in my eyes.

I silently thanked God for giving me the courage to speak up that day, and for using me to help Him change Carlos's heart.

      Hot Apple Cider with Cinnamon

Miss Gardiner's Birthday

Historical Fiction

Joanna Clark Dawyd

Alice Gardiner sat by herself in a chair against the parlour wall, hands lying idle in her lap. She'd been beating herself at checkers, but the game lay half-finished on the table next to her as she harboured blue thoughts. She had another birthday today. Born in 1883—on a clear June night, or so her mother had told her ages ago—she was now 86. But instead of being happy about it, she felt old and lonely. She, who had been one of Dr. Gardiner's girls—the life of Toronto's social scene at the turn of the century—was now an old maid reduced to playing checkers alone to keep her mind active.

To be sure, she was usually still the life of the party, but today she felt no desire to socialize with her housemates, who were sure to offer her many happy returns of the day.

She looked over at Mr. Pike, who was only 70 years old but seemed much older. He drooled as he dozed in his chair before the fire, the day's newspaper slipping from his fingers to the floor. Mrs. Lloyd, age 81, sat in the recliner next to him, knitting furiously and arguing aloud with the husband she'd buried 20 years before. The other residents of the house normally rested in their rooms at this time of day, so the large sitting room was otherwise empty.

When Alice was young, she'd proudly imitated the proverbial lilies of the field that "toiled not, neither did they spin."[1] Dr. Gardiner's daughters had their mother's beauty and money, and just enough of their father's brains to keep the boys guessing. They didn't need to learn any useful skill. Even the handwork that was common among ladies—such as knitting and embroidery—was called old-fashioned among her set.

Now Alice's hands were so gnarled by arthritis that they couldn't learn anything new, but she often thought it would be nice to know how to make the lovely sweaters and afghans Clara Lloyd was always sending to her grandchildren. Not that Alice had any grandchildren.

Oh, she'd had plenty of beaus when she was young. In fact, she could have told stories of her many offers of marriage that would make her poor young suitors' ears burn with embarrassment had they heard. *Yes,* Alice thought, *I must have been too particular about the men.* One by one, they'd dropped away.

Alice didn't notice at first that all her friends were settling down to marriage and family while she was earning a reputation for being hard to please. Her sarcastic wit, once listed among her many attractions, had been too much for some of them. Her being so hard to please had taken care of the rest. Until one day she found herself middle-aged and alone, still living in her childhood room in her father's—now her brother's—house, and faithfully teaching Sunday school each week at the same church in which she herself had been baptized.

Alice had contented herself with her accidental lot in life. She became the ideal maiden aunt, doting on her numerous nieces and nephews, never admitting—even to herself—a longing for children of her own. She found beauty and peace in long walks in the city's parks, and mental stimulation in reading good books, going to the theatre, and attending dinners with old friends. Most of the time, she was optimistic, taking joy in her availability to serve the community through her church, which would not have been possible to the same extent were she focused on her own husband and children.

She had always frequented the library, and when she found she needed something more to do, she took a job there. All in all, she was happy in her single life and could usually ignore the whispers from her soul, saying it needed deeper companionship.

When Alice was 70, and still feeling very young, her widowed brother sold the big house she'd lived in all her life and moved to Alberta to live near his son's family. Alice could have moved in with one of her sisters, but she instead elected to stay in her old neighbourhood. She moved into a large house down the street that had newly been turned into a nursing home—but perhaps retirement residence would be a more accurate name, since most of the residents required only minimal nursing care. The interest from her inheritance, scarcely touched over the years due to Alice's frugal nature and library income, nicely covered the fees for room and board. Alice had been comfortable there over the past 16 years, pleased with the house's manager, Ms. Elizabeth Jones, and the care of the nurse and the other household staff. But today, as she reflected on all she might have had, she was in no mood to appreciate the good things her life had given her.

"Excuse me." A man's voice broke into Alice's thoughts, and she looked up. A stranger stood before her.

"May I join you for a game of checkers?" His face had such a boyish look of hope that Alice found she couldn't refuse him, despite her morose frame of mind.

"Of course. Have a seat." She waved her hand at the chair across the table from her.

The man sat down and swept the remains of Alice's solitary game off the board. "I'm Geoff," he said, beginning to set up the new game. "Geoffrey Beasley."

"Alice Gardiner."

"I know. I asked the nurse to point me to the prettiest lady in the house. She told me all about you." Geoff had a slightly British-sounding accent. He cleared his throat. "Red or black?"

"Red." Alice was always red. Ignoring the prick of irritation she felt over being the topic of gossip, she said, "Shall I assume you know everything about me and we'll just chat about you?"

Geoff chuckled. "I'm sure she left one or two things out." He moved his first piece.

"Only because she didn't know them, I'm sure." Alice moved hers.

For the next few moments, the only sounds were the clicking of the checkers and the crackling of the fire—Mrs. Lloyd apparently having decided to give her dead husband the silent treatment.

Alice pretended to be as absorbed in the game as Geoff appeared to be. Instead, she slyly studied her opponent. Grace Moody, one of the residents who seemed to hear everything, had told Alice yesterday that the new resident moving into room number four was 90 years old. With his thick, pure white hair, and his smooth skin, he looked much younger. His neatly trimmed moustache and the impeccable clothes on his slight build gave him a distinguished look.

Click-click-click.

Alice pulled her thoughts back to the game. A triple jump. "Hey! Are you sure that's fair?" She gave a playful scowl.

Geoff chuckled. "Of course it is. As you'd know if you were paying attention. Keep your mind on the game, love. We've got plenty of time to gaze at each other."

Alice's cheeks grew hot, and she chided herself for blushing—at her age! "Perhaps I was trying to figure you out." She made her move. A single jump. "Since no one told *me* all about *you*, you'll have to tell me yourself."

"Well," Geoff said as he shifted in his chair, "like your father, I was a doctor. Practised in Barrie 'til last year when my daughter made me retire."

"You kept working until you were 89?"

"I did. And she—my daughter that is—didn't want to retire herself while her old dad was still ticking along."

Alice couldn't keep from smiling. "How many children do you have, Geoff?"

"Three. Ruth, Janet, and Davy. Their poor mother died when Davy was only 15. But we got along all right."

A few more moves clicked across the board. Black. Red. Black.

"Grandchildren?" Alice asked, nudging her red checker onto its new square.

"Oh, scads of 'em. Nine, I think." Geoff flicked a glance toward the ceiling, thinking. "No, ten now; Davy's got a young wife and they have three now. Four great-grands too."

"Why did you never remarry?"

"Oh, I'd done it once—that was enough for me." Geoff winked at Alice. But then his expression softened. "Too busy, I think. Maybe I was afraid to make a poor choice. But now I rather wish I had taken a chance."

Alice heard the loneliness in his voice and felt it mirrored in her own heart. Then she scolded herself. *Enough wallowing!*

Sitting up straight, she smiled perkily. "So what brought you here, Geoff?"

Geoffrey studied the checkerboard for a moment. "Oh, I asked a friend of mine where the prettiest ladies live and he told me 'Toronto,' so here I am!" His move on the board was accompanied by a low chuckle. "King me!"

Alice decided not to point out that he had used that "prettiest ladies" line already.

Later Alice stood in her room tucking the last wisps of her thick dove-grey hair back into place. She wore it long—no modern bob for her—and did it up in pin curls every night, arranging the resulting ringlets each day. She still followed her mother's advice to be ever prepared to look her best. That's why she detoured up to her bedroom to freshen up before dinner every evening. As she slicked on a fresh coat of pale pink lipstick—she had given up her signature red once she passed age 65—Alice thought about this Geoffrey Beasley. He was interesting. And he did like to flirt, that was certain!

She hoped her new friend would help to liven up the place. They hadn't had any fresh excitement since Alan Moody and Grace Munro had married last fall—each of them 70 years old! Well, they seemed happy.

Finished with her primping, Alice looked straight at her mirrored reflection. "Well, Alice," she said aloud, "as of today, you are eighty-six years old. But that does *not* mean you can't have a little fun. Go enjoy your birthday."

Pretending she had on one of the long evening dresses she wore in her twenties instead of comfy blue polyester slacks and supportive lace-up shoes, Alice turned away from the mirror and flounced out of the room and down the stairs. She paused in the hall to select a record of soothing classical music. Lifting the polished wooden lid of the old Victrola player, she nestled the record into place and heard the soft crackle as she placed the needle gently at its edge. That done, Alice entered the dining room a bit more sedately, the last one there, as usual. The five other residents already chattered companionably around the antique oval table, with Geoffrey in her usual seat.

"There you are, my dear!" Geoffrey was the first to greet her. "Mrs. Lloyd was just telling me all about her husband. He sounds like a fascinating fellow." He turned back to Clara, who was seated next to him at the elegantly set dining table. "Is he coming down for dinner? I hope he'll tell me about his years of travels."

Clara opened her eyes wide. "Oh, well—I don't know, really." She was clearly flustered. "He's away just now. Has been for quite some time..." Her voice trailed and she gazed down at the salad plate in front of her.

Alice pulled out the empty chair and sat across the table from Geoff. He winked at her. "You look perfectly lovely, Alice."

"Really, Geoffrey, the way to a woman's affections is not through winks and compliments." Alice's brow furrowed sternly for a moment as she scolded. Then she smiled. "But thank you all the same."

Mr. Roger Pike, who had been a missionary, cleared his throat. "Friends, let us give thanks."

Alice and the others bowed their heads while his deep voice rumbled. Roger's prayers were always short, letting his hungry housemates get at the food while it was still hot. Alice was grateful; she had forgotten all about her usual afternoon snack while playing checkers with Geoffrey, and now she worried that her belly's protests would be heard.

Having been raised in the best society, Alice had impeccable table manners. Her silver fork rested lightly in her hand while she took dainty bites and pretended not to be watching the newcomer. Geoffrey's lighthearted flirtations with Clara Lloyd and Grace Moody gave her ample time to study the man. She was pleased to see that his manners were nearly as polished as her own.

Dinner passed through its three courses with more friendly banter between Geoffrey and Alice. While not entirely neglecting the others at the table, Alice was drawn toward Geoff's bright and affable optimism as much as to his still-handsome face.

She suspected that, had he been one of her suitors all those years ago, he would have enjoyed her teasing high spirits more than the stuffy young lawyers and medical students she had known as a debutante. They had been always so eager, so amiable, that she'd had a hard time conversing with any of them beyond the usual pleasantries.

After the meal, crowned by a delicious birthday cake and the traditional off-key serenade, the others drifted away, but Alice and Geoff stayed at the table. Heedless of the housekeeper clearing dishes around them, they shared the highs of their lives with each other. Geoff told of his sudden uncharacteristic shyness the first time he met the girl who would be his wife, and the pranks of his college days. His pride in his children was evident when he spoke of them and their accomplishments and families. He related a few of the cases he was pleased with, where his patients got well in spite of all predictions.

Alice told of her own pranks, learned from her two older brothers and scorned by her sisters; of her relationship with her beloved father, who seemed to always have time for his youngest daughter; of her devotion to the library where she had spent so many hours; of her love of reading; and of the deep emotions that overcame her when holding her first niece, so small and helpless.

"Yes." Geoff nodded. "Nothing can compare to those feelings. But you know…" His eyes crinkled at the corners when he grinned. "I once believed that babies were delivered in the leather bag the doctor carried."

"You didn't," Alice said.

"My mother and I went to visit her sister, who was having a baby. I was about five or six at the time. They sent me outside to play in the yard. I wasn't out there long when the doctor rushed past carrying a large black bag. A few hours later, after I'd had a glorious afternoon making mud-pies, my mother got me washed up and brought me inside to meet Aunt Sue's new baby. It was a tiny red wrinkled thing. I thought it was wrinkled from being stuffed in the doctor's case." Geoff laughed, his guffaw infectious, making Alice laugh too.

Geoff's smile slowly faded as he looked into Alice's eyes. "May I ask, love, why did you never marry?"

Alice was tempted to brush off the question with a clever quip and a laugh as she had countless times before. But the earnest sincerity in her companion's eyes made her pause.

She took a deep breath before answering, slowly and thought-fully. "I suppose I—I simply never found anyone I wanted to marry. I wanted someone to stand alongside me, not to be my master, nor to be hen-pecked. Someone strong enough to take some teasing and dish it back, yet gentle enough to cherish me. As the years passed, I realized I was getting older and stopped looking."

"You know," Geoff patted her arm. "Love isn't only for the young."

Alice smiled. "I know. But I came to an age that made me realize I needed to stop pining for what I didn't have, and enjoy my life as it was. So I did. I've really had a lovely life." She stood abruptly. "Have you seen the gardens yet?"

"Not yet." Geoff stood too. "Will you give me a tour, my dear?"

"Come along." Alice moved around the table, meeting Geoff in the doorway. She placed her fingers in the crook of his offered arm and they went out the side door.

"I like to take visitors around the gardens," Alice said softly. "I've been here so long, I feel as if they belong to me." She grinned, "They may as well belong to me. The gardener does whatever I tell him. This lily garden here, that was my idea. I love to smell their heady scent as soon as I step outside. And on clear, still nights the smell drifts right to my window upstairs."

"They're lovely," Geoff said. Their shoes padded softly against the wide and level concrete pathways as they walked.

"I love lilies," said Alice, "I wore one on my dress or in my hair to every party I went to when I was young. I wanted to be unforgettable—the girl with the lily." She sighed, and was silent for a moment. "But roses have always been my favourite."

They had turned the corner around a low, stone wall. Before them was a riotous profusion of roses.

Alice continued speaking, almost to herself, "Not the prim and proper type that can't handle a cold winter, but the almost-wild heirloom varieties. Some of these cultivars date back to medieval England."

The roses climbed trellises, sprawled around benches, and intertwined through the beds so it looked almost as if one bush bloomed in a whole spectrum of shades, from pristine white—glowing now in the dusk—through sunny yellows, sweet pinks, and deep velvety reds.

Alice released her hold on Geoffrey's arm and sat on one of the benches. It was the best spot for watching the moon rise.

"I never feel quite as old and lonely among the roses." Her voice was soft and she bent to caress a blossom, embarrassed by the quaver in her voice. She did not look up, although she felt the bench creak as Geoff sat beside her. He took her hand, smoothing his fingers over its swollen joints.

"Alice," he began, "we have no need for loneliness."

When she finally looked up, she found him gazing thoughtfully at her, with no trace of that boyish teasing she had enjoyed all day.

"It's a pity you didn't come around when I was young enough to marry."

"We're young enough yet, love."

"Oh, Geoff." Alice leaned her head against Geoff's shoulder and a tear trickled down her cheek. Together, they watched the bright, full moon rise above the trees.

1. Matthew 6:28

Your People Will Be My People[1]

Nonfiction

Christine Kenel-Peters
with Marguerite Cummings

It was almost one a.m., but I couldn't sleep.

"Mom… Mom!" I whispered imperiously, knowing my mother was still up and would hear me. "Please… can I get up? Can I get dressed? Aren't we leaving soon?"

It was pitch dark, but my nine-year-old voice was full of excitement. I hadn't slept at all.

My mother entered the room quietly, not wanting to wake up my older sister.

"Don't worry, Christine," she spoke softly. "I'll make sure we don't miss that ferry. A promise is a promise, right?"

I was ecstatic. In a few hours, I would be seeing "real" First Nations people for the very first time!

It was the summer of 1974, and we were headed for Manitoulin Island, the largest lake island in the world, a well-known beauty spot on Lake Huron. My Swiss-born parents loved to take our family on camping trips throughout our province of Ontario. For me, this particular excursion was a special treat.

"This island has one of the largest First Nations communities in Canada," my parents had explained, knowing my growing passion for First Nations. "I've booked the first ferry crossing in the morning," my mother had added with a smile, "so we'll have all day to explore."

These words were playing in my head as I continued tossing in bed. All day! My Grade 3 teacher, whom I loved, had taught our class at length about these incredible "Indians" (as we called them then[2]). I imagined them as a strong, beautiful people who loved the

Hot Apple Cider with Cinnamon

land, nature, and their families. *Do they still ride horses? Will I see a real teepee?*

Finally, an hour or so later, it was time to get up. After an epic nighttime drive, we made it just in time for the first ferry.

However, we had barely arrived on Manitoulin Island and driven off the ferry at the southern docks when disaster struck: our brand new car broke down. We were stranded, right on First Nations reserve land.

As my parents sat, crestfallen, at the reserve garage, waiting to have the car repaired, a small group of Ojibway children immediately became curious about my two siblings and me—not because we were white, I learned, but because we were about the same age. Peeking around the corner, they finally approached our family.

"Can you come and play with us?" they asked shyly. "We want to play tag!"

I glanced at my mother. After a moment, she replied, "Sure." She'd let us play outside with friends many times in our neighbourhood. "Go right ahead!"

I spent a wonderful morning playing with these new friends. I felt so happy running around with them! My parents always made sure we were well mannered and well dressed—but these children were loud and boisterous; I was almost envious of their messy, tousled hair, ragged clothes, and bare feet, as we scampered and laughed together, playing endless games of tag and hide-and-seek around the buildings nearby.

And yet, even in my joy that day, I felt something was wrong. Why were so many windows broken? Why was the paint chipped on all their homes? And why was there so much junk everywhere? I could see many broken-down vehicles. Even to my young eyes, the church and school looked old and neglected. The contrast to the life I knew was dramatic.

Moreover, this didn't match at all what I had expected from First Nations—picture-book perfect, with their tame horses, soft moccasins, and neat teepees.

I couldn't help but wonder why the real First Nations children I had just met were so different. *Maybe their parents are very sad and don't feel like taking care of these things.*

Hot Apple Cider with Cinnamon

I never forgot that day. It was to be the first milestone in a lifelong journey of love for First Nations.

As I grew older, my passion for First Nations continued. I dragged my family to pow-wows, eager to experience firsthand what their life and culture were all about. Whenever I had a choice, my school projects were either about First Nations or about Switzerland, my parents' home country.

At 19, wanting to broaden my horizons, I decided to live and work in Switzerland for one year. Until then I had been familiar with a very comfortable lifestyle. However, while I was in Zurich, through a remarkable chain of events, I came to know Christ in a way that completely transformed my outlook and priorities in life.

That experience was a turning point. Once back in my native Canada, I became intensely involved with my family's German Lutheran church. My newfound faith prompted me to take part in many outreach activities and short-term mission trips, both in Canada and abroad. This period in my life culminated with three years as a full-time missionary with Youth With A Mission, working in Scotland, on the Caribbean island of Saint Croix, and in North Africa.

Most of my time was spent with the marginalized—people living on the streets, ignored or rejected by society. I was deeply moved by their needs, yet I also felt I could relate to them easily, share their jokes, and identify with their views. Showing them compassion became my priority.

On numerous occasions, I would come across homeless Aboriginal people—indigenous people on a remote island or First Nations people on the streets of large Canadian cities. Invariably I would feel drawn to them as if by a magnet. I vividly remember being mistaken for a First Nations woman myself—probably due to my dark hair, dark eyes, and high cheekbones.

"Are you *sure* you are not First Nations?" a First Nations chief once asked me in Calgary.

"Yes, I'm sure!" I laughed in reply.

How proud I felt to resemble the people I loved!

At age 27, having travelled the world, I felt an urge to return to Canada once more. I sought God's guidance and, on my arrival, I connected with a Toronto mission that reaches out to the homeless and needy: Yonge Street Mission. The director asked if I would meet regularly with a group of teen girls from a troubled housing project. I would be doing most of this work at the community centre run by the mission in the heart of Toronto. This volunteer position felt like a perfect fit, and I accepted.

On my very first evening, the custodian came to check on me. "So—who is this new face on the block?" he asked with a cheeky smile.

My eyes immediately caught his long wavy hair, the twinkle in his eyes, and his First Nations features.

"Hi, I'm Christine. And who are you?" I replied, holding his gaze and unexpectedly feeling my cheeks get hot.

His name was James, and he was 30, broad-shouldered, and muscular. I found James very engaging and I loved his keen sense of humour. We spent much time that fall taking my group of girls on outings, including a hiking trip to Algonquin Park in Ontario. James turned out to be a licensed canoe and kayak instructor and, to my amazement, seemed to know everything about the outdoors.

As I got to know him better, I discovered that James had learned survival skills the hard way. For about two years as a young teen, he had lived in a cabin in the bush just west of Algonquin Park, with no electricity or running water. Then at 17, he had been left to fend for himself on the streets of Toronto. He'd eventually found his way to Yonge Street Mission and accepted Christ. His story was compelling. His life had clearly taken a new turn.

James was full-blooded First Nations, born to parents of the Caldwell Band, also known as "the Chippewas of Point Pelee and Pelee Island," which is in the very southernmost tip of Canada on Lake Erie, bordering the United States.

As our trust and affection for each other grew, we started attending a First Nations church in Toronto together. I immersed myself in First Nations ways and customs. I also continued to appreciate James's humour and how perceptive he was of people. His insights and faith were a constant source of encouragement.

We were married the following year, in November 1993, in a unique celebration orchestrated by three pastors: the pastor from Yonge Street Mission, the Ojibway pastor from our First Nations church, and the Afro-German pastor from my Lutheran church.

My love journey with First Nations had reached another milestone and turned into a full-scale adventure.

Just a few months after our wedding, James found out that he had type 2 diabetes. The news was unsettling, as we were just finding our feet as a young couple. This challenge was the first of many severe difficulties to come over the following years.

Meanwhile, James had taken work as a building contractor. Our son, Jonah, was born, then our daughter, Naomi, two years later—our two most precious gifts. We settled in Richmond Hill, just north of Toronto, where I had lived all my childhood.

The diabetes slowly started affecting James's eyes and kidneys. In 2007, the specialists told James he was going blind. This was devastating news.

Any hope of recovery was crushed the following year, when surgery on his left eye failed. James retained limited vision in his right eye but was unable to return to his work as a contractor or take other employment.

James began spending increasing amounts of time listening to the Bible and other audio books, and praying. By God's grace, our faith and family became stronger.

I took various jobs to try to make ends meet. In 2011, I started work as an administrative assistant at the large church we had begun to attend as a family: Bayview Glen Church.

One evening near the end of October 2011, I returned home from work as usual and began preparing dinner. I turned on the television but focused on my other tasks, paying little attention to the news. However, the corner of my eye suddenly caught images of a First Nations reserve. Curious, I put down what I was doing and went closer to the TV.

The name of the reserve was plastered on the screen: Attawapiskat. I had never heard of it before. They said it was a remote community in northern Ontario.

Theresa Spence, chief to the Swampy Cree living on the reserve, had just declared a state of emergency.

As alarming images flashed in the background, the news spokesperson described the crisis in the community. Due to a number of factors, including recurrent river flooding, many houses had gradually become uninhabitable, and the situation was worsening. Numerous families were living in trailers, sheds, even tents, with inadequate bathrooms, no running water, or no electricity. With winter and bitterly cold temperatures approaching this subarctic region, disaster loomed.

As the newscast ended and I went back to preparing dinner, I was deeply troubled. I shivered as I pictured young children in the drafty shacks I'd just seen, with the wind whistling and temperatures dipping to –30°C[3].

The phrase "Love your neighbour as yourself"[4] kept running through my mind. This wasn't some faraway country—it was my own province of Ontario! How could I show my love for my neighbour in this bleak situation?

Sending money wasn't really an option—we had very little, and the newscast hadn't mentioned any aid agency.

I remembered the Ojibway children I'd played with as a nine-year-old, and the sadness of their living conditions. Memories of the many other First Nations people who had welcomed me warmly over the years came flooding back. They felt like my own family. My people.

I fell asleep that night knowing I had to find a way to help.

Early the next morning, at my desk in the church office, I quickly did some research. *Where was this reserve again?* I looked on the internet, found Attawapiskat on the map—way up in northern Ontario, near the shore of James Bay. It was hundreds of kilometres from the nearest city, in a territory completely unfamiliar to me and my family. Then I sat back. *What next?*

Suddenly I felt a nudge to call a good friend, Terri Lamarche, who lived in downtown Toronto. Although I hadn't spoken to her for some time, I remembered her well from the First Nations church our family had attended for many years.

Terri was an "Elder," which is a term of great respect used for wise, older First Nations people. During my almost 20 years of marriage to James, I had turned to Terri and other Elders many times for advice. Terri was kind, compassionate, and helpful, always willing to talk through and help with any issues put before her.

Terri answered the phone with her customary enthusiastic greeting.

It was hard to believe that she was nearly 70 and had severe health issues—she was always full of life, glamorous-looking in her matching leopard-print outfits and fashionably dyed hair! Just hearing her voice lifted up my spirit.

We spoke for a while about our families; then I dived in.

"Terri," I asked with some trepidation, "did you watch the news last night? They were talking about a crisis in a northern reserve—I'm not sure how you pronounce the name. Do you know anything about this place?"

"Of course!" she exclaimed. "It's Attawapiskat. My mother was from Attawapiskat. Didn't you know?"

My mouth fell open: Terri—connected with the very same reserve? I knew that Terri was Cree and came from northern Ontario, but I wasn't at all familiar with the dozens of reserves in that remote area. What a coincidence!

"As it happens," she continued, "I wasn't actually born in Attawapiskat. My mother had tuberculosis. She was sent to a sanatorium 600 kilometres south, and that's where I arrived. Then I was with my grannie in Moosonee until my mom got better. But I still have cousins in Attawapiskat. And," Terri continued with a laugh, "it's pronounced 'Atta-*WA*-pis-kat'! It means 'People of the parting of the rocks.'"

Our discussion quickly turned to what the people of Attawapiskat might need most.

  Hot Apple Cider with Cinnamon

"I think it's a great idea to try to help them. Count me in!" Terri told me eagerly.

She went on to tell me that she had already been in touch with Rev. Ross Maracle,[5] a well-known figure among First Nations in Canada, to discuss the needs of Attawapiskat.

Together with Mohawk friends, Ross was planning to send a shipment of warm blankets, clothing, and Christmas gifts for the children.

"So," Terri said, "I think we'd better concentrate on collecting food—you know, the non-perishable kind."

"Sounds like a good plan, Terri," I agreed with a twist of apprehension. I had never organized a food drive before. "I can look into getting some food boxes together."

Terri and I ended our conversation in prayer, asking God for help in the many tasks ahead of us.

After putting the phone down, I glanced up—the pastor for seniors had walked into the church office, on his way to a pastoral meeting, and caught the tail end of my conversation.

"So—what was all this about?" he enquired, with a kind smile. "It sounded pretty serious."

I told him about the crisis situation at the reserve.

He was quiet for a moment.

"Leave it with me," he said finally. "Maybe we can do something to help."

My heart beat faster as he disappeared into the meeting room.

When he came out some time later, he had a broad smile.

"Great news, Christine! The church is right behind you in this initiative. We can announce it from the pulpit, and you can distribute flyers—whatever you think will work best to get that food collected. How does that sound?"

I could hardly contain my excitement. Within 24 hours of watching the newscast and being nudged into action, not only had I received enthusiastic affirmation from Terri, with her insider knowledge of Attawapiskat, but my church had given its full backing for a food drive!

I had taken a small step of faith, and now I felt like a new door was opening wide, with friends rallying around in support. *Thank you, Lord,* I prayed as I contemplated the next step.

As I related the events to James and our teenage children at home later, they chimed in with enthusiasm.

"What a great idea! We can help pack the boxes," said Jonah.

"Yeah—we've never done this before, but we *do* know God can take care of things, don't we?" commented Naomi.

We were all surprised at how little we knew about this remote community of Attawapiskat.

"Sounds like this needs a lot of prayer," concluded James. He was keenly aware of the needs of First Nations, but equally concerned that his limited vision would make it harder for him to help out. "I'll certainly do what I can."

A short time later, Terri and I tackled the next challenge as we studied the map together.

"It seems like an awfully long way," I told Terri. "I'm not sure my little car is going to make it there and back. Should we be hiring a van?"

Terri laughed. "Christine, you can't drive there. The only road to Attawapiskat is an *ice road* in the winter—for big trucks and the like. I'm not even sure it's made yet."

I was shocked. "What! No regular roads? But why not?" I glanced at the map and frowned. "I just don't understand—this is still Ontario."

"That's right," Terri replied in a serious voice. "But that's the reality up there in the North. No roads." She paused for a moment. "Oh—but now I remember! I have a contact at Air Creebec. They might be able to help us."

"You mean, 'Air Quebec'?" I asked, mystified that I hadn't heard about that airline before.

"No, no," Terri laughed again as she corrected me. "Air *Cree-*bec! It's completely owned and operated by First Nations people. I know someone who works there. They have planes going regularly between Attawapiskat and Timmins. Yes, that might work. I think that if we can get food to Timmins, Air Creebec might be willing to fly it to Attawapiskat, especially if it's to bring help in a crisis."

Timmins! I glanced at the map again. Timmins was about 500 km south of Attawapiskat, and 700 km north of Toronto. *At least it sounds more manageable than going all the way to Attawapiskat.* I was already plotting the route in my mind.

To our delight, Air Creebec immediately gave us the go-ahead to send 50 food boxes. Now we had a specific target to achieve.

However, it was already November, and it soon became clear that there wouldn't be enough time to organize a large-scale food collection in time for Christmas. I felt frustrated and disappointed. *How are the people of Attawapiskat going to survive the winter?*

As the holidays approached, Terri and I were relieved to hear that many organizations, religious and secular, had stepped up to help: Ross Maracle launched an Attawapiskat Compassion Outreach; several churches sent up supplies; even the Red Cross coordinated an appeal and intervened.

Nevertheless, we realized that the needs of the troubled Attawapiskat community would continue for some time. Terri and I resolved to resume our efforts in the new year, while James continued to pray.

"How I wish I could fly to Attawapiskat with these food boxes, once we've collected them," Terri reflected during our next phone conversation. "I feel it's important to tell these people that this food comes with our love, the love of Jesus."

Terri sighed. The air fare was clearly out of our reach. "At the very least, I'd want to drive with you to Timmins airport, to thank the staff at Air Creebec in person and explain to them why we are doing this."

"Now that I think of it," Terri continued, her voice suddenly sounding concerned, "what about the other end? Surely we shouldn't just leave the food boxes unassigned at the airport in Attawapiskat. Imagine the chaos!"

"You're right." I shuddered at the thought. This was something we hadn't considered. "Perhaps we can connect with specific people in Attawapiskat to let them know the food is coming?"

I decided to search the internet for churches in Attawapiskat, and to my delight, found two. No one answered at the Catholic Church, but when I called the Pentecostal Church, a man named Stephen Stoney answered the phone.

I introduced myself.

"We are collecting food for your community," I explained, "and we are looking for someone to take care of the boxes once they arrive—to ensure the food reaches people who need it."

"Praise God!" he exclaimed. "We've been praying for God to supply the needs of our community—and food is definitely one of them! My wife, Cathy, and I would love to help."

Stephen explained to me that he and his wife were from the First Nations reserve of Fort Severn, the most northern community in Ontario. They had come to work as teachers at the elementary school on the Attawapiskat reserve and were also pastoring the Attawapiskat Pentecostal Church.

Step by step the plan was unfolding. We felt that God had provided just the right connection once again.

At my request, Pastor Stephen sent me a list of Attawapiskat families in need, including people's ages. My heart broke as I saw that this list included many young children.

Armed with that information, I designed some flyers to insert in the weekly church bulletin. And so, early in 2012, the call for donations went out to the congregation of Bayview Glen Church.

Each Sunday in February, James took up position by a designated table in the foyer. Instantly recognizable with his buckskin jacket, neatly-tied hair, and white cane, my husband stood as a powerful, living symbol of his people, and a keen reminder of the purpose of the donations. Though nearly blind, James eagerly greeted and thanked the many families and individuals dropping off contributions in response to the appeal.

James was often accompanied by Jonah and Naomi.

On February 26, Terri herself came to speak to the congregation. Together, she and I stepped up to the platform and showed pictures of the harsh conditions that families in Attawapiskat were facing. We then described the astronomical cost of groceries in such a remote community.

Imagine my surprise when I arrived at church the next day to find the desk in my office surrounded by food bags, boxes, and parcels of every description, filled to the brim with food items, diapers, and other items on the list!

Our initial goal had been to fill 50 office-type filing boxes. However, we quickly surpassed that target, and items continued to arrive. Our team of volunteers zealously pitched in, and in a short time, we had over 100 boxes packed full with non-perishable groceries of every description.

Clearly, my car was going to be too small to carry them all.

We marvelled at God's provision as one church couple offered the use of their midsize van for the drive to Timmins. Then a custodian remembered the church owned a small trailer, normally used by the youth group. We gladly accepted the offers.

Terri phoned Air Creebec several times to ask nervously if they would allow "just a few more boxes." Finally, they said, "One hundred and twenty-five, no more!"

I counted all the boxes that had piled up in the back of the church office. There were *exactly* 125.

On Thursday, March 29, 2012, about ten days before Easter, we were ready. With the 125 boxes of supplies packed tightly inside the van and trailer, and with much trepidation, I was going to tackle the 700-kilometre, nine-hour drive from Toronto to the airport at Timmins. Terri was all set to accompany me.

We planned to drive first to North Bay, which was about half way, and stay overnight at the home of a friend. Then we'd drive to Timmins the next day, unload the boxes, and drive back to Toronto. Easy!

Since I worked at the church, we agreed to meet in the church parking lot around 4 p.m. My excitement mounted as Terri arrived, along with her little dog and seven bags. We jammed her belongings inside the van, set her dog on her lap, and got on our way, chattering like two school girls on their first field trip.

I quickly settled into driving the unfamiliar vehicle, trailer in tow, grateful that the van owners had had it thoroughly serviced ahead of the journey, and had worked closely with the custodians to secure the trailer.

We'd barely driven five minutes when Terri fell silent, then asked quietly, "Christine, does this van run on diesel?"

I glanced at her. She looked pale. "Yes, Terri," I replied. "Why?"

"You know about my liver, right?"

I held my breath as I remembered that Terri had many health concerns.

"I just cannot handle the diesel fumes," Terri whispered. "They make me feel really sick. I may even fall unconscious—and that wouldn't be much help to you, would it?" She smiled weakly.

I gripped the wheel, feeling ready to crumble.

Terri, like many First Nations I had observed, showed no sign of sorrow, anger, or frustration. In a remarkable attitude of complete surrender, she concluded, "I think I'll have to stay put in Toronto. You just go on without me." Seeing my face, she added, "You have my blessing, Christine. You know I'll be praying for you all the way."

Heartbroken, knowing how much this trip meant to Terri, I turned the van toward my house, which was only a few minutes further north.

My husband stood there, silently taking in this turn of events, as Terri bravely stepped out of the van and I left her and her little dog in the care of my mother and daughter. "James," I said, "you'd better come with me. There's no way I'm making that journey alone."

James just smiled and—to my astonishment—pointed to his overnight bag, which was already packed and ready to go!

I knew he had been praying for the project all along, but what I hadn't realized was that James had received complete assurance from God that he was going to make this trek with me. James had kept quiet about this in front of Terri, since he knew how much she wanted to be part of this initiative for her people. And the few times that he had spoken to me about his conviction that he would come, I had just dismissed it as wishful thinking. Yet here he was, ready, in complete obedience to God's call.

We set off again, in awe of God's provision at each step of the way.

The rest of the drive to North Bay went well. Happy memories flooded back as we stopped for a short break in Huntsville, where James and I had had our honeymoon. Later that evening, Terri's friend Sylvia, an Ojibway Elder, warmly opened her North Bay home to us for the night.

As I've found is often the case when I'm in the company of First Nations people, laughter and storytelling abounded around the kitchen table as we shared a meal, accompanied by bannock[6] and black tea. Sylvia had lived through many hardships, but her spirit of thankfulness shone through.

James and I arrived in Timmins early the next afternoon. As we approached the hangar for Air Creebec, I noticed that James was very still, listening intently. His eyes could barely see the barren landscape around us, but he could hear the planes roaring overhead. My heart beat faster, dispelling all feelings of tiredness after two long days of driving. Giddy with emotion, my mind retraced each step of our journey. The end was almost here.

Two young men from the airline helped us unload our van and trailer. We watched in appreciation as they placed all 125 boxes on three wooden pallets and skillfully got the entire shipment shrink-wrapped.

"How much weight do you have here?" one of the young men asked, as if it was a normal business shipment. Of course, we had no idea. The men laughed as they weighed the shrink-wrapped load.

"Do you know how much it would normally cost to ship this amount of weight to Attawapiskat?" the young man asked us casually. We looked at him in wide-eyed ignorance. Both men chuckled. "Thousands of dollars!" Our mouths fell open.

As we completed the paperwork and procedures, we were struck again by the gracious attitude of the airport officials.

"We can't guarantee your boxes will be there for Easter, you know," they told us. "Your boxes are flying free—we've got to give priority to paid items. But we'll do what we can."

"Of course, we understand," we replied. "Thanks for your help!"

Humbled, James and I left the airport amazed at the way God had made this entire journey possible.

A short time later, back in Toronto, we heard that the boxes had indeed arrived in time for Easter.

Since that time, our church has hosted six similar donation drives, with generous contributions from our congregation and, on occasion, other churches in the community as well. Every single time, the shipment has reached its destination before the target date. Moreover, after that first journey, a member of the church offered the services of his truck company for each 700-km trek from Toronto to Timmins—at no cost.

Thanks to the internet, I've been able to get to know many people living in Attawapiskat. I've seen pictures, not only of almost everyone attending Attawapiskat Pentecostal Church, but also of many other people living on the reserve. We've shared recipes, exchanged jokes, and prayed for one another. I feel deeply loved by this community as they have opened up their hearts to me, my family, and my own community here.

It all hinged on one small step of faith, back in October of 2011, when I heard the news story and acted on what I believed God was asking me to do—love my neighbour as myself. This step knit my own immediate family together more closely, unleashed incredible generosity from many in my church family, and swung open new doors of friendship and understanding.

Being part of this process has been an amazing experience, and a deep confirmation of the lifelong love and respect that God placed on my heart for the First Nations people—a people who have truly become my own.

As I pursue this journey of love, my prayer is that my heart will continue to listen, and I will continue to have the courage to obey, as God nudges me on to the next adventure.

1. Ruth 1:16

2. When used to refer to indigenous people of Canada, the term "Indian" is now considered outdated and potentially offensive. Since the 1970s and '80s, it has been gradually replaced in Canadian usage by "First Nations [person]." If used at all in this context, the term "Indian" should refer to someone with "Indian status," which is a very specific, tightly defined legal term. For a more detailed explanation of terminology, see:

http://www.aadnc-aandc.gc.ca/eng/1100100014642/1100100014643 (Canadian government website, accessed January 24, 2015);

http://indigenousfoundations.arts.ubc.ca/home/identity/terminology.html (University of British Columbia website, accessed January 24, 2015)

3. −30° Celsius is about 22° below in Fahrenheit.

4. Mark 12:31

5. Rev. Ross Maracle was the host of the *Spirit Alive* television broadcast for 20 years (1988–2008) and the founder of several other First Nations initiatives. He died in a tragic car accident in 2012 (age 66), having done much to help Attawapiskat. Maracle was half-Mohawk, half-Scottish, and lived for a long time in Deseronto, next to the Tyendinaga Mohawk Territory, on the northern shore of Lake Ontario, between Belleville and Kingston, Ontario.

6. Bannock is a type of pan-fried, unleavened flatbread. Indigenous peoples around the world have traditions of bannock through many centuries.

The Letter

Nonfiction

Nikki Rosen

Just before I found the letter, I had been in my basement apartment playing with the idea of taking my life. For the past 13 years, all I'd done was shoot dope into my arms, three and sometimes four times a day, and struggle with a serious eating disorder. Anything I ate I threw up. I had no reason to live.

My life began to fall apart after they diagnosed my mother with terminal cancer when I was nine years old. A few weeks before my 13th birthday, she died. Soon after that, my older sister packed her bags and left home. This meant I was left alone with my father, who had always terrified me because of his uncontrollable rages. I had no one any more to shield me from his hatred and brutality.

"I love you," my father would tell me. Then he'd beat me and call me filthy names.

"I love you," he'd say. Then he'd lock me alone in the car for hours in the worst part of town.

"I love you," he'd tell me. Then he'd shove his fist in my face and force me to eat even when I kept throwing up.

"I love you," he'd say. Then he'd hold me down on the bed and hurt me.

I started taking drugs after my mother became ill, but at 13 I began shooting up. It helped calm my fears and numb the pain. Soon after I turned 17, I ran away after a vicious beating.

I lived on the streets, convinced I could make it on my own. I learned to fight the perverts and crazies, but inside, I felt alone, lost, scared. Drugs gave me courage and a sense of being in control, but my moods became erratic and my behaviour wild.

One day, a concerned friend took me to meet a guy she believed could help me.

"I'll take care of you," he said, "and give you a safe place to live."

I was young and naïve. I trusted him. But once I entered his house, I became his prisoner.

"I love you," he told me. Then he held me down and raped me.

"I love you," he said. Then he punched me so hard my spleen ruptured.

"I love you," he told me. Then he locked me in a cold, dark room and refused to let me go.

The days melted into weeks and then into months. Summer gave way to fall and then to winter. Snow fell as temperatures plummeted below zero. I tried to leave, but he locked me in an upper room in a back coach house. I managed to pry the lock open.

I had no boots or shoes or warm clothes but, desperate to be free, I somehow managed to climb over the six foot high iron fence that he had erected around the property.

I was free, yet I wasn't. The images of what had taken place in that house played over and over in my mind. I wandered the streets with an awful ache in my gut. I felt worthless and alone. No one knew what had happened to me, and shame kept me from saying anything. I was convinced nobody cared if I was hurt or safe or scared, and I didn't care either. I started living wild, on the edge, out of control.

I dulled the pain the only way I knew how—by shoving needles into my arms, getting stoned, throwing up, and using sharp rocks and razor blades to cut my arms until they bled. The dope helped me to not think or feel. Especially to not think. Seeing the blood and feeling the pain reminded me I was still alive.

A social worker convinced me to let her help me get off the streets. She found a basement apartment for me, and arranged for monthly welfare cheques.

Still, I couldn't kick the drug addiction or break free from the horrible memories. Living life alone as a drug addict held no promise that things would ever change for the better. Suicide seemed the most viable option for putting an end to my misery.

And then I got "the letter."

Around 11 o'clock that morning, I went upstairs to get the mail.

I found the letter, consisting of two handwritten pages, shoved inside my mailbox. There was no envelope.

Although my name wasn't on the pages, it seemed obvious that someone wanted me to read the penned words. I read the first line.

"Hi. I needed to write this to tell you something important, something you need to know."

Curious, I kept reading.

"You're loved," the note said. "Greatly loved."

"Right." I muttered under my breath. "Some jerk is playing a sick joke." I flipped to the end to see who had written the letter. It had been signed, "A Friend who cares."

I scratched my head, trying to think which of my friends might have done this. Like me, though, they were all living in their own misery and struggling to make it from one day to the next. I couldn't see any of them putting it in my mailbox, never mind writing it.

I went back to reading. "I know you feel alone, that nobody cares whether you live or die, but you're wrong. I care. Deeply care."

Chills rifled through my body. *Who had sent this letter? How did they know about my situation and the desperation I felt?*

The writer went on to say, "I died for you and I would do it again in a heartbeat. That's how much I love you."

I choked on those words. *Love me?* All I knew of love is that it hurts. Everyone in my life who had claimed to love me had left me alone, empty, and damaged.

Annoyed by the nerve of the person who had stuck this in my mailbox, yet also curious, I read the next line. "When I died, I took your pain, all of it, and also the shame. I did it so you can live free."

Anger now replaced my confusion. I racked my brain trying to think of who could have written this and what they wanted from me. But no one came to mind.

Exasperated, I shoved the papers in my pants pocket and hurried back downstairs to the apartment. Once inside, I locked the door, pulled out the letter, and read it straight through from the beginning to the end.

"I'm here watching over you. I've always been with you even in those dark and terrifying moments. You're of great worth to me. I truly love you."

A part of me wanted to crumple up the pages and burn them, but the words had slipped inside my heart. I clutched the letter to my chest and, for the first time in a long time, tears spilled from my eyes. I wanted to believe what the letter said, and that whoever had written it actually did care for and love me.

In the days and weeks following, I read and reread that letter many times. Although I was confused as to what it actually meant, and still wondered who had sent it, the message kept me from giving up and gave me enough hope to keep on fighting.

It would take months and another miraculous experience before I discovered the truths written in that letter.

I was at a local park when I met a girl who invited me to what she called a "camp meeting." I had no idea what that was, but I wanted to get out of the city, so I agreed to go.

While I was at the camp, I had a seizure because I hadn't taken any drugs since leaving home. Those who had invited me on the trip took me to the hospital. In Emergency, while lying on a gurney getting oxygen, I heard a voice say, "Pray in My Name."

I sat up and whispered the name "Jesus." Instantly, I felt as if someone had turned a key in a lock, causing the chains wrapped around me to fall off. I felt flooded with peace and joy.

Since that day, I've never touched another needle.

Not that everything has been easy. At first, I didn't trust Him to stay. I thought His love was conditional on what I did or didn't do. And I didn't think He'd forgive me for the things I couldn't stop doing, like throwing up and cutting myself. But He did. Again and again and again.

Some days I tried to force Him to leave. I screamed and demanded that He go away and leave me alone, like everyone else had done. He never did. He stayed and waited until I was ready, until I felt safe. He loved me regardless of what I said or how I acted.

Looking back now, I think the wires in my head had become all mixed up when I was a kid. I thought that what had happened to me was normal, that everyone lived on the edge, fighting to avoid getting beaten, like people in a war zone, in total chaos, confusion, and tension. And I believed that the awful things that happened to me were because there was something wrong with me.

I had no idea that they had no right to do what they did. All I knew was that it made me crazy and made me want to punish myself in ways that almost killed me. But I learned that real love doesn't hurt; instead it comforts and brings healing and relief.

God's love changed me, took away the fears, and padded me with hope to hold on, to stay in the game, to never give up. He gave me the courage to walk free. His kindness softened my heart. His gentleness quieted the rage. His love dissolved the hate. He never judged, forced, or violated me in any way. He accepted me as I was, with all the anger, hatred, and addictions. His love remained a constant, and in time became an anchor for me to hold onto no matter what storm I was in.

I slowly began to change from the inside out. I found myself wanting to make Him happy and do the things I knew would please Him. I wanted to emulate Him and show kindness and love to others as He had shown to me.

The hardest part was forgiving those people who had hurt me. I had wanted revenge for what they had done, but I told myself that if God could forgive me, I could do the same for others.

Years have passed since I received that letter. I never did find out who wrote it and dropped it in my mailbox. Sometimes I've wondered if the person who placed it there was like me, someone who had lived broken, alone, and afraid, and then been touched by God's love. Perhaps God had changed that person's life and he or she wanted to make a difference for someone else.

I wish I could tell that person that their act of faith, kindness, and love made a huge impact on my life. The only way I know to show my gratitude is to pass on the love they sent me that day in "the letter."

It's strange about love. It hurts at first when you're not used to it. It hurts so much that even though you hunger for it, you're afraid to feel its pain.

Love is an amazing thing. It gives courage and freedom. What I can't or won't do because I'm afraid—love makes me able to do. If someone I love needs me to do it, or wants me to, then I'll do it. I'll do it for them. Simply because I love them.

Love has power to push me beyond my own limitations and make me do things that are terrifying and seem absolutely impossible.

Feeling touched by love—safe, accepted—has greater power than any words. I had a radio interview yesterday. When asked what made the difference in turning my life around, I knew. It was the touch of His love.

Love made the difference. Love that waited, love that never forced me to be or do anything, a gentle and accepting love that met me right where I was. In the dark. In the pain. In the shame.

And even more impactful than my loving someone is having someone love me. Knowing I am loved has this strange power—it becomes a motivator that pushes me to live my best life and reach for my dreams. Just as abuse and trauma change who we are and how we live our lives and move in the world, so does love.

The touch of God's gentleness made the difference. It showed me that love, kindness, and forgiveness free us in ways that nothing else can. I knew force, threats, and fear, but this was different. Kindness softened my heart. Gentleness quieted the rage. Love dissolved the hate.

Before that day at the hospital, I had always equated love with violence, fear, abandonment, and neglect. But real love is different.

"I love you," God said. Then He patiently waited until I was ready to trust him.

"I love you," He told me. Then He broke the hold of the drug addiction.

"I love you," He said. Then He calmed my anger and hatred.

"I love you," He told me. Then He healed my heart with His gentle touch.

"I love you," He said. Then He freed me from shame and fear.

  Hot Apple Cider with Cinnamon

On Drowning

Connie Inglis

When life accosts with hopelessness and woe,
When strength of mind and arm you can't employ,
And sorrow pulls you in its undertow
May the God of love fill you with His joy.
Amidst the rise and fall of endless waves
There still is rescue for the crying heart;
An Anchor firm, unmoving, He who saves,
Limitless grace and love He will impart.
Beware the one who seeks to blind your eyes
With grit and murky water to deceive;
Hug anchor's hope, believing not the lies;
Trust the promise, not circumstance's grave.
Drowning does not mean resignation of
Your life, if you are drowning in His love.

What's Next?

1. Visit our website and we'll give you a special gift:

http://hotappleciderbooks.com

2. While there, sign up for our reader updates to get:

- Special offers
- Information about author signings
- News about upcoming books
- Reviews and endorsements
- Information on how to get bulk copies of these books at a discount

3. Did you enjoy this book? Let our writers know.

- Post a comment on our website or Facebook page.
- Write a short review and post it on Amazon, Barnes & Noble, Goodreads, your blog, or any place else you frequent.
- Tell other people about the book. Better yet, buy copies to give as gifts to friends and family who would enjoy them.
- Buy the writers' other books. Or get them from your library.
- Connect with the writers whose work you like by signing up for their newsletters, following them on Facebook, Twitter, or other social media.
- The writers will appreciate it very much.

Editor and Writers

N. J. Lindquist

http://www.njlindquist.com

Photo by Stephen Gurie Woo

N. J. Lindquist is an award-winning author, an inspiring speaker, and an empowering teacher. Her published work includes 20 books and one play as well as numerous columns, articles, and short stories. N. J. writes in a variety of genres: memoir, opinion, discipleship, nonfiction, coming-of-age fiction, mystery, and fantasy.

N. J. is passionate about empowering writers from the Canadian Christian faith community. In 2001, she co-founded The Word Guild and served as its executive director until January, 2008. She also directed the Write! Canada conference for 11 years. N. J. continues to post advice and instructional videos on her website for writers, www.writewithexcellence.com.

In 2007, N. J. realized that an anthology of true stories, fiction, and poetry would be the perfect way to showcase the work of Canadian writers who are Christian. That led to the publication of the Hot Apple Cider Books.

N. J. has taught workshops for writers in every province of Canada except Newfoundland (one of these days!) as well as in the United States. She also speaks to adults and teens on leadership, creativity, and other topics.

Born in Saskatchewan and raised in Manitoba, N. J. lives in Markham, Ontario, close to her four sons and their families.

LoveChild: Reflections from a Former Ugly Duckling, Part 1
(That's Life! Communications)

As J. A. Menzies – *Shadow of a Butterfly: The Case of the Harmless Old Woman* (MurderWillOut Mysteries)

As Alleyn Shaw – *My Brother's Keeper: A Second Chance for Shane Donahue* (That's Life! Communications)

Ruth Ann Adams

http://ruthannadams.com

Ruth Ann Adams is a high school English teacher, Sunday School superintendent, mother of five and pastor's wife. One of her most recent publications is a story entitled "Charles Holloway: Man of Mystery," in *Promises of Home: Stories of Canada's British Home Children* by Rose McCormick Brandon. Ruth Ann is addicted to cats and British history. Her passion is to bring God's love and encouragement to others. Ruth Ann has a blog named *5 X Mama*. Originally from Owen Sound, ON, Ruth now lives in Dartmouth, NS.

A. A. Adourian

http://www.aaadourian.com

A. A. Adourian loves to learn about God and write about how the Holy Spirit can change our hearts. She's always asking God for more faith to trust Him, and He gives her plenty of practice! A librarian by profession, with more than a decade of experience in the field, A. A. is a skilled researcher and the author of numerous business-related reports in a corporate environment. She was first published in *A Second Cup of Hot Apple Cider,* and continues to thank God as He challenges her to make Him known both by how she lives and what she writes. A. A. makes her home in Toronto.

Brian C. Austin

http://www.undiscoveredtreasures.org

Brian C. Austin is a writer and speaker. His work includes print and audio poetry, nonfiction articles, historical fiction, and dramatic monologue. Brian is an active member of The Word Guild and contributed several poems to *Hot Apple Cider: Words to Stir the Heart and Warm the Soul*. He's spent many happy hours working in bookstores and organizing church libraries. Brian lives near Durham, ON.

Muninn's Keep (Word Alive Press)
Laughter & Tears (Word Alive Press)

Glynis M. Belec

http://www.glynisbelec.com

Glynis Belec, an award-winning freelance writer & children's author, faces each day with hope and thanksgiving. She rejoices daily and is constantly reminded about looking at the world through child-like eyes. Glynis loves capturing life in words and can't wait for tomorrow so she can feel inspired all over again. Glynis lives in Drayton, ON.

Jailhouse Rock (Concordia Publishing)
Hopeful Homer (Angel Hope Publishing)

Vilma Blenman

http://writerteacher.wordpress.com

Vilma Blenman is a teacher and counsellor with the Toronto District School Board. She has two pieces in the award-wining Canadian anthology *A Second Cup of Hot Apple Cider*, and two more in *A Taste of Hot Apple Cider*. In 2013, Vilma published *First Flight*, an eclectic collection of poetry. She also tied for first place in the Writers Community of Durham Region annual summer slam competition, delivering a powerful performance of her poem, "Fat Girl Feelings." In 2014 she co-edited a published collection of students' stories and recipes in the literary cookbook, *S.I.S.T.A. Soulfood: Delightful Recipes & Recollections*. She lives with her family in Pickering, ON.

Bill Bonikowsky

http://www.billbonikowsky.com

Bill's experience includes the editing of *Alpha News* for Alpha Ministries Canada, and editing of *Report to the People* for Greater Vancouver Youth for Christ. Bill was a contributing writer for the *NIV Life Application Bible* and was published in *A Second Cup of Hot Apple Cider*. Bill lived in Guelph, ON before moving to BC in 1974. He now makes his home in Surrey, BC. He has three sons, nine grandchildren, and a wife (Joy) in heaven.

Grace K. Chik

http://gracekchik.wordpress.com

Grace K. Chik was born and raised in Guelph, ON. She currently lives in Mississauga with her husband Keng Hon "Tim" Yee. Her writing goal is to encourage others with heart-felt stories. Some of the themes that particularly interest her are blessing, reconciliation, and forgiveness—especially toward those who aren't able to reciprocate.

Photo by Dr. Tricia K. W. Woo

Season's Blessings for You: A Collection of Christmas Stories (Word Alive Press)

Bobbie Ann Cole

http://www.love-triangles.com

Bobbie Ann Cole writes, speaks, and teaches about her experiences as a Jewish Christian. She also helps people hone their own faith stories and dare to share. Her latest book is *Love Triangles: Discovering Jesus the Jew in Today's Israel*—a blend of memoir, travelogue, historical document, and investigative journalism. It follows on from where her miraculous coming-to-faith story, *She Does Not Fear the Snow*, an Amazon #1 bestseller, leaves off. Bobbie divides her time between Canterbury in her native UK and New Brunswick, Canada.

Lynne Collier

http://lynnecollier.com

Lynne Collier is a Lay Associate Pastoral Counsellor and Kingdom Purpose Coach. She's written a personal reflection about raising her son, who's on the Autism Spectrum. It won third place in the 2012 God Uses Ink Novice Writers Awards. Her second book is a collection of ideas for hosting a Middle Earth Shire party. Lynne is passionate about tending her garden and seeing people discover their purpose in God's Kingdom. She and her husband live near Bowmanville, ON.

Raising Benjamin Frog: A Mother's Journey with her Autistic Son (CreateSpace)
Hosting a Shire Party: Costumes, Food and Games (CreateSpace)

Marguerite Cummings

http://margueritec.wordpress.com

Marguerite Cummings has a distinctively international background. Born in Belgium into a French-speaking family with roots in Austria, Belgium, Poland, and Romania, she moved to England in her late teens. There, she completed an Oxford degree, attended Bible college, trained as a technical writer and editor, and worked in computing. In 1998, she moved to Toronto, Canada. Marguerite was thrilled to be part of the bestselling anthology *A Second Cup of Hot Apple Cider*. She has also designed two reader's guides and co-edited two discussion guides for the Hot Apple Cider book series.

Joanna Clark Dawyd

http://www.toaprettylife.com

Joanna Clark Dawyd is a writer, editor, and blogger. But all that has to be squeezed into the corners of her life as a wife and a mother of two. Her long-term goal is to be a novelist, but she's temporarily altered that ambition for the sake of actually finishing something. When not blogging about parenting, home, writing, and the rest of her life, she struggles to compose articles and short stories. Joanna lives in Edmonton, AB.

Catharina den Hartog-Terry

Catharina den Hartog-Terry was born in the Netherlands, raised in Canada, graduated from Oral Roberts University, and met her sweetheart of 42 years in Jerusalem. She and Leonard raised seven children, and they are presently raising their newest grandchild, Esmeralda. A freelance writer, Catharina loves creating stories of hope and encouragement. She co-authored *Real People—Real Stories*, a booklet published by her church. It contains true stories of people who have discovered the reality of our awesome God!

Beverly G. DeWit

http://www.bevdewit.weebly.com

Beverly DeWit is an internationally qualified Upper Elementary Montessori teacher, artist, and freelance writer. Her artwork is on display at Express Yourself Art Studio Inc. in Lion's Head, ON, where she lives. Beverly's work has been published in medical journals and medical newsletters, and on blogs and websites. She's also had work published in various church publications. She has led various women's ministries and enjoys speaking to women. She is the wife of a senior pastor.

Mario Dimain

http://www.photographersforchrist.blogspot.ca

Mario Dimain is a husband, a father, and a grandfather. He spends his retirement years doing what he loves—enjoying the beauty of God's creations. Between times with his family, he spreads God's Word through photography and creative writing. Mario writes inspirational articles and short stories. His Christ-centred short fiction, "Screaming Silence," won a place in the published *Aspiring Writers 2013 Winners Anthology*. A happy Filipino immigrant, Mario has lived in Scarborough, ON for forty years.

Patricia Anne Elford

http://stillwatersanddancingwings.blogspot.ca

Patricia Anne Elford, OCT, B. A., M. Div., is a professional member of The Word Guild and InScribe Christian Writers' Fellowship, educator, clergyperson, poet, enthusiastic freelance book and article editor, and award-winning writer. She has been published in literary journals, newspapers, periodicals, anthologies, worship publications, and online. With four book manuscripts under development, Patricia—wife, mother, grandmother and cat's domestic servant—leads a full, God-nourished life in the Ottawa Valley.

Grandmothers' Necklace (Epic Press)

Lisa Elliott

http://www.lisaelliottstraightfromtheheart.webs.com

Lisa Elliott is an award-winning author, inspirational speaker, pastor's wife, and mother of four. She's often described as "refreshingly real" as she passionately shares the life-changing truths and principles from God's Word "Straight from the Heart." She has appeared on Christian television and radio, and contributes to *Just Between Us* Magazine. She and her husband live in London, ON.

The Ben Ripple: Choosing to Live through Loss with Purpose (Word Alive Press)
Dancing in the Rain: One Family's Journey through Grief & Loss (Word Alive Press)

Angelina Fast-Vlaar

http://angelinafastvlaar.com

Angelina Fast-Vlaar is an 18-year cancer survivor and begins each day with thanksgiving. Her writing includes nonfiction books, articles and poetry. She has won three first-place awards for writing. Widowed twice, she walked with her second husband through a decade-long struggle with dementia. In her upcoming book, she hopes to encourage other caregivers. She makes her home in St. Catharines, ON.

Seven Angels for Seven Days (Castle Quay Books)
The Valley of Cancer (Word Alive Press)

Maureen Fitzpatrick

Maureen Fitzpatrick won first prize for her poem "Peace" and second prize for her short story "Adieu" in a National Newspaper Competition in Guyana, South America. She produced a House Journal and a radio program for the Bauxite Industry, and published a booklet "The Guyana Bauxite Years of Achievement." She had four booklets published for the Institute of Applied Science and Technology. From Guyana, Maureen is based in Toronto.

A Cry for Love (Watermark Press)

Christiana Flanigan

Christiana Flanigan is a writer residing in Mono, ON, and is a member of The Word Guild and the Headwaters Writers' Guild. Her love of writing began at age 12 when she received her first journal. Christiana has had short stories published in two of the Chicken Soup for the Soul series. For the past five years, she has been a regular contributor to *Sideroads of Dufferin County* magazine. She holds two diplomas from the Institute of Children's Literature.

Doris Fleming

Doris Fleming—author, life-coach, and co-founder of Creative Expression Outlet—finds that putting words to paper has become an act of worship; as she writes, she senses God's pleasure. Currently, Doris is writing the sequel to her first novel, creating devotionals for a weekly radio spot, and developing prompts for young writers. Encouraging fellow-writers along the sometimes-arduous journey toward publication yields her profound enjoyment. Born in Alberta, Canada, Doris lives and works with her husband Art in Wallace, Idaho.

Seeds in the Wind (Lighthouse Publishing)

Carol Ford

http://carolfordassociates.wordpress.com

Carol Ford is a speaker, career coach, and writer. One of her interests is in sharing her adoption reunion story with women's and senior's groups. As a contributor on Hope Stream Radio, she gives advice on work life. From Newmarket, ON, Carol volunteers with The Word Guild and leads a local writers' group which has written a new book for writers.

As the Ink Flows: Devotions to Inspire Christian Writers & Speakers (Judson Press)

Ramona Furst

http://www.ramonafurst.com

Ramona Furst is a writer and artist who lives in North Bay, ON. Her mission statement is "to serve God well and to bear witness, through her writing and her art, to the glorious God moments she has experienced." A wife, mother, and grandmother, Ramona also has a heart for missions and has participated in several missions trips to Africa and South America. She's a member of The Word Guild, Inscribe Christian Writers' Fellowship, and the Canadian Society of Children's Authors, Illustrators, and Performers (CANSCAIP).

Kelsey Greye

https://www.facebook.com/kelsey.g.friesen

A western Canadian pastor with a passion for people, Scripture, and theology, Kelsey Greye loves being part of God's work in and through the local church. She has a strong affinity for rainy days, a good murder mystery, and a strong cup of tea. Kelsey is the author of three novels: two historical romances and a romantic suspense.

A Thread of Truth (Word Alive Press)
All That Remains (Wesbrook Bay Books)

Laureen F. Guenther

http://reeniesresources.blogspot.com

Laureen F. Guenther, a freelance writer, elementary school teacher, and lifelong learner, wrote Sunday school curriculum for Faith Alive Publications and now writes regularly for newspapers and a writers' magazine. Laureen aims to love God with all her might, and to encourage and comfort everyone He places in her path, particularly those with disabilities or other challenges. She teaches and writes from her home near Calgary, AB.

Photo by Pamela Photography

Rob Harshman

Rob Harshman has been a social science teacher for more than 40 years and has traveled to more than forty countries. He is married, and has two married daughters and a grandson. Rob's hobbies include travel, gardening, and photography. He has been a contributor to the Chicken Soup for the Soul series, and plans to continue writing short stories from his home in Mississauga, ON.

Wendy Dewar Hughes

http://www.wendydewarhughes.com

Wendy Dewar Hughes is an award-winning author of inspirational suspense and sweet romance novels. Her nonfiction books include spiritual and inspirational topics, coloring books, and illustrated journals. Wendy is a writing and publishing coach, and a professional artist whose artwork appears on book covers and gift products sold throughout the world. She lives in BC's Fraser Valley.

Picking up the Pieces (Summer Bay Press)
Sketches from the South of France: Postcard-Sized Coloring Projects for Adults (Summer Bay Press)

Connie Inglis

http://www.dougconnie.com

Connie Inglis has lived life to the full with her family as an overseas missionary, literacy worker, and teacher. She is passionate about serving minority language groups, being a grandma, and writing—especially poetry. Her life experiences are a testament to God's goodness and love, and she is thankful each morning for the gift of life. Connie lives in Alberta.

Linda Jonasson

http://alinefromlinda.blogspot.com

Linda Jonasson is an elementary school teacher and a writer. Her newspaper articles about history and social issues have appeared in *Maranatha News, Christian Courier,* and *Brantford Expositor.* Two of her short stories were published in *Promises of Home: Stories of Canada's British Home Children* in July, 2014. Currently, Linda is seeking a publisher for her book, *I'm Just Daisy,* about her British Home Child great-grandmother. Linda is married with two children and lives in Brantford, ON. She blogs daily about history, home and writing.

Marianne Jones

http://www.mariannejones.ca

Marianne Jones is a writer and retired teacher from Thunder Bay, ON. She and her husband Reg have two daughters and two gorgeous granddaughters. Marianne has varied interests, and her four books include a children's picture book and a YA fantasy, a collection of poetry, and a cozy mystery. She is proud to have three of her poems installed at Prince Arthur's Landing at the Thunder Bay Marina Park.

Great-Grandma's Gifts (Split Tree Publishing)
The Serenity Stone Murder (Split Tree Publishing)

Photo by Lorna Lillo
Photography

Bobbi Junior

http://www.bobbijunior.com

Bobbi Junior's passion is to use story to show how God brings value to our suffering. Through memoir, she explores caregiving, grief, disability, and other life experiences, with an honest sharing of mistakes made and victories won. Bobbi has won awards for her book, *The Reluctant Caregiver,* and her short story, "Tell Me About Today." She also creates weekly episodes for "Not Me, Lord" on HopeStreamRadio. com. Bobbi lives in Edmonton, AB.

The Reluctant Caregiver (Word Alive Press)

Photo by Amy Cooper

Christine Kenel-Peters

http://christinekenelpeters.wordpress.com

Christine Kenel-Peters is a Swiss-Canadian who has lived most of her life in the suburbs of Toronto. As a young adult, Christine came to a deeper level of faith which transformed her heart, leading to full-time missions work for several years in the Caribbean, Scotland, and North Africa. Christine and her family now attend and serve at their local church, where she is employed as an administrative assistant. Christine and her husband are passionate about Aboriginal issues and are both open to speaking engagements.

David Kitz

http://www.davidkitz.ca

David Kitz is an actor, award-winning author, and an ordained pastor with the Foursquare Gospel Church of Canada. His love for drama and storytelling is evident to all who have seen his Bible-based performances. He has toured across Canada and the United States with a variety of one-man plays for both children and adults. Born and raised in Saskatchewan, David now lives in Ottawa, ON.

The Soldier, the Terrorist & the Donkey King (Essence Publishing)
Psalms Alive! (Forever Books)

Elizabeth Kranz

https://www.linkedin.com/pub/
elizabeth-jensen-kranz/103/176/828

Elizabeth often heard the question posed to her five children, "What do you want to do when you grow up?" Since she had given up gainful employment to mother them full-time, she wondered what she would do when they grew up. What would God want her to do? Well, they're up and out and now she writes about them, Biblical characters, and the canoeing adventures she has with her busy, talented pastor husband. She lives near the tiny community of Killaloe, ON.

Marcia Lee Laycock

http://www.marcialeelaycock.com

Marcia writes from Alberta, Canada, where she lives with her pastor/husband and two golden retrievers. She was the winner of The Best New Canadian Christian Author Award for her novel *One Smooth Stone,* and is a columnist with a wide following for her devotional column, *The Spur.* She recently won the 2014 Word Award for her YA fantasy. Marcia also speaks at women's retreats and one day events.

A Tumbled Stone (Word Alive Press)
The Ambassadors (Helping Hands Press)

Les Lindquist

http://leslindquist.com

Les Lindquist took early retirement from his IBM career as a change consultant a few years ago. Since then, he has been tackling the challenges of tremendous change in the publishing industry. In addition, he is now focused on two book projects of his own. In his spare time, Les invests in helping Canadian writers who are Christian reach their potential. Born in Saskatchewan, he lives in Markham, ON, where he swims regularly (and competes in swim meets), and enjoys spending time with his grandkids.

Photo by Stephen Gurie Woo

Frieda Martens

Frieda Martens is a retired school teacher who enjoys writing about cooking and her experiences as a teacher. Two examples are "The Art of Baking Pies" (*Manitoba Cooperator*) and "Teaching Merle" (*Avant Magazine*). She has also published two cookbooks. Frieda is passionate about teaching English as a second language to university students and immigrants in Manitoba, where she lives, as well as to second language teachers in Ukraine.

Precious Wild Berries (Art Bookbindery)
Precious Grains (Art Bookbindery)

Heather McGillivray-Seers

Heather McGillivray-Seers is busy turning challenges into stepping stones during this season of her life, as she delves deeper into the treasuries of God's Word. These discoveries are tucked snuggly between the pages of her daily journal, which she refers to often to be sure she's really living out what she's learned. Unbeknownst to anyone else, poems, stories, and other ideas continue to plague her, and she commits them all to her heavenly Father, Saviour, Shepherd, and Best Friend for safe keeping. Heather lives in Quebec.

Heidi McLaughlin

http://www.heartconnection.ca

International speaker, author, and columnist Heidi McLaughlin believes there is nothing more beautiful than people who know they are loved by God. Heidi guides people into this truth through her speaking, mentoring, thought-provoking articles, and intimate conversations over a steaming cup of strong coffee. She lives amidst the beautiful vineyards of West Kelowna, BC.

Beauty Unleashed: Transforming a Woman's Soul (VMI Publishing)
Sand to Pearls: Making Bold Choices to Enrich Your Life (Deep River Books)

Sally Meadows

http://sallymeadows.com

After 25 years juggling her creative passions with a professional career, Sally Meadows took the plunge in 2013 to write prose and music full-time. A two-time national-award-nominated singer/songwriter, Sally has contributed to several anthologies, written nonfiction articles, and authored two children's books. She continues to follow passionately wherever God takes her from her Saskatchewan home.

Photo by Esprit Photography

Beneath That Star (Word Alive Press)
The Two Trees (Your Nickel's Worth Publishing)

Ruth Smith Meyer

http://www.ruthsmithmeyer.com

Ruth Smith Meyer, a writer and speaker raised in the Stouffville area, now alternates living between Ailsa Craig and Listowel, ON. She has published two well-received adult novels, a children's book (*Tyson's Bad Sad Day*), and, recently, her memoirs. An inspirational speaker, Ruth addresses a variety of topics, including how to face death, dying, and the grief journey in a positive way.

Not Easily Broken and *Not Far from the Tree* (Word Alive Press)
Out of the Ordinary (Word Alive Press)

Laura Aliese Miedema

http://laurabookma.wordpress.com

Laura Aliese Miedema loves the Word and works in two storehouses of words, Colchester-East Hants Public Library and Immanuel Baptist Church Library in Truro, Nova Scotia. She studied English words at Crandall University and Colchester Christian Academy. Her words won first place in The Word Guild's 2012 God Uses Ink Contest. You can find her at the Metro Christian Writers Group, the Word Nerds Teen Writing Group, or on Pinterest (www.pinterest.com/lauraaliese/) and Twitter (@LauraAliese).

Darcy Elizabeth Neal

Darcy Elizabeth Neal uses words as a way of exploring the world, of sounding the depths of the soul, and of reaching out to God and other people. A poet and freelance writer, her work has appeared in various publications including *Focus on the Family Magazine*, *Children's Ministry Magazine*, *Quebec Chronicle-Telegraph* and *The Muskokan*. She and her husband live in Quebec City. They have three grown children and one grandchild.

Violet Nesdoly

http://violetnesdoly.com

Violet Nesdoly uses her prize-winning fiction, nonfiction, meditations, and poetry to do what she is passionate about—bring the Bible to life. Her debut novel *Destiny's Hands*, a Bible fiction, was a finalist in the 2013 Word Awards. Violet lives with her husband in Langley, BC. When she's not writing or reading, you'll probably find her, camera in hand, enjoying one of the local nature trails.

Destiny's Hands (Word Alive Press)

Shelley Norman

Shelley Norman draws inspiration for her writing not only from The One who gave her the gift but also from the family farm she operates with her husband, their animals, and the children who attend her home childcare. Shelley has had more than 50 short stories published in various magazines, literary journals, and anthologies in Canada and the US. She also has one published children's book.

Bruce County Counts (The Brucedale Press)

Judi Peers

http://judipeers.wordpress.com

Judi Peers is an author, speaker, and engaging Bible study leader. She has written several children's books and Bible studies, as well as contributed stories to award-winning anthologies. When Judi is not working with words, she can be found weeding her garden, travelling with her husband Dave, or enjoying family and friends on the shore of the Otonabee River in Peterborough, ON.

Niki Allday Photography

Playing Second Fiddle: God's Heart for Harmony Regarding Women and the Church (Word Alive Press)

Heather Rae Rodin

Heather Rae Rodin serves as Executive Director for Hope Grows Haiti, which helps bring medical, educational, nutritional, and housing assistance to Haiti. A freelance writer, Heather has always had a passion for story. She has recently published the true story of a Haitian man who was dedicated to Satan as a baby, but found God. When not working in Haiti, she enjoys speaking to women's groups, making presentations for the mission, and time spent with her large and growing family. Heather and her husband Gord live on an acreage near Peterborough, ON.

Prince of Vodou: Breaking the Chains (Westbow Press)

Nikki Rosen

http://www.write2empower.webs.com

Nikki Rosen uses her writing to empower others to reach for their best. Nikki is the author of *In the Eye of Deception: A True Story,* winner of the 2010 Word Award for life stories, and *Dancing Softly*, which was shortlisted for the same award in 2014. Nikki has won a number of short story contests and has been published in various anthologies and magazines across North America. She lives in Burlington, ON.

In the Eye of Deception: A True Story (Gentle Recovery)
Dancing Softly (Gentle Recovery)

Rose Seiler Scott

http://roseseilerscott.com

Rose knew in fifth grade she wanted to be a writer, but took a few career detours, including teaching piano and bookkeeping. Eventually, family history drew her back to writing and resulted in her first novel. She believes truth is expressed through stories, especially through the greatest story of all. Rose lives in Surrey, BC, with her husband Andy and their two youngest children.

Threaten to Undo Us (Promontory Press)

S. M. Shigemitsu

http://cassisa.blogspot.ca

Born to Japanese immigrants in Alberta, where she currently resides, S. M. grew up with stories about Japan and God's faithfulness. As a native-speaking English teacher, God gave her opportunities to teach in Mongolia, Japan, and Bangladesh where He taught her His faithfulness and love. Her hobbies are reading, writing, and drawing. She never leaves home without a book to read. This is the first time her writing has been published.

Adele Simmons

http://adelesimmons.wordpress.com

Adele Simmons is an award-winning writer and editor published in many formats including books, journalism, television, scriptwriting, songwriting, and poetry. Also a keynote speaker and singer, Adele teaches public speaking, creative ministries, and music. She hails from the west, but spent her career life in Quebec and Ontario in business management, marketing, mental health, and college teaching. Adele lives near Whitby, ON.

Janet Sketchley

http://janetsketchley.ca

A key theme in Janet Sketchley's writing is that whatever happens, Jesus will be there. Janet lives in Nova Scotia, where she writes Christian suspense novels and blogs about faith and books. She loves Jesus and her family, and enjoys adventure stories, worship music, and tea. Fans of Christian suspense are invited to join Janet's writing journey through her monthly newsletter: bit.ly/JanetSketchleyNews.

Heaven's Prey (Redemption's Edge book 1)
Secrets and Lies (Redemption's Edge book 2)

Martin Smith

Martin Smith spends nine-to-five working at David C. Cook Distribution Canada, but is also busy as President of the Gospel Music Association of Canada, a not-for-profit association whose mission is to promote the growth and ministry of Christian music arts in Canada. In his spare time, Martin dabbles in community theatre in Brantford, ON. Martin has acted, directed, and written several plays, including *The Strong Hand Of Love, The Other Noise,* and *Baked Muffins With Dates.*

L. June Stevenson

Former special education teacher, mental health consultant, and editor, June Stevenson says, "I had a dream to be a famous writer." Today she is content to be at least a prolific author of daily devotions, poetry, theological articles, and greeting card verse. June is an award-winning writer published nationally and internationally, both in secular and denominational magazines. In 2014, her first song won the Terence L. Bingley Award. Now retired, June enjoys freelancing and spending time with her two children, five grandchildren, and her muse and life partner, Terence, in Ajax, ON. "I like to work through issues in my writing in order to clarify to what God is calling you and me."

Beverlee Wamboldt

http://www.amazon.com/-/e/B013PUAD58

Beverlee Wamboldt, of Dartmouth, Nova Scotia, is "Mom" to two adult children and "Nana" to five young adults. She starts each day seeking God's peace and guidance. Since retirement, along with her husband she has travelled throughout Canada and the United States and visited Great Britain and Europe. Her short story "The Memory Tree" was published in *Chicken Soup for the Soul: O Canada The Wonders of Winter.*

Ruth Waring

http://www.ruthwaring.com

Author, speaker, and workshop leader, Ruth Waring encourages others to discover the value of "Writing Our Yesterdays" through her seminar "Yes! There is a Story in You." She has established writers' groups in London, ON, and Lindsay, ON, where she now lives with her husband Doug. Ruth is passionate about mentoring, leading a women's Bible study, and sharing the love of Christ through speaking.

Come Find Me (Word Alive Press) finalist in the 2010 The Word Awards
Then Came a Hush (Word Alive Press), the sequel

T. L. Wiens

http://tlwiens.wordpress.com

T. L. Wiens lives in the hills along Lake Diefenbaker, SK, with her husband and two youngest children. Her book, *Where a Little Rain Comes Down* was chosen to be one of 30 novels out of 60,000 featured at the New York Library Association Trade Fair. She recently published her third novel, *In Search of Truth*. She is a member of Inscribe Christian Writers' Fellowship and Saskatchewan Writers' Guild.

Where A Little Rain Comes Down (Xlibris Publishing)
In Search of Truth (Dream Write Publishing)

Carolyn R. Wilker

http://www.carolynwilker.ca

Carolyn R. Wilker, of Kitchener, ON, finds beauty in creation in every season. You'll often see her, camera in hand, taking pictures of things in nature, her grandchildren, friends, and family. Many of those selections accompany her blog, "Storygal," at https://storygal.wordpress.com, where she writes about life, love, and gardening.

Once Upon a Sandbox (Hidden Brook Press)
Big Ideas for the Big Stage, contributor and editor (Speaker's Think Tank)

Ray Wiseman

http://www.ray.wiseman.ca

Ray Wiseman of Fergus, ON, began writing seriously in the early 1980s following careers in electronics and ministry in Canada and South Africa. Ray has written eight books, appeared in two anthologies, and penned over 1,000 editorials, newspaper features, and columns. Ray leads a team of writing experts who critique manuscripts for new authors.

When Cobras Laugh, with co-author Don Ranney, MD
(OakTara Publishers)
Write! Better: A Writing Tip for Every Week of the Year (WordWise)

Carmen Wittmeier

http://www.carmenwittmeier.blogspot.com

Carmen Wittmeier completed her MA in English at the University of Alberta in 1999. She has taught English literature at several colleges and worked as an editor, writer, and reporter. Her current passion is advocating for children trafficked into the sex trade. Carmen lives in Calgary, AB, with her two daughters and their growing collection of pets.

Affirming the Birth Mother's Journey: A Peer Counselor's Guide to Adoption Counseling (Trafford)

Brenda J. Wood

http://heartfeltdevotionals.com

A motivational speaker and author, Brenda is a true alphabet girl because she's written about experiences with abuse, bulimia, cancer and her husband's death. While the topics sound heavy, Brenda's sense of humour lightens her work. She much prefers a good read and a warm fire to any outdoor activity!

The Pregnant Pause of Grief: The First Trimester of Widowhood (Word Alive Press)

Gentle Humour with Jesus (Heartfelt Devotionals Press)

Acknowledgements

I'm delighted to have another opportunity to showcase work by some Canadian writers who are Christian.

Thanks to my husband and business partner, Les Lindquist, for not only going through the submissions with me and helping me make the selections, but for actually doing a fair bit of substantive editing and checking over pretty well everything I sent out.

Thank you to everyone who sent in submissions. There were so many good stories, and I wish I could have used them all.

Thank you to the 60 writers whose work was chosen to be in *Hot Apple Cider with Cinnamon*. Thank you for putting your stories into words, and thank you for not getting too upset when I started messing with those words. When I sent my edits out, I figuratively prepared to duck. It always surprised me when, instead of yelling at me, many of you actually thanked me for doing it!

Thanks to Audrey Dorsch of http://www.dorschedit.ca/ who did the final copy edit and caught a number of things that had been missed.

Thanks to Krysten Lindquist for her help with the author photos.

Thanks to all the contributors who checked the final drafts and sent in anything they caught. Thanks in particular to Adele Simmons, Judi Peers, Patricia Elford, Laureen Guenther, Marguerite Cummings, and Claire de Burbure who were a huge help in finding random glitches.

Thanks to Sheila Wray Gregoire who, in spite of being super busy, generously agreed to write the foreword to this book.

Thanks to those who wrote endorsements for the book—especially given how busy they are and the short time-frame they had!

And thanks most of all to the readers who told us how much they enjoyed our first books and gave us the courage to undertake putting together another book.

My prayer is that each person who reads this book will benefit in some way from the words and ideas on these pages.

N. J. Lindquist

More Books You Might Enjoy

A Taste of Hot Apple Cider

16 heart-warming stories and poems from 15 writers

Trade paperback and digital

"Through poems, fiction, and nonfiction alike, [the writers] remind readers that the struggles we face are common to everyone. Their honest descriptions of wrestling with cancer, caring for and losing aging parents, dealing with a spouse's dementia, moving beyond one's fear to tell neighbours about Jesus, and more, show us that hope is very much alive."
—from the foreword by author Grace Fox.

Available from most bookstores and online

http://hotappleciderbooks.com

Hot Apple Cider

44 stories of hope and encouragement from 30 writers

Trade paperback and digital

"A collection of short stories, poetry, and wisdom seeking to heal and mend the soul of the reader after difficult and stressful situations.... Highly recommended..."
—*Midwest Book Review*

"This is a book to sample, to savour, and to share."
—**Maxine Hancock**, PhD, Professor Emeritus, Regent College

Winner, five The Word Awards

Winner, Church Library Association of Ontario One Book/One Conference

Available from most bookstores and online

http://hotappleciderbooks.com

A Second Cup of Hot Apple Cider

51 stories of hope and encouragement from 37 writers

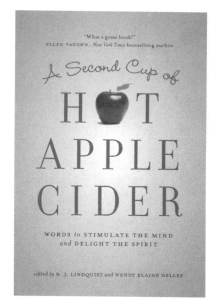 

Trade paperback and digital

"Some books surprise you with their ability to take your breath away.… Be sure to buy more than one, for you will probably have the urge to share this gem of a collection with others."
    —Faith Today

Winner, thirteen The Word Awards

Winner, Christian Small Publisher Gift Book of the Year Award

Winner, third place, The Book Club Network, Inc. Book of the Year Award

Available from most bookstores and online.

http://hotappleciderbooks.com

Publisher

That's Life! Communications

Books that integrate real faith with real life

That's Life! Communications is a niche publisher committed to finding innovative ways to produce quality books written by Canadians with a Christian faith perspective.

http://thatslifecommunications.com

We'd love to hear your comments about this book or any of our other books. Please post a comment on our website or write to us at:

comments@thatslifecommunications.com